WIZARDS
of WALL STREET

WIZARDS of WALL STREET

MARKET-BEATING INSIGHTS AND STRATEGIES FROM THE WORLD'S TOP-PERFORMING MUTUAL FUND MANAGERS

KIRK KAZANJIAN

Author of **NYIF GUIDE TO MUTUAL FUNDS**

NEW YORK INSTITUTE OF FINANCE

NEW YORK • TORONTO • SYDNEY • TOKYO • SINGAPORE

Library of Congress Cataloging-in-Publication Data

Kazanjian, Kirk.
  Wizards of Wall Street / Kirk Kazanjian.
    p. cm.
  Includes index.
  ISBN 0-7352-0154-4 (cloth)
    1. Mutual funds—United States. 2. Stocks—United States. 3. Investments—
  United States. 4. Investment advisors—New York (State)—New York—
  Interviews. 5. Stockbrokers—New York (State)—New York—Interviews.
    6. Stock exchanges—New York (State)—New York. I. Title.
HG4930.K394 2000
332.63'2—dc21   99-086110

Photographs of James Callinan, p. 65, Barbara Ries Photography © 1999; Amy Domini, p. 121, Timothy Greenfield Sanders; Neal Miller, p. 189, Seth Resnick © 1997; James Oelschlager, p. 241, David A. Shoenfelt Photography.

Printed in the United States of America

10   9   8   7   6   5   4   3   2

This publication is designed to provide accurate and authoritative information in regard to the subject matter covered. It is sold with the understanding that the publisher is not engaged in rendering legal, accounting, or other professional service. If legal advice or other expert assistance is required, the services of a competent professional person should be sought.

   . . . From the Declaration of Principles jointly adopted by a Committee of the American Bar Association and a Committee of Publishers and Associations

Although the information and data in this book were obtained from sources believed to be reliable, neither the author nor the publisher assumes responsibility for their accuracy. Under no circumstances does the information in this book represent a recommendation to buy or sell stocks or funds.

ISBN 0-7352-0154-4

NEW YORK INSTITUTE OF FINANCE
An Imprint of Prentice Hall Press
Paramus, NJ 07652

Visit us at www.phdirect.com/business

NYIF and NEW YORK INSTITUTE OF FINANCE are trademarks of Executive Tax Reports, Inc., used under license by Prentice Hall Direct, Inc.

To my mom, Linda Kazanjian,
whose continuous love and support
have always made me feel immensely rich

CONTENTS

INTRODUCTION

More than 63 million Americans invest in mutual funds today. Chances are, you're one of them. The industry now boasts more than $6 trillion in assets. Despite the growing popularity of indexing in recent years, most of this money is in actively managed funds. What's ironic is that a majority of all stock funds consistently *underperform* the unmanaged market indexes. For instance, over the past three-, five-, and ten-year periods, fewer than 10 percent of all equity fund managers have been able to beat the Standard & Poor's 500 index. Those who have are part of a rare breed. They are experts with a keen eye for knowing when and what to buy and, just as important, when to sell. They are the *Wizards of Wall Street*.

Because active managers in general have done so poorly, mutual funds have been getting an increasingly bad rap in recent years. Part of this is due to the incredible bull market, which has propelled a handful of high-profile stocks to amazing levels. As a result, many investors seem to believe mutual funds are too boring. Why own a fund when you can buy Microsoft and earn 50 percent a year? Or so the thinking goes. Of course, the media focus on stocks that have done well. The truth is, many more have performed miserably. If you were in the right individual stocks, making money was easy. Otherwise, that seemingly boring mutual fund would seem like a pretty good deal.

Adding fuel to the fire are the numerous Internet-based discount brokerage firms that don't make much money from selling funds. They want traders to buy and sell individual stocks at a rapid-fire pace. These brokers have made it their mission to glamorize individual stock speculating and day trading, to the point of implying that investors are crazy to trust their money to a fund. Of course, in a bull market everyone looks like a genius. And, by the way, the online brokers have (perhaps not mistakenly) forgotten to report the findings of various surveys showing that anywhere from 70 to 95 percent of all day traders (and I suspect individual traders in general) lose a significant amount of money.

If all that weren't bad enough, active fund managers have been bedeviled by the amazing performance of the Standard & Poor's 500 index over the past five years. Few active fund managers have been able to outperform this bogie, especially since 1993. As a result, assets have been pouring into S&P 500 index funds, prompting an ever increasing flood of articles about why people should steer clear of actively managed funds. What's interesting, and predictable, is that these same magazines were calling index funds "inferior to active" just a few years back. Like the general public, the press tends to follow performance and tout what is hot. But are they right this time? Should people abandon active funds in favor of indexing and individual stocks? My answer is quite simple: absolutely not.

It's true that of the 13,000-plus mutual funds available today, most are dogs. I would guess that some 12,800 aren't worth buying. But there are a handful of brilliant fund managers who outperform their peers, benchmark index, and yes, even the S&P 500 on a consistent basis. They are the *Wizards of Wall Street*, managers who have stood the test of time and proven their ability to pick great stocks. You're about to meet them in the pages that follow.

Keep in mind that in this book I don't focus on conversations with media celebrities. These Wizards all have the performance to back them up. In fact, some of these managers never talk to the press. They're too busy making money for their shareholders.

To be crowned a "Wizard," each fund manager must have outperformed the S&P 500 on an annualized basis for at least the past five years. In many cases, they have done it much longer. Some, such as Kevin Landis and Warren Lammert, are relatively new to the business, yet have clearly demonstrated they are at the head of the class among today's new generation of fund managers. Others, such as Robert Torray and James Oelschlager, have been doing a brilliant job of standing out from the crowd on Wall Street for decades. Then there's William Miller, who has an unmatched record of having outperformed the S&P

500 each year for nine straight years. That performance outshines legendary Fidelity Magellan manager-turned-TV-pitchman Peter Lynch's record, making Miller the reigning king of equity fund managers.

The purpose of this book is several-fold. First, for those of you who already own funds, I wanted to give you an up-close look at some of the best managers in the business today. If you don't own funds run by at least some of these experts, you probably should. This book will help you determine which manager's style makes the most sense to you. Second, even if you're not interested in funds and instead prefer to pick individual stocks, this book will show you how the industry's sharpest minds do it. You'll learn firsthand about the techniques these gurus have used to outsmart both the indexes and their colleagues. Third, this book will give you an inside view of the fund industry. You'll discover what it's like to start a fund, what impact a flood of assets can have on your performance, and much more. Finally, I believe you'll find this book to be just plain fun to read. These managers all have great stories to tell and amazing experiences to share.

The interviews, presented in alphabetical order, all follow a pretty similar path. We start off discussing the managers' backgrounds and how they got into the business. We then move into investment processes and uncover the secrets of their success. We wrap it all up by talking about their current observations of the industry and some of the lessons they've learned along the way.

There are a total of 18 Wizards featured in this book. The truth is, there aren't many more managers in the entire fund universe who meet my stringent requirements. These masters have a mix of styles and specialties. There are large-company growth managers, such as James Oelschlager, Ronald Canakaris, Spiros Segalas, and Howard Ward; value-oriented managers, such as William Miller and Robert Torray; small-company experts, such as James Callinan, Richard Lawson, and Neal Miller; and managers who specialize in certain market sectors, such as technology-guru Kevin Landis, communications-expert Bruce Behrens, and financial-services pro Christopher Davis, whose father and grandfather both made a fortune in financial stocks as well.

Having spent much of my professional career analyzing Wall Street money managers, I can tell you that the key to selecting an excellent mutual fund is finding one run by a top-notch manager. If past performance continues to be an indication of the future, these *Wizards of Wall Street* will continue to stay at the head of the class among managers as we enter the 21st century.

While all of these managers have slightly different techniques and specialties, there are many traits they seem to share. At the end of the book, I have summarized these traits. I have also outlined 10 keys to beating the market, which I have distilled from interviewing these living legends.

I hope you enjoy my conversations with these managers as much as I did, and I wish you much future investment success.

—Kirk Kazanjian

PART ONE

THE WIZARDS OF WALL STREET

DAVID ALGER

FRED ALGER MANAGEMENT

Fred Alger Management is a legend on Wall Street. The firm has turned out some of today's brightest and most respected portfolio managers since its beginnings in the 1960s. Today the company is run by the founder's little brother, David Alger. While the investment shop's past has at times been as volatile as the high-flying stocks it tends to favor, life for David and his company has never been better. The 56-year-old manager oversees 16 funds and numerous private portfolios representing more than $13 billion in assets. His best-performing fund, Spectra, is the firm's only no-load offering and has the best record of any diversified fund over the past ten years. He also runs several other funds that have been at the top of the charts for the past three and five years. Ironically, Spectra has been available to the public only since 1996. Before that, it was a tiny $8 million closed-end fund that traded on the New York Stock Exchange.

If David hadn't made his brother angry as a college student, he might not be where he is today. As a kind of apology for taking out too much aggression on his brother, Fred Alger provided his sibling with a stock tip that turned out to be right on the money. David was instantly hooked. Although he started out working for another investment firm, he somewhat reluctantly joined his brother's company several years later. He's been at the firm's office in New York's World Trade Center ever since.

Despite David's reputation for having a heavy hand and favoring smaller stocks, most of his gains have come from owning large companies, such as Microsoft, Pfizer, and Home Depot. In fact, David says he's never focused solely on smaller names, although his early success with the Alger Small Cap fund is what initially focused the spotlight on his firm's fund family.

David is the author of the book *Raging Bull,* which is a good description of his current outlook for the market. He believes the Dow will pass through 20,000 in the next few years, and he is also a major proponent of Internet stocks.

Kazanjian: *Your family has a long political history in Michigan.*

Alger: Yes. My father, Frederick Alger, Jr., ran unsuccessfully for governor in 1952. He was then ambassador to Belgium. My great-grandfather was governor, senator, and Secretary of War under President William McKinley, and a general in the Civil War, Fifth Michigan Cavalry.

Kazanjian: *Was your family wealthy? They must have been pretty well-to-do, since you went to boarding school from the seventh grade on.*

Alger: No. It's an ironic story. My great-grandfather, Russell Alger, was an immensely weathly lumber baron in Michigan. He made an enormous fortune. Sadly, my grandfather lost most of it during the Depression. What was left, my father spent. Indeed, I grew up in a very privileged way. We had a huge house with lots of servants. My family is quite prestigious in the state. But, in reality, all the money was gone. I don't know how my father would have gone on had he lived another ten years because he had basically spent everything. He died when I was 23. My mother died earlier. I wasn't left with anything to speak of. While I had a privileged upbringing, I was left out on my own in my twenties with a tiny inheritance. I grew up with a silver spoon in my mouth, but they took the spoon away. Every dime I have in the world now is money I've made on my own.

Kazanjian: *Was it your brother, Fred, who first got you interested in investing?*

Alger: Yes. My brother is nine years older than I am. He got interested in investing in business school. Fred established our firm in 1964. I was still in college at that point. Actually, I thought I wanted to be a criminal lawyer. I had no interest whatsoever in the stock market. Then, in 1965, I went from Milton Academy to Harvard, where I was an American history major. That year I came down to visit my brother. He and I had a bit of a disagreement because I'd stayed in his apartment with a young lady. Fred and his wife got very angry with me. Later, instead of apologizing, he gave me a stock tip. I borrowed some money from my girlfriend, and we invested it in the stock. It did extremely well. I thought, "Wow, this is really easy! Why do I want to be a lawyer?" I changed my career plan at that moment and worked in the investment business during the summer. I eventually went on to business school at the University of Michigan. From that point on I was completely hooked by the stock market. That's all I could think about. I decided I wanted to work in New York after graduation, although not necessarily with my brother.

Kazanjian: *The original plan wasn't to join your brother then?*

Alger: Not at all. In fact, neither of us wanted to do that.

Kazanjian: *Where did you start?*

Alger: As a securities analyst at the Irving Trust Company. The firm was starting to really ramp up its active money-management effort. They hired a bunch of young MBAs to be analysts. It was a wonderful job because they gave me enormous latitude. Before us, they had no other analysts. I became the senior oil, retail, and special-situations analyst. I got to play around with a lot of money, even though I had very little experience. A year later, I was hired away by a research boutique that no longer exists. I was very lucky because I hit on a stock that made me slightly famous, Milgo Electronics. It was the hottest stock of 1969.

Kazanjian: *How did you discover it?*

Alger: I don't think I did. Someone probably told me about it. The company made modems, and no one had ever heard of modems in those days. I helped popularize the concept. I simply sold the story. In those days, the market was so hot, you didn't really need numbers. It was a bit like Internet stocks today. You just needed a one line story. The story was that Milgo makes a box that lets one computer talk to another computer. People thought that was the greatest concept they'd ever heard. The stock went up many, many times. It got me a lot of notoriety. I was offered a lot of jobs, including director of research of a large investment-banking firm. That was pretty amazing, considering I was just 25 and had only one good stock pick. I turned it down because, to borrow from Groucho Marx, I didn't want to join a firm stupid enough to hire me as director of research. I didn't know enough. In 1971, Fred Alger Management, which was still quite small, was trying to ramp up its research efforts. Almost sort of warily my brother hired me.

Kazanjian: *What did he hire you to do?*

Alger: To be an analyst.

Kazanjian: *What's your title today?*

Alger: My official position is president, CEO, and chief investment officer.

Kazanjian: *The firm itself has a great history of cultivating a lot of very successful analysts.*

Alger: That's true. Among the better known ones are Tom Marsico (who now runs Marsico Capital Management), Helen Young Hayes (manager of $25 billion in international investments for Janus), Tony Webber (skipper of the Alleghany Veredus Aggressive Growth Fund), and Warren Lammert (another Janus manager who is also featured in this book).

Kazanjian: *Fred Alger Management started in the go-go sixties and has a great reputation. How did it become what it is today?*

Alger: The firm has gone through three iterations. The first was from 1964 to the mid–1970s. During that time, we subadvised some funds, but principally managed money for rich individuals. We were very small, five guys in a room managing less than $100 million. In the mid–1970s, after ERISA was passed, all the large corporations started looking around for people who could run money well. They hired us as a pension manager. Pretty soon cash was pouring in. We ramped up to a high of $3 billion. We had two small closed-end funds, but by 1986, we were almost purely pension fund managers. We had very good performance most of the time. We did a lot of unique things in the 1980s. We started our own training program, which trained some of the people previously mentioned. We began our own headhunting firm for analysts. We completely integrated our computer system. But, at the heart of it, we have always been research-oriented growth stock pickers. In 1986, we decided to diversify our business. We wanted to go into the mutual fund industry, so we launched the Alger Fund. The launch was accompanied by a large advertising campaign. It was probably the worst advertising campaign in history. We spent $17 million, and it actually cost us business. It hit just about every wrong note you can hit. It was really a disaster. The idea was the SEC had just permitted performance advertising. We decided this was a loophole we had to take advantage of because we had great performance. We went on TV with an ad campaign that my brother liked more than the rest of us. Its slogan was "A Genius for Managing Money." One of the things we discovered along the way was that you can call yourself just about anything and you'll find a support group. I mean, if you're a child molester, you'll find a support group for that. But the one thing you can't say about yourself is that you're a genius, because then everybody will hate you. The ad campaign was considered much too glitzy and showy. People really responded badly. Moreover, our existing base of clients took offense. They felt we were leaving the pension fund business for this sort of retail mutual fund business. I guess they thought that made us less serious. We started losing clients. Then came the crash of 1987. We lost two-thirds of our business. Our assets went down from more than $3 billion in 1986 to just over $1 billion in 1990.

Kazanjian: *Purely because of performance?*

Alger: Performance fell off in 1987, and 1988 was very much a value stock year so we didn't bounce back much. It was a very bleak time for the company. Then a miraculous thing happened. Our small-cap fund was the number-one fund in America in 1989. Suddenly we got an enormous amount of press and money started coming in. A couple of years later, we went heavily into the variable annuity business. This whole thing ended our ten-year reign as a pension fund manager and began our period as a mutual fund manager. We've grown to about $13 billion under management, of which all but $2 billion is in one form of mutual fund or another. We run three separate families of funds plus an offshore fund and a separate no-load fund called Spectra.

Kazanjian: *It sounds as if these are the best of times for the firm.*

Alger: The last two years have been excellent for us. We've had very good performance.

Kazanjian: *How many funds do you oversee now?*

Alger: Sixteen.

Kazanjian: *You're a busy guy.*

Alger: I'm co-portfolio manager on all our funds. Each one has a very talented portfolio manager who works with me. I can devote only about half my time to the investing side of the business. Thirty percent is marketing, and 20 percent is administrative.

Kazanjian: *When you first joined the firm did working with your brother go well?*

Alger: No, it didn't. It was very shaky. Due to my early successes, I expected to be treated as an equal. He thought I was a wet-behind-the-ears kid who needed to be worked to death, paid nothing, and treated as harshly as possible. He wanted to shake out of me any ideas I might have that I knew something about the stock market. Those two views of the world clashed quite a lot during the first five years. After that, we started to get along extremely well. The rest, as they say, is history.

Kazanjian: *Is your brother involved in the firm's day-to-day operations?*

Alger: Day to day, no. He's retired. He's still chairman and the largest shareholder. He hasn't made investment decisions for many years. He basically turned all that over to me in 1989.

Kazanjian: *Why did he leave?*

Alger: A number of reasons. One was that I had essentially taken over the investment and marketing functions. He was just doing the administrative side. Second, I guess he felt it was time to retire. He wanted to live abroad. He is an expatriate and lives abroad most of the year. He got divorced and remarried, and I think there was a certain element of starting a new life elsewhere. He now lives in Geneva, Switzerland.

Kazanjian: *How many people do you have at the firm?*

Alger: About 170.

Kazanjian: *Of that, how many are analysts?*

Alger: Research personnel, if you throw in everybody, would be nearly 20.

Kazanjian: *I know you have an apprentice-analyst program at Alger. How does that work?*

Alger: In the old days we used to hire nothing but undergraduates. Now we hire both people with BAs, MBAs, and also those from other careers. They go to work on a team with a senior analyst. At first they mostly do spreadsheets, go to meetings, take notes, and report back what they've found. It's a lot of grunt work. After a year or two, depending on the analyst they're working for, we make them take the CFA series [a series of three tests leading to the designation of Chartered Financial Analyst]. After passing the level-two exam, they take on more responsibility. They're not recommending stocks, but they're doing most of the work. Once they become a CFA, they are promoted to a full analyst.

Kazanjian: *Why is the CFA designation so important to you? Most of the managers I've interviewed don't have it, and they've certainly been very successful.*

Alger: It's important because when we started the program, we hired only undergraduates. Since they didn't have MBAs, or even business degrees, we needed some metric to ensure ourselves that they really had accounting and the basics of security analysis down pat. We felt the CFA was a good proxy for an MBA.

Kazanjian: *Are the opportunities for young analysts increasing on Wall Street, and will they dry up once the market turns sour?*

Alger: I think the opportunities are vast. What we see now, of course, is people paying very big salaries. It's getting more competitive to get good people. These kinds of things always follow in line with the market.

Kazanjian: *What's a typical day like for you?*

Alger: It depends on whether I'm focusing on the stock market or marketing. There are entire days when I am consumed with giving speeches, appearing on television, traveling to see potential clients, and meeting with clients. When I don't have a lot of marketing obligations, I concentrate on the market. I meet with all the portfolio managers, go over their portfolios, and listen to their stock ideas. I have veto power on all new stock ideas. Analysts come in with ideas; I listen and pass judgment on them. Often I'll spend time on the computer looking at all the portfolios and asking a lot of questions. Then I'll hang out by the trading desk for a couple of hours. I have a station up there. I want to see if anything really good or bad happens to the market.

Kazanjian: *You have final say on everything?*

Alger: Yes, on every stock we buy.

Kazanjian: *You talked about marketing. Today we've almost turned mutual fund managers into celebrities. The only way you get assets is by doing marketing and keeping a high profile. What do you think of this fund manager as a rock star mentality?*

Alger: I'm not so sure that it's quite as bad as it once was. In the 1960s, it really got out of hand. I think today's fund managers, even the well-known ones, are less flamboyant than they were back then. But this is a business. People want to know who's investing their money. I spend a lot of my time talking to financial planners and brokers. When I'm at a conference, these people all want to have pictures taken with me or books signed by me. I find it a little strange. They say, "It's really important to my client that I know you personally." For example, I'm especially popular in Germany, where we distribute our funds. I've gone on tours of Germany, and every single broker will line up to have his picture taken with me.

Kazanjian: *Let's talk about your investment approach. You're primarily associated with small-caps. Perhaps that's because of your early strong performance in that asset class.*

Alger: Actually, it's a total misunderstanding. We're not exclusively small-cap managers at all. In fact, probably only 20 percent of our funds are small-caps. Our growth fund, which focuses on large-caps, has done considerably better than our small-cap fund in recent years. You're right, though, our small-cap fund did well in 1989, so people do think of us that way. But it's not accurate. We're an aggressive growth manager. Our approach has been the same since 1964. We want to buy stocks of America's fastest growing companies. We're a domestic-only growth stock manager. We are interested in all market cap ranges. We're also great believers in bottom-up research. We have our own research department, which is very expensive to maintain. What it really means to us is that if you have better research, in the long run you're going to win. That's really our philosophy. We don't buy foreign stocks. If we do, it's less than 5 percent of any portfolio.

Kazanjian: *Do you not buy foreign because you don't believe people should own foreign, or because it's not your area of expertise?*

Alger: A little bit of both, actually. It's not our area of expertise, but we're also very excited about what's been going on in the United States. We think America's got the most vigorous economy. We think we're the world's technology leader, and that lead is accelerating. America has the broadest and deepest market with the most transparent accounting system. We don't see much reason in the long term to invest anywhere else when there are so many great companies in the U.S.

Kazanjian: *You have several funds at the top of the charts over the past five years. Do they all hold the same stocks?*

Alger: No, they don't. In fact, there are some pretty big differences.

Kazanjian: *In terms of finding stocks, do you look for the same characteristics in both small- and large-caps?*

Alger: Basically, yes, although the smaller the company, the faster we want it to grow. A very large company growing at 40 percent per year is hard to find, but most smaller companies have to be growing that fast in order to survive.

Kazanjian: *Let's talk about your process of putting the portfolio together. How do you start?*

Alger: It's done on a bottom-up basis. The analyst teams each follow a group of 50 to 150 companies. Their job is to find the best stocks in that group. They essentially make stock recommendations to me and the other portfolio managers.

Kazanjian: *Are the groups divided by industry sector?*

Alger: Yes. Some follow more industries than others. We either accept the recommendations and buy the stock or turn them down. The recommendations are very quick and to the point. There's nothing written. It's all verbal. If we like the stories, we put them in the portfolio right away. It's done within minutes after a stock is approved.

Kazanjian: *What traits does your ideal stock have?*

Alger: It's got to be growing rapidly, at both the top and bottom line. We do valuations on a stock-by-stock basis. When an analyst recommends a stock, he or she has got to make a case for the valuation of that stock. We call it the target multiple—the multiple they would like to see the stock sell at in order to make the expected gain. Once we establish that target multiple, we enter it in the computer so we can track how that stock is doing against its target. We call it "potential appreciation," or how much additional appreciation we believe is left in the stock. We follow, rank, and sort all of our companies by potential appreciation. Once it reaches the stated target, we make a decision as to whether we ought to sell or hold. We also have very powerful software that enables us to look at each portfolio in many different ways from the top down. We call it the hourglass method of management—looking at it from both the bottom up and top down.

Kazanjian: You set a price target on every stock before you go into it?

Alger: Precisely.

Kazanjian: *Can you give me an example of a recent stock that you bought to show how this process works?*

Alger: Express Scripts is a mid-cap company. We bought the stock at $62. Our target price is $95 to $100, predicated on 35 times 2000 earnings of $2.30 per share, with a little extra added because of the company's Internet component. We enter that target into the computer, and the computer tracks how the stock is doing each day. Once the price gets to $100, the potential appreciation, in our view, goes down to zero.

Kazanjian: *Is there a point where you would upgrade the price target?*

Alger: We might. Once it gets down to a level of low appreciation, we have a discussion with the analyst and decide what to do. For instance, we are talking about Cisco Systems right now. It is currently trading at 60 times earnings. Our target is 70 times earnings.

Kazanjian: *Does that mean you'd probably sell once it got to 70 times earnings?*

Alger: Not necessarily, but we would review it closely. We might even cut back on part of the position, since it's a great company.

Kazanjian: *What happens when you set a price target but the stock goes down, not up?*

Alger: I'm a big believer in technical analysis. I take the charts of all our holdings home over the weekend and grade them. If a stock is plunging and has a bad chart, we consider selling. On the other hand, if the chart isn't bad, we might use that weakness as a buy point.

Kazanjian: *You obviously do a lot of selling. Your turnover, at around 100 percent, is higher than most funds. Are there other reasons you sell, or is it strictly a price target discipline?*

Alger: If there's any fundamental shortfall we'll sell right away. If our analyst set certain objectives for the stock, and it doesn't meet those objectives, we'll sell. I'm not a believer in dragging companies through their problems. Once they get their problems worked out we can go back into them. That doesn't mean we sell if it's a penny below the whisper number. That's kind of stupid. But if it's a meaningful shortfall, in terms of earnings or other results, we'll sell and look at it later when the problems are solved.

Kazanjian: *Do you take taxes into consideration before making a sale?*

Alger: No. In an ideal world you would, but I'm not going to avoid harvesting a gain just because of taxes.

Kazanjian: *A lot of managers I've interviewed say you want to buy and hold good companies for a long time. Is that thinking wrong?*

Alger: No, that's ideal. That's perfect. But there are two important points. One, there are very few great companies one can hold for many years. Second, you don't know when you've found one. If a stock shoots way up and gets ahead of itself, you can't be certain it's going to become a great growth stock long-term.

Kazanjian: *Is there any stock right now that you could look at and say I want to buy and hold this company forever?*

Alger: I don't think so.

Kazanjian: *How many stocks do you own at any given time in your funds?*

Alger: It depends on the fund and the size of the portfolio. We take tinier positions in the small-cap funds, so we may own 100 or more companies in those accounts. In the large-cap funds, it might be more like 60 to 80 names.

Kazanjian: *You clearly believe in diversification. You also use leverage.*

Alger: We use it only as a flywheel. If we lose assets due to redemptions, we use leverage to avoid having to liquidate the portfolios. We don't intentionally leverage the funds, even though we have the right to by prospectus.

Kazanjian: *Are there certain sectors that you're focusing on at this point?*

Alger: We always have between 25 and 45 percent of our holdings in technology.

Kazanjian: *Is that on purpose, or merely because those stocks happen to meet your criteria?*

Alger: Certainly the faster growing areas of the market are in technology, so that's what we want to concentrate on.

Kazanjian: *You wrote in your book,* Raging Bull, *that you thought health care was the place to be as an investor.*

Alger: Yes, but right now we're very low in that sector. Drug stocks got very expensive given their growth rates, and we felt we should sell them. There's a good example of an entire group of stocks that met our price target multiples.

Kazanjian: *Your large-cap funds have performed better than your small-cap funds. Do you expect that trend to continue in the future?*

Alger: I think mid-caps will do better going forward. Small-caps will eventually do well, but it will take time. Large-caps will also continue to do well.

Kazanjian: *How much of an impact does your market view have on your portfolio design?*

Alger: It has some influence by osmosis. We like to think of ourselves as bottoms up stock pickers, but clearly my market view permeates how analysts look at their stocks.

Kazanjian: *Do you raise cash if you're bearish?*

Alger: We'd have to be very bearish to raise cash. We would have to expect a profound drop, 25 percent or so, even to contemplate such a thing.

Kazanjian: *Do you meet with companies?*

Alger: Our analysts meet with companies all the time. I personally meet with companies occasionally. The management of our biggest holdings come in to meet with us once a year.

Kazanjian: *So, it's not strictly a numbers game. You do want to get to know the company?*

Alger: Absolutely. I want to know their products, their management, and their competitors. We like to think we know our companies better than anybody.

Kazanjian: *Individual investors don't have access to management, nor to your analysts. How should they go about researching companies?*

Alger: It's hard. I think one of the best bits of advice for an individual investor comes from Peter Lynch, which is buy the stocks of companies you know and like.

Kazanjian: *Even then, you've got to do some additional research into the company, right?*

Alger: Of course.

Kazanjian: *What should you be looking for?*

Alger: You need to look at so much stuff. You have to do a complete analysis—check out their balance sheet, income statement, and make their future earnings projection out at least five years. You have to talk to their competitors, suppliers, all of that. It's a lot of work for an individual to do.

Kazanjian: *The conventional thinking is that with the Internet all this information is available to individuals. Is that not true?*

Alger: I don't know. I'm on the Internet a lot, and it may be available somewhere. But you've got to know how to look for it and put it together in a way that makes some sense.

Kazanjian: *Does that mean you think individuals are better off in funds?*

Alger: No question, especially for their serious money. I recognize that individuals like to amuse themselves by speculating in the market, but to me that's more of a form of entertainment than serious investing.

Kazanjian: *What's the most common reason a stock becomes a loser?*

Alger: The fundamentals are bad. You thought it was going to grow by 30 percent, and it's growing by 20 percent. Very rarely is it because of a high valuation.

Kazanjian: *Do you try to cut your losses quickly?*

Alger: When a stock is dropping, there are two possible responses. It could be a great opportunity to buy more, or it could be doing poorly because someone knows something you don't. I don't think there's a hard-or-fast rule about it. You have to know the company and what is probably driving it down. You have to look at the chart and get a sense of whether this is a real breakdown or just a pullback.

Kazanjian: *Let's talk about the Internet. You've said that it's misunderstood by investors, and you seem to be very enthusiastic about it. What do you like about the Internet and what kinds of companies are you interested in?*

Alger: Only companies that I really think are going to add value and will be around five years from now. The Internet is growing very fast, but it's going to grow even faster, partly because large corporations are really moving fast into the space. This is good news and bad news. It will move the market along even faster than before. By the same token, companies must be well financed, well managed, and have very good products to do well. They're not going to be up against other small Internet startups. They'll be up against large corporations. The biggest example is in the financial services area. The big banks jumped in right away and have already taken away 90 percent of the market.

Kazanjian: *What kinds of companies would you be buying then?*

Alger: Companies that have a really good product and know what they're doing. The Ciscos, Amazons, Yahoos, and such.

Kazanjian: *In other words, you're willing to own both the e-commerce and infrastructure companies?*

Alger: Certainly.

Kazanjian: *Given what you just said about the competition increasing and the big guys getting into this, doesn't that mean the e-commerce leaders of tomorrow will be much different from the leaders of today?*

Alger: Yes, quite possibly. That's where you have to be very careful.

Kazanjian: *Earlier you said the Internet was misunderstood by investors. What did you mean by that?*

Alger: I think there are two things people don't understand about the Internet. One is the speed at which it is going to grow over the next five years. I think everybody acknowledges it will grow fast. I don't think anybody really understands how fast. Second, I think the profits and losses of these Internet companies are misunderstood by Wall Street. The main costs of an Internet service or e-commerce company are advertising and marketing. You can throw only so many dollars into those areas. As their advertising and marketing budgets flatten out, there will be tremendous leverage, greater than people expect.

Kazanjian: *With competition being as intense as it already is, won't it be hard for companies to make money?*

Alger: No. I think some people will make enormous amounts of money.

Kazanjian: *Let's talk about Amazon.com. You like the stock, but a lot of folks say there's no way to possibly value it, including Warren Buffett.*

Alger: Internet stocks are very hard to value, no question about it. But there are numerous ways to value Amazon. One is to make some projections into the future and then discount them to present value. That's certainly one way of doing it.

Kazanjian: *Explain what you mean by that.*

Alger: Amazon and AOL both have the same basic characteristics and are going to earn a lot more money than people think in five years. That's because a great majority of their spending is on advertising. Consumer advertising and promotion expenses will stay flat. That will give them more leverage than people are willing to attribute at present.

Kazanjian: *But users of the Internet are becoming so price conscious. Many of these companies are selling items below cost, including Amazon.*

Alger: That model won't survive.

Kazanjian: *Are you predicting it will change?*

Alger: Yes. E-commerce companies will still substantially underprice bricks-and-mortar stores, but people who sell things at or below cost won't survive.

Kazanjian: *For years, you've said you don't like concept stocks. Don't you think these Internet start-ups are concept stocks?*

Alger: No, I don't. Most of the stocks we own make money, although there are a couple of exceptions. Amazon is one. I don't think the Internet is a concept. The Internet is a reality. It's here. There are 85 million people on it.

Kazanjian: *How about the big bricks-and-mortar stores? Will they be able to make inroads on the Internet, or are they too late?*

Alger: I think some will, though not necessarily the big ones. For instance, Williams-Sonoma is ideally structured to be on the Internet. I'm sure Wal-Mart will do well, too. The victims won't be the big chains. It's perceived that Amazon and Wal-Mart will ultimately square off for control of the world. I don't see it that way. I think what these companies are doing is sucking the life out of every small strip mall in America, plus a whole bunch of mom-and-pop stores.

Kazanjian: *We talked about how you do a lot of trading. What do you think of the day traders?*

Alger: I think they should view it as an amusement, like going to Las Vegas. They're not really going to make money. Trading stocks is a very demanding business. It will tear your heart out because you'll do well for three months, then you'll have one or two really terrible trades and lose all your money.

Kazanjian: *You certainly trade a lot. Do you consider yourself an investor or a trader.*

Alger: I'm an investor. My turnover would be a lot higher than 100 percent if I were a trader.

Kazanjian: *I alluded earlier to the book you wrote in the early nineties,* Raging Bull. *Are you still a raging bull?*

Alger: Absolutely. I think the market's going to double again by 2004 [which would put us well above 20,000].

Kazanjian: *In the book, you predicted the Dow would get to about 6,000 by the end of the 1990s. We've pretty much doubled that.*

Alger: What's interesting is that my expectations were very jazzy at the time.

Kazanjian: *What will it take to get us to Dow 20,000 in the next few years?*

Alger: The Internet, among other things. I thing productivity will continue to increase. Consequently, inflation will remain under pressure and even come down. Superimposed on this is the Internet, which I believe is the biggest deflationary force ever to hit the world. It's going to dramatically reduce prices over the next three years. I suspect that by the end of three years we'll have zero inflation or even negative inflation. Once you have that, and it's recognized by the market, bonds will have an enormous rally. I wouldn't be surprised to see a 4 percent long bond. When you get there, all the metrics clearly show the stock market will double.

Kazanjian: *Do you expect this to be a straight rise up, or will there be bear markets along the way?*

Alger: There will be bear markets, as there always are.

Kazanjian: *What would cause you to change your opinion? In other words, what could derail that bold prediction of yours?*

Alger: Any surge of inflation. My view of inflation is pretty aggressive. If I'm wrong, that would cause me to change my view. Also, international calamity would dampen the outlook.

Kazanjian: *If a bear market were to come along, would you take action or ride it out?*

Alger: It depends on how profound I thought it was. If I thought it was going to be around 20 percent, like in 1998, I'd stay put. If I expected a sustained bear market, I would obviously have to take some action.

Kazanjian: *Would you ever go to 100 percent cash?*

Alger: No, never.

Kazanjian: *How did you react during the 1973–74 bear market?*

Alger: In dismay. That was the only market that I really felt was profoundly depressing.

Kazanjian: *Have you changed your investment approach over the years, since you've been at Fred Alger, or have you always invested the same way?*

Alger: Since I've been here, things have definitely changed. We have computers and all sorts of tools we never had before. But the basic premise is the same. We're looking for good companies with good products growing very quickly, with creative management doing energetic things.

Kazanjian: *People seem to be talking more about fund expenses these days. Your funds are pretty expensive across the board. John Bogle, chairman of the Vanguard Group, has been critical of people like you who charge loads and high annual expenses. Do you think people should be concerned about these charges, as Bogle implies?*

Alger: John Bogle talks about this stuff because he's pushing index funds, which have extremely low expenses. What really matters is the net rate of return you get on your investment after expenses are deducted. I'd certainly be willing to pay someone 60 percent a year in fees if they could increase my money by 1,000 percent a year. You'd be a fool not to. Fees are irrelevant. What is relevant is what kind of return you are getting after fees are deducted. After all, when you look at mutual funds, that is your performance measurement. Mutual funds take the fees out before they calculate your performance. The performance of mutual funds is all net of fees. Who cares what the fee is as long as you're getting an adequate return? Vanguard will argue that since 80 percent of managers don't beat the S&P, you shouldn't pay high fees for an inferior return. I agree. But for those of us who are in the 20 percent bracket, who do beat the S&P, what difference do fees make?

Kazanjian: *What about sales loads? A lot of your funds are sold through brokerage channels?*

Alger: All of our funds are load funds with one exception, Spectra, which is a no-load fund. I think a lot of people need advisers to help them set up a plan to achieve their goals. If you're using a planner, he or she deserves to get paid. That's what the load is all about.

Kazanjian: *Why did you decide to make Spectra no load when you converted it?*

Alger: Spectra was always unique. It was a closed-end fund we managed as far back as 1974. We never opened it up because we didn't have the capability to do the back office to service an open mutual fund. After the Alger Fund was up and running, we had that capability, so we opened up Spectra. We made it no-load because we thought it would be interesting to see if we could have a no-load product. We don't want to make our regular channel angry so we haven't really advertised Spectra very much. You'll notice if you look in the paper that it's not included among our funds. It's separate. We've done that intentionally because we don't want to get the brokers upset. That fund has been very successful. It has the best record of any fund over the past 10, 15, and 20 years.

Kazanjian: *Do you believe in indexing at all for investors?*

Alger: No, not really. I always like to believe that people should try to do better than the averages. After all, over time people *should* do better than the averages.

Kazanjian: *Why do so many fund managers fail at that endeavor?*

Alger: I think it really speaks to the nature of the S&P 500. The index is constantly being revamped and keeps improving because the committee is always upgrading to better companies. Plus, so much money has gone into passive investing that it creates a bias for the S&P. Because of that, I think the S&P will remain pretty hard to beat. You could say the game's a little rigged.

Kazanjian: *How do you invest your own money?*

Alger: I don't invest in stocks at all. I gave that up a long time ago for two reasons. One, every time the SEC comes in here for an audit, the first thing they want to see is my personal account. The penalties for being crosswise with my clients are so severe it's not worth it. Second, the great bulk of my net worth is tied up in my ownership of this firm. Since the firm's assets are invested in the funds we manage, I'm indirectly invested in the market.

Kazanjian: *So bring us full circle to where we started. You talked about how you grew up in a life of privilege. Are you back there again now?*

Alger: You mean do I live luxuriously? No, not exceptionally so. We have a house out in the country, which is pretty nice. But my wife, two daughters, and I live a very quiet, family-oriented life. We're not very flashy at all.

Kazanjian: *Whom would you say your funds are most appropriate for?*

Alger: I think our funds are appropriate for everyone. If you take our performance composite, which is not funds but individual accounts, going back to 1976, we've had only three down years, which is pretty good.

I got to see David's celebrity status in action at a recent conference for financial planners in San Francisco. He made a guest appearance at the Alger Fund's booth for one hour and was flocked by brokers looking to be chummy with this star manager. It reminded me of fans gathering to get their favorite rock star's autograph.

David gets defensive when people tag him as a small-cap manager, even though that is the area of the market where he first made a name for himself. Lately, however, he's been finding most of his big winners among much larger names. He may also be investing in the Internet more aggressively than his peers. So far, this bet is really paying off.

When it comes to finding good stocks for his many portfolios, David has one primary requirement—rapid growth. Price is less important, as long as the company's earnings continue to deliver. He's also about the only Wizard who closely follows technical analysis, although it's interesting that he uses it more to confirm his fundamental research than as the sole basis for stock selection. ■

BRUCE BEHRENS

ALEX. BROWN INVESTMENT MANAGEMENT

How has Bruce Behrens been able to steer a seemingly stodgy investment for widows and orphans to chart-topping returns for more than 15 years? Through a combination of timing, luck, an eye for value, and a willingness to keep up with change. Bruce manages the Flag Investors Communications Fund, which is distributed by broker-dealers and financial planners around the country. The fund began in 1984, following the divestiture of the old American Telephone & Telegraph Company. As Bruce explains in the interview, it was conceived as a marketing gimmick for those who didn't know what to do with their AT&T stock following the breakup, but the performance has been no joke.

Bruce has consistently dialed up impressive results. The fund's annualized return since inception is a full 4 percentage points ahead of the S&P 500. The fund was originally called Flag Telephone Income, to reflect the portfolio's general mandate of buying dividend-paying phone companies. But over the years, Bruce began evolving his portfolio to make way for the new communications companies of the 21st century, including Internet providers such as America Online, which is currently the fund's top holding, and high-tech names such as Lucent Technologies.

To reflect this evolving structure, the word "Telephone" was recently removed from the fund's name and replaced with the more generic "Communications." The fund's objective now is to invest in "companies that are engaged in the research, development, manufacture, or sale of communications services, technology, equipment, or products." The income mandate has also disappeared, although the focus on value remains the same.

Bruce added comanager Liam Burke to his team in 1997. Both work out of Alex. Brown Investment Management's Baltimore office. And even though the communications area has been ringing up incredible profits for investors for more than a decade, this 56-year-old manager sees plenty more gains to come in the new millennium. He also sees an industry dominated by a few major players who will leave all of their smaller competitors in the dust.

Kazanjian: *Tell me how you first got interested in the stock market.*

Behrens: I was not one of those prodigies who loved investing and ran little businesses out of my house as a kid. But when I was 17, my dad paid me for painting our house with $1,000 of stock in Russ Togs, an apparel company. It was acquired by Liz Claiborne a few years ago. I followed the stock as it went up and down throughout college.

Kazanjian: *Did that experience prompt you to major in business?*

Behrens: No. I majored in economics and minored in psychology. I decided I didn't want to either be a clinician or zap rats. Business was more interesting. I then went straight to get an MBA at the University of Michigan. I had Vietnam breathing down my neck and wanted to marry my girlfriend, so I went right to grad school.

Kazanjian: *Did you start working in the investment field right away?*

Behrens: After grad school, I went right into the investment-research department at Citibank. Citibank was highly organized and wanted to attract people either as analysts or portfolio managers. I ultimately wanted to manage portfolios but thought it was better to be an analyst to really learn that trade first. They weren't happy with that, but accommodated me and let me work in research for one-and-a-half years. I then moved over to the investment management side.

Kazanjian: *You mean they wanted a fresh-faced kid like you to start managing money right away?*

Behrens: As somebody's assistant. Don't forget this was a bank environment, so you had to follow highly prescribed stock lists. I didn't think that was a logical way to do it. I thought if you were going to be a stock picker you ought to learn how to analyze companies first, instead of just reading what your research department told you.

Kazanjian: *Did you move on to the institutional investment advisory side?*

Behrens: Yes. We managed medium to small institutional accounts for foundations, endowments, personal holdings companies, and some high net-worth individuals. I finally went into the pension department and was there from 1968 to 1972. Citibank's approach was to train people to be managers in all areas, not technical specialists. They took one of our great analysts and had him go to work in a consumer finance operation in Australia. It rounds you out as a business manager, but doesn't exactly keep you in the investment field.

By this time I knew I wanted to pick stocks. Citibank was not the place to focus on that so I started looking around. There was a little innocuous ad in *The Wall Street Journal* for a middle-Atlantic bank holding company that was creating an independent investment management operation from ground floor. I wrote off to this blind-ad post box and said, "You're looking for an analyst. I'm more of a portfolio manager, but can certainly do general analysis. It strikes me if you're starting out you need these skills." I got a letter back from Equitable Bank in Baltimore. I was thinking middle Atlantic was something like Chapel Hill, North Carolina. I came down for an interview. The were starting with what they called Investment Counselors of Maryland, a subsidiary of Equitable Bank. They felt they had to get out of bank personnel hierarchy to have an independent investment management group. They were also giving a piece of the action as part of the compensation. I was 28, and that entrepreneurial opportunity was very appealing. After a series of talks, I and two others started managing the firm. We had a great fourth quarter in 1972 and thought we were really smart. Then we got into a two-year bear market, the worst in the postwar period. I would say we had good relative negative numbers in 1973–74. It was a humbling learning experience. I did a lot of soul searching, in terms of my investment philosophy. At the urging of one of my associates, Jim Hardesty, I went back to the well and reread the work of Ben Graham. I

remember being in New York for a conference in the summer of
1974. Graham and Bill Ruane, who's now with the Sequoia Fund,
both spoke. I really got charged up. We formulated a much more
value-oriented investment philosophy at that time. Citibank was a
growth stock operation.

Kazanjian: *You said you had good relative performance. How bad was
it?*

Behrens: From peak to trough when the Dow was down 50 percent,
we were probably down 25 to 30 percent. That was relatively good,
but pretty darn hard if that's the only record you have to go out and
market yourself with. People don't want to pay you to lose a quarter
of their money.

Kazanjian: *What happened next?*

Behrens: I was with Investment Counselors of Maryland for five years.
We were really captive to the bank, and I was still itching for something more entrepreneurial. I joined a one-man firm, Corbin Associates, where I literally had an equity interest. We had a lot of very
small accounts and ran them like a mutual fund. We had somebody
write a computer program for us so we could spread trades evenly
across accounts. Our focus was almost all on research. It was a very
eclectic stock-picking process with no real philosophy to it. I did that
for a couple of years. Then Dorsey Brown, who runs our operation
here at Alex. Brown Investment Management, enticed me to join him.
That was in 1981. We all work as analysts/portfolio managers and
manage many accounts.

Kazanjian: *What qualified you for inclusion in this book is your amazing work running the Flag Communications Fund. What was the ori-
gin of that?*

Behrens: In 1983, AT&T agreed with the government to divest into
eight different companies. Jim Price, a partner of Alex. Brown and
one of the original panelists on *Wall $treet Week With Louis
Rukeyser* saw that so many people owned only AT&T and were
going to go from a single stock that was like mom and apple pie to
eight companies in a new competitive world. He realized they were
going to need some guidance. This was a marketing opportunity.
They created this fund, and salesmen throughout Alex. Brown wore
little blue buttons that said, "Do you own AT&T?" We got together
$64 million in a tax-free exchange. People tendered their AT&T stock

for shares of the fund, which we managed with the same conservative objective of somebody who might have owned AT&T.

Kazanjian: *So, it was a solution for people who had AT&T but didn't know what to do after the breakup. They could just buy this fund and you would take care of all the seemingly tough decisions.*

Behrens: Yes. We'd decide what to sell and might gradually diversify. It had the added appeal that it was a tax-free exchange.

Kazanjian: *How were you able to get Uncle Sam to allow that?*

Behrens: The exchange funds were just starting. If people had a huge position in Xerox or IBM with a low-cost basis, they could add it to some funds in a tax-free exchange. The IRS cracked down on several funds because if they stayed open ended and more stock came in, you eventually diluted the gain of the original holder, who would never have to pay taxes on those gains on a per-share basis. Once we did the initial offering, we couldn't sell new shares because that would allow cash to come in. At the end of five years, and this is just a custom, you can reapply to open the fund, which we did in 1989. The irony of the whole thing, and one of the reasons the IRS approved this move, is that there really weren't many gains in the AT&T stock that was put into the fund in the first place.

Kazanjian: *How did you get tapped to run the fund?*

Behrens: The firm needed somebody to manage it. In my one-year stint as a pure analyst at Citibank, one of the things they stuck me with was utilities because they knew I wasn't going to be in research that long. Alex. Brown decided telephone stocks were a kind of utility, so they asked me to run it.

Kazanjian: *When you started this fund, I assume you were trying to run it as a vehicle for widows and orphans.*

Behrens: Yes. It was an equity-income fund. We literally had 7 to 8 percent yields on stocks in 1984. We also thought there would be an evolutionary change and the industry could become reasonably attractive. This was an unusual opportunity to invest in a large industry with a $200–$300 billion market capitalization that was about to undergo significant change. You had seven fairly equally sized companies, plus AT&T, that were financially sound with strong business franchises, brand names, capable management, and highly recurring cash flow. Even though it was going to be open to competition in

time, we could see the power of incumbency would be strong for a
long time.

What's interesting is that everybody thought AT&T was the one
with all the sex appeal. We thought it was the most vulnerable to
competition. When the breakup occurred, 28 percent of the value was
in AT&T, with 10 to 11 percent in each of the regional Bells. We sold
AT&T down to about 3 percent in the first year. For the first few
years, we didn't think you'd be able to distinguish among the regional
Bells that well, so we went with the cheapest. We heavily weighted
four of the cheapest and sold off those that seemed to be more popular. For instance, everybody said Nynex was in a big city and was
going to be awful. Therefore, people sold it off and it was cheaper.
That's one of the names we built up. People loved Pac-Tel and Bell
South. We trimmed those off to smaller holdings. We looked for
value disparities in the first few years and were constantly telling
shareholders that there was a real evolution going on. These stocks
were selling at about a 35 percent discount to the S&P 500, yet had
much better earnings. The S&P's earning growth at that time was basically flat. The regional Bells were growing 7 to 9 percent a year,
sometimes more. That was partly because they were allowed some
rate increases. They also cut costs, because they were finally incented
to do so. You saw a lot of cost cutting, layoffs, and so forth. It had a
marvelous impact on margins. As I spent more time on this industry, I
realized this was a more attractive area than I originally thought. It
truly has been fabulous. We've fought off all those who wanted to
change the fund and make it more diversified because we feel this is a
unique opportunity.

Kazanjian: *You've called this "a sector fund with a difference." What
does that mean?*

Behrens: Several things. Many sector funds focus on small companies.
Here you have stocks with huge capitalizations. They are financially sound with some of the characteristics Warren Buffett would
like, including a franchise and positive cash flows. We don't run any
other sector funds here. This one is unique in an area that's full of
opportunity.

Kazanjian: *People think of telephone stocks as being really conservative, dividend-generating instruments. But looked at over time, your
fund has significantly outperformed the S&P 500, which contains
much more aggressive companies.*

Behrens: We've done better from the get-go. Earnings for these companies went up so much during our first few years up and running. You also had big dividends, and the S&P wasn't going anywhere. It was a real opportunity that people didn't anticipate.

Kazanjian: *You recently changed the name and focus of your fund to take advantage of the fast-paced changes in the telecommunications area. Did you see all these changes coming?*

Behrens: In preparing for this interview, I went back and read all of our annual reports for the past 15 years. We really were constantly evolving. One of the first things we articulated that seemed very clear to us in terms of the opportunity was that you had an industry with unit growth, that was growing faster than the gross national product. There is hardly a country in the world where telephone usage, measured by minutes of use or calls, isn't growing faster than the GDP. You also had all these new technologies that were changing the way this business was going to operate. When AT&T was a pure monopoly, it didn't bother to take advantage of these changes. We began moving from analog to digital switches to handle calls. Wireless didn't start for several years but we saw the early cellular phone experiment. Then you had fiber optics starting to branch into the long-distance network with these multiple advances in capacity. You essentially were getting much more productivity out of that same fixed-cost base because of the addition of technology. That resulted in a declining unit cost and expanding volume. Then you had additional features and functions. Call waiting was developed during the 1980s. Then came a whole series of services a digital switch could provide, such as call forwarding, call return, call waiting, and eventually voice mail and caller-ID.

Kazanjian: *All of these added services are pretty profitable for the phone companies, aren't they?*

Behrens: Extremely profitable. They come on top of your basic business. They have almost no marginal cost associated with them.

Kazanjian: *Do you think the original divestiture of AT&T was a good idea?*

Behrens: Yes, I do. It was a real good idea for customers because otherwise I don't think you would have been able to get the company out of its inertia. People complain that the regional Bells drag their feet, and they do. They're capable and competitive, but when you have close to a monopoly, you need incentives to change what you're doing. Deregulation is allowing that to happen. For instance, the regional Bells are now being allowed to provide enhanced services.

Kazanjian: *That's true. But there are so many companies competing for this business today. It's very confusing for consumers to figure out. How will this eventually wind up?*

Behrens: You had big players in the past and you'll have big players in the future. But they'll be different. When the original breakup occurred, you had all these equivalent companies operating in different regions. The only thing that got separated was local and long distance service. Initially, it was easier to get into long distance because of the lower capital required.

Today, with all the mergers and acquisitions, we're going back to the point where everything is vertically integrated, from long-distance to local service. But each company can go into the other's territory. I think we're going to end up with four or five large competitors. One will be AT&T, which will use the cable line to get into the home for local service and will also be able to do what it calls "fixed wireless." That's like cellular, but you have a station in your house and run all your extensions off it. You go from the central office wirelessly to your home, so the streets don't have to be dug up to run wires. For less dense neighborhoods they'll come in with wireless; in dense neighborhoods they'll come over with cable. It's going to be a fully integrated operation, with long distance, local, and wireless.

SBC Corp. [formerly Southwestern Bell], in combination with their earlier acquisitions of Pacific Telesis, Southern New England, and now Ameritech, will cover 60 percent of the nation, but will have 70 percent of the Fortune 500. Because they can follow their customers to the other 30 percent of the country, they can justify spending the money to wire out or buy local independent wire operations in other cities and bring competition to the other regional Bells. Most companies don't want to be in a field of dreams and just build something and hope someone will sign up. You're going to have AT&T and a couple of the big Bells do mergers and offer fully integrated services. I think the best of the current bunch is WorldCom, which merged with MCI. US West is also a major player. You'll have enough of an oligopoly that everybody realizes you've got a big fixed plant and don't want to compete purely on price, because that will drive everybody down. It's like the chemical industry. If somebody builds one more ethylene plant, you suddenly have too much supply and prices fall. Phone service is not a commodity today. In time, it could be, but I really believe that's a 20-year or more proposition.

Kazanjian: *You see these mergers and acquisitions continuing then?*

Behrens: I do, but not at as fast a pace as the last couple of years. I think from here on it's going to be just more of the fringe add-on product. The big moves are 50 percent or more over and will settle in over the next couple of years.

Kazanjian: *You mentioned four big companies—AT&T, Southwestern Bell, US West, and WorldCom. Would you own all four today?*

Behrens: I think the whole group is going to do reasonably well. MCI WorldCom is more expensive, but the earnings are growing so fast that in two years the multiple will be reasonable. It's our favorite right now. We're very focused on managements that really get the job done. Bernie Ebbers at WorldCom has been a master of that. People joke and say that he was originally a coach. I guess early on we all did things that were less sophisticated. But his ability to keep team managers on board through his acquisitions is great. He makes the right kinds of decisions and has avoided areas of the business you don't want to be in.

Kazanjian: *Today's phone company is no longer just the phone company. It's the phone company, Internet provider, and cable company. Is that the wave of the future?*

Behrens: They will definitely be the big communicators. Bundling products is what everyone thinks is the Holy Grail. I don't feel that strongly about it, but it does make a lot of sense. You will keep your customers and reduce what they call "churn" [people logging off to try another carrier] if you tie them up with more products on one billing system. That's been touted as the big concept for a number of years, and it has been difficult to implement. If AT&T can get your long distance and sell you local service on a combined bill, it can then provide your cable TV, connect you to the Internet, and maybe sell you wireless service on a common bill. You're going to be reluctant to log off any one service because of the convenience.

Kazanjian: *Isn't there a risk that these companies are getting into too many things? Companies often get in trouble from becoming so diversified.*

Behrens: I agree with you completely that we've seen so many mistakes in industry from diversification. But it's usually because they buy unrelated business. All of these communications businesses have a fairly common denominator and are going for the same customer. The high-end long-distance user has a lot of communication needs. He or she uses the Internet, call waiting, call forwarding, paging, etc. We talk about ourselves as being technology agnostic. I think successful companies have to be that way. Technology can be bought. It's really managing your customer and your customer's need. We're looking for people and companies that understand that equation.

Kazanjian: *What about the long distance resellers who want us to dial 10–10-whatever or sign up with them for cheaper rates. Will they eventually fall by the wayside?*

Behrens: Yes. I think in every case they've been transitory parasites.

Kazanjian: *Have telephone stocks gone from being stocks for widows and orphans to being more suitable for aggressive investors?*

Behrens: I think the big regional Bells are still selling at a discount, although less of one. Other areas of communications have been very strong performers and are definitely growth stocks. But, yes, they're more aggressive than before and should continue to perform well.

Kazanjian: *What do you think of the company that started all of this, AT&T?*

Behrens: AT&T is a very unusual situation for us. We managed that stock well in the 1980s and early 1990s, but not since 1997. We underestimated the difference Mike Armstrong would make.

Kazanjian: *You sold the stock in 1997.*

Behrens: In fact, our last sale was close to the bottom. As the company's shares took off, we didn't jump back in. I have been slowly taking another position but am kind of mixed. I feel that strategically the right things are going on, yet the execution is a risk. The burden of executing this is very big.

Kazanjian: *You recently had a huge position in America Online, calling it a par excellence company. Do you expect AOL to get into other forms of communications too?*

Behrens: I'm quite confident they will do some deals with a company like AT&T but I'm more interested in the AOL service combined with the high-speed access. I think the company is very smart because it allows all of its partners to share in the action. AOL brings so many customers to the party. It dominates this field, in terms of the number of people who deal with the company. It owns Netscape, CompuServe, and ICQ, which is an internationally popular Website for communicating with people. AOL probably has 100 million customers if you look at all the places people are using one or more of its services.

Kazanjian: *You changed the name of your fund last year. What was the reason for that?*

Behrens: We brought the dividend yield of the fund down gradually because the phone companies themselves stopped growing their dividends and instead were spending money in new areas. We had to go to shareholders and say, "This is not your father's Oldsmobile." It was an evolving change. We couldn't get the income dividends we used to, but got so much more in capital appreciation nobody complained. We had to recognize this was not a dividend-paying industry anymore. It was in a growth phase. We changed the name to recognize that, from the Flag Investors Telephone Income Fund to the Communications Fund. Income and telephone are out. When we did that, we probably didn't change the portfolio more than 10 percent in the next year because it had already evolved in little steps.

Kazanjian: *You've always had a pretty concentrated portfolio.*

Behrens: We typically own 30 to 35 stocks. We don't own a little bit of everything. We own just what makes sense to us.

Kazanjian: *What makes sense to you going forward?*

Behrens: I like companies involved in computer networking, such as Novell and Sun Microsystems. We're going to have telephone service over the IP, which is Internet protocol. All these fields are crossing over into one another's territory. The successful companies will continue to be the ones with the customers, regardless of what they deliver. Companies also have to evolve and offer complementary services.

Kazanjian: *What about cable companies?*

Behrens: We have managed cable stocks poorly. We were right to stay away from them for a very long time. But when Bill Gates made an investment in Comcast, we didn't feel it was that meaningful. He's thrown a billion here, a billion there around pretty easily in the past because he needs friends and he didn't have a whole lot in this area. We didn't see his investment in cable as much more than that. We were wrong. Then, as the stock prices went up, we didn't buy. I think part of our value investor heritage is that once a stock gets expensive, we refuse to chase it. Many times that's a great strength. I look at every dollar we invest and ask what's my expected return on it? Just because it's run up and it's in our sector, I do not feel as if I have to own it.

Kazanjian: *Are you now buying any company involved in communications?*

Behrens: By charter, 65 percent is in the telecommunications field. That could even include media. But I think it's going to continue to have a fairly heavy weighting in traditional telephone companies and closely related products, be it software, hardware, content, or distribution. We've also always held noncommunications stocks, such as Xerox, IBM, and Kodak, for the yield. We no longer have the yield mandate.

Kazanjian: *What are the specific characteristics of your ideal company?*

Behrens: First we look at value. We articulate our investment philosophy as "flexible value." This means we are stock pickers, fundamentalists, and don't invest from the top down. We're flexible and don't have any rigid constraints. So many value managers say, "I will buy only at a low PE and sell at a high PE." They sat out of half of this bull market. That's inexcusable. Ultimately, for us, it comes down to determining the discounted cash flow available on the investment. There are a lot of ways to get that. Sometimes you have to look much further into the future, like with AOL. Other times, as in a more mature business that may be liquidating, buying back stock, or reducing the equity capital, it's more immediate. We like companies that have barriers to entry, proprietary names, and proprietary products. Many times they have huge market shares that they can leverage. Then we look for good management that operationally really knows how to run the business and is financially sophisticated. We also want them to own substantial stock and behave in the share-

holder's interest. So the ideal company has great business characteristics, great management, and sells for a reasonable price. As an old
friend says, "I'll buy a great company at a good valuation or a good
company at a great valuation," meaning cheap. That's what we want
to do.

Kazanjian: *Why do you own so few names?*

Behrens: We try to concentrate our dollars in the best ideas. All of the
ideas are on a continuum. There are probably five you absolutely
love, and another 10 to 15 that are good but maybe not that different
from one another. We really don't believe in the Noah's ark approach
where you have two of everything until you get a whole zoo of stock.
Part of this focus is allowing the winners to run. Traditional value
managers bail out way too soon. There aren't that many great businesses with great managements. I'm going to err on the side of holding them even if they get ahead of themselves. For instance, AOL got
too far ahead of itself and got to be a huge position in the portfolio.
We put only 3 percent of the portfolio in it originally. Our cost was
around $4 a share.

Kazanjian: *At one point AOL was almost 24 percent of the portfolio.*

Behrens: If we hadn't cut back on it, AOL would have been around 30
percent.

Kazanjian: *When do you sell a stock?*

Behrens: It's subjective. We don't believe in any hard, fast rule of
thumb. With AOL the more we got to know that business, just like
the whole telecom industry, the more we liked the various aspects of
it. If you would have asked me my selling point for that stock two
years ago, it would have been a lot lower than it is today. We've allowed ourselves to keep adjusting that. I don't think that's a lack of
discipline, because we always keep asking that question. I think it's a
matter of being willing to try and be objective by constantly asking
what makes sense.

Kazanjian: *Which companies, if any, have you owned in the portfolio
since day one?*

Behrens: One is SBC Communications, Inc. We feel this has been by
far the best managed of the regional Bells. Their financial management is great, and their chief executive has made a few big decisions

well. When SBC announced it was merging with Ameritech, we bought a lot of Ameritech to own more SBC. [Southwestern Bell and Pacific Bell are also subsidiaries of SBC.]

Kazanjian: *What is your vision of the future for the whole communications industry, and how can investors profit from that?*

Behrens: I think you'll see more mergers between domestic and international telecommunications companies, especially as the big guys grow and become more global. It's such a natural. Communications has no boundaries. The players will continue to dominate until the infrastructure loosens. There will be an ongoing marriage between service providers and telecommunications equipment makers, particularly in the heavy switching area, primarily through mergers. I think you'll have companies that offer more computerized equipment and software to drive the growth in networking. There are also some real niches in here. I own a company called Black Box Corporation, which is a distributor of smaller, less sophisticated telecom equipment. Every time you wire an office with a network you must have little plugs, switches, and commodity-type routers. Black Box has a huge catalog of these thousands of parts. What sets it aside is it has developed a wonderful call-in tech-support service area. Whether you're doing it yourself or have your company technicians installing something, you can call these guys and they'll tell you what you need, how to hook it up, etc. We view the satellite business as being attractive. We also distinguish ourselves by saying no to a lot of things we don't understand. If we can't get our arms around it, we'll just avoid it. I'd rather miss an opportunity than actually lose real dollars.

Kazanjian: *What about wireless?*

Behrens: I think it's a tool to accomplish the basic function of communications. We owned AirTouch, which we thought was high quality. [That company has since been purchased by Vodafone.] We also own companies like PageNet and SkyTel, which have highly integrated ways of sending messages.

Kazanjian: *In the future, will we all be walking around with little palm-sized computers with wireless phones, Internet access, and pagers, all in one?*

Behrens: Absolutely. If you stop and think of how you communicated five or ten years ago, it's just breathtaking how everything continues to change, get smaller, and become more convenient. I've got a Palm

Pilot and wouldn't be caught without it. It synchronizes with my computer and calendar at the office. I'm not a gadget geek. This is new to me. I've evolved with this stuff. My comanager, Liam Burke, follows all these technologies.

Kazanjian: *You also manage diversified private accounts. What percentage of the total do you allocate to the communications sector in these portfolios?*

Behrens: From 15 to 30 percent. In these accounts, I own mostly AOL, Ameritech, Cincinnati Bell, and MCI WorldCom.

Kazanjian: *You haven't mentioned the foreign telecommunications companies, many of which are at least partially privatized. Are you attracted to them?*

Behrens: People like foreign telephone companies because they're usually the biggest stock on a given country's exchange and are an easy way to play the country. The most I've had in foreign stocks is about 15 percent back in 1993. Today I'm down to around 6 percent. Here again I felt free to say no to these companies, even though the world was beating a path to our door, saying we'd miss something by not owning them. The biggest problem I've had with many of the big foreign stocks is that they sell only part of the company to the public. The government still keeps a piece to sell later. There is a certain initial success with the stocks because they price them low enough to attract people and give them a good taste so when they sell the second piece, investors will be eager to buy more.

Kazanjian: *People talk about how most of the planet doesn't have a phone. Will the major players in the United States be able to profit from that?*

Behrens: We have 10 billion people in the world, and a pretty high percentage don't have a phone. The problem is a lot of these people don't make enough to afford telephone service. Still, there's no question it's going to be one of the highest growth industries in most countries.

Kazanjian: *Will companies like AT&T and MCI WorldCom be able to take advantage of that opportunity?*

Behrens: Somewhat, but frankly they're not too interested in being pioneers until the market is really ready to pay them for it. They're going after the big cities in Europe, Latin America, and elsewhere where they can build out and tie it in with big customers. Development in smaller countries will be slower. That's where you'll probably leapfrog technology. Telefonos de Mexico had a problem because if it strung a lot of copper wire, it would all be stolen and resold.

Kazanjian: *Your fund is a sector fund. If an investor has a portfolio of diversified funds, do they really need a telecommunication sector fund, or do most general funds have proper exposure here already?*

Behrens: This is a viable group. It's like the mainframe computers of the 1960s, in terms of its importance to the economy. I think you want to have some telecom exposure in every diversified portfolio. Having said that, I literally discourage investors from owning this fund as their single holding. That was acceptable when it was more of a widows-and-orphans fund, but I don't think it's appropriate today.

Kazanjian: *What percentage is? Perhaps 10 to 15 percent?*

Behrens: Maybe even 20 percent, depending upon the level of valuations in the marketplace.

Kazanjian: *If you're an individual investor choosing individual telecommunication stocks, how many should you buy for proper diversification?*

Behrens: It depends on your level of sophistication and what homework you do. In a more traditional portfolio, you probably want around four stocks.

Kazanjian: *Is there anything else about your investment approach you'd like to add?*

Behrens: This fund has definitely evolved over time. Managing it has been a very satisfying experience, both personally and professionally. Often as a general portfolio manager you're moving from group to group and stock to stock. Something you liked five years ago may not be attractive anymore, and you lose some sense of continuity with your industry sectors. Having followed just one sector, I have seen how one-issue oriented Wall Street is. It will say it's either all cable TV or all telephone. Then it's long distance versus local, wireless versus landline, etc. What's really going on is a whole melange of different things. I've developed a real appreciation for how fickle and frankly irresponsible Wall Street can be. Following the telecommunications industry has been breathtaking. In the telephone area, you've had huge changes in technology, regulation, and rewriting the structure of the industry through the divestiture of AT&T, then the cable act, and the telephone act. Supposedly, the FCC someday won't even be regulating this industry. We just try to use a lot of common sense in business judgment. By doing so, we have been able to anticipate some of these changes in advance and have profited from them.

Who would have thought that investing in stodgy telephone stocks could be so profitable? A friend of mine who used to work at a major discount brokerage firm was telling me how he chuckled each time supposedly novice little old ladies would come in with their many stock certificates that resulted from the breakup of AT&T. They would innocently ask, "Are these things worth anything?" Often, they were worth hundreds of thousands, if not millions, of dollars. If only all investments could be this boring!

It seems that even Bruce has been surprised by how well the telephone companies have done over the years. I'm not sure anyone could have predicted how fast these corporations would evolve and grow. Even today, these companies are continually merging and changing their stripes. There is no such thing as a pure "telephone" company anymore. All of the big players are now communications powerhouses.

Although Bruce is arguably now more of a "technology" than a "utility" manager, he's really just kept up with the changing face of the phone companies. After all, corporations like MCI WorldCom are likely to make more money from their involvement in the Internet in the years to come than on long-distance calls, no matter how often you may choose to phone your friends and family. ■

GLEN BICKERSTAFF

TRUST COMPANY OF THE WEST

Back in 1994, while attending a family get-together, my cousin suggested I look into a stock fund managed by a guy named Glen Bickerstaff. He claimed it had consistently trounced the S&P 500. "What's the name of this fund," I asked. "I'm not sure," he replied. "But it's a Transamerica fund." I immediately went home and did a search on both Glen Bickerstaff and Transamerica, but couldn't find a single match. It turns out this fund did exist, but it was available only to employees of Transamerica, including my cousin, as part of their retirement plan.

Fortunately, the folks at Transamerica realized that the rest of the public would also be interested in tapping into this Fund's great record. So when the company launched its own retail fund in October 1995, Glen was selected as its manager. After two successful years at the helm of Transamerica Premier Equity, Glen hopped across town to manage money at the Los Angeles-based Trust Company of the West. In addition to running separate accounts, which have a minimum requirement of $100 million, he runs the TCW Galileo Select Equity Fund.

Technically, Glen doesn't qualify to be among my panel of Wizards, since he's been running a retail mutual fund only since October 1995. (I was demanding a published record of outperformance dating back at least five years.) However, his long-term public record is so good, I made a slight exception in this case. After all, he has outperformed the S&P 500 11 of the 12 years he's been running money, falling behind only slightly in 1989. I don't know of any other manager with a record like that, including Peter Lynch. Had Glen's fund been offered to the public sooner, he might be the most popular fund manager around.

What's unusual is that, for the most part, this 43-year-old is self-taught and has done a brilliant job of making money ever since he got into the business. His secret, he says, is concentrating in a small number of names and buying only those companies with a demonstrated record of success.

Kazanjian: *It's always fun talking to a fellow USC Trojan. When did you first start learning about the stock market?*

Bickerstaff: In high school. We played a stock market game where we tracked stocks over the course of a semester. I grew curious about investing in general. I was looking for a way to make my money work for me as opposed to the other way around. In college, I took securities analysis and other courses that got me pointed toward the stock market. I always thought it would be fun to be the person who got to make the key decisions and to be considered an expert in an area. In investing, analysts typically concentrate on a sector or industry and become the experts in their areas of focus. As a portfolio manager, it's really a question of whether you can distill all that information, add your own analysis, and make the best investment decisions over a long time period.

Kazanjian: *Did you major in business in college?*

Bickerstaff: I did. I got a business degree at USC in 1980. Finance and business economics were my areas of emphasis.

Kazanjian: *What was your first job?*

Bickerstaff: I started in the trust investment department at Security Pacific Bank as a research analyst. I followed different industry groups and made recommendations to the portfolio managers. That was interesting, but I wasn't in a position where I could make the ultimate decision. There's a natural tendency for analysts to want to become portfolio managers, since, as a manager, you're the one pulling the trigger. I eventually got the chance, in 1983, to manage money at the bank's spin-off investment firm in San Diego. You never stop being an analyst, though, because you're analyzing businesses to put in your portfolios. Since I'm not the world's best delegator, I always wanted to have a hand in the analysis. I ultimately got a chance to manage money primarily for individuals. That was valuable because there's nothing more humbling than having a meeting with the individual whose assets you're managing and getting the impression very quickly that this is real money from real people. It's important that you take it very seriously.

Kazanjian: *What happened next?*

Bickerstaff: I spent about 18 months at a start-up firm in Orange County. One of the two partners was a friend of mine going back to high school. That firm was small and was growing slowly at the time. I joined Transamerica in September 1987. That's when my track record really begins because ever since I have continuously been managing comingled portfolios and separate accounts.

Kazanjian: *What were you hired to do at Transamerica?*

Bickerstaff: To be the principal equity manager for an insurance company separate account. It was a comingled product that was available to outside qualified plans. About a year later I was given the domestic equity portion of Transamerica Corporation's own pension plan. The insurance company separate account continued to grow pretty significantly. It was then made an option for Transamerica's own internal 401(k) plan. In 1995, we formed a new family of mutual funds, and the flagship fund was cloned from the insurance company separate account that I'd managed going all the way back to 1987. It was called Transamerica Premier Equity Fund.

Kazanjian: *You left Transamerica to join Trust Company of the West in 1998. What was the reason for the change?*

Bickerstaff: A dramatically better opportunity came along that met all my criteria. I didn't have to leave southern California, and TCW provided a great platform on which to grow and be successful at both the mutual fund business and investment counseling business. We had very little, if any, exposure to investment counseling at Transamerica. We had no marketing to institutions. Moving over here was a way to capitalize on the enormous level of resources that TCW makes available to its portfolio managers. The infrastructure is here to grow the assets we manage while continuing to generate outstanding returns. I don't think those opportunities would have been available at Transamerica.

Kazanjian: *TCW manages money mostly for large institutions. What's your minimum for an individual account?*

Bickerstaff: It's $100 million for institutional portfolios. Our TCW Galileo Select Equities Fund has a $2,000 minimum.

Kazanjian: *In fact, you came over to manage the TCW Galileo Select Equity Fund. TCW is not that well known as a fund family to the general public?*

Bickerstaff: We're trying to establish a much bigger presence. We have had expertise in the institutional area for many years. We're making this same offering available to individuals through the funds.

Kazanjian: *Where did you initially learn how to invest?*

Bickerstaff: That question has two different answers. I believe very strongly that a good portion of being successful at this is your own makeup and personality, what you emphasize, what you value, things like that. The other part of it is more specific to how you apply those things and what characteristics you look for in businesses. Some of that was clearly learned on the job because the more businesses you look at, the more you can differentiate a good one from a bad one, or a great one from a pretty good one. I came to this business with a certain collection of analytical, strategic, and psychological skills that I think have worked to my benefit . Along the way I picked up a lot of specific business analytical skills.

Kazanjian: *Do you think you were a good investor when you first arrived at Transamerica, or were you still learning on the job at that point?*

Bickerstaff: I think you're always learning, but I had a pretty good model in my mind for how this should work. It really was structured around a core philosophy that I've had for quite a while, which is that real wealth is created in the stock market by owning great businesses for long periods of time and effectively participating in their success year after year. If you look backward at some of the great wealth that's been created in the stock market, it has happened in individual stocks that have gone up many times over many years. I've always thought you should be moving your portfolio toward identifying and owning as many of those stocks as you can with the full understanding that there aren't a lot of great businesses out there. What characteristics are there in businesses that make them tremendous long-term success stories? I've grown to view the managements of businesses, their track record, and their ability to effectively recreate their success or reinvent themselves as being very important. One expression I use is you look for patterns of perfection. You can do that in any field. You look for people who have been successful and find out why they were successful. Then you ask if it's something that's likely to be repeated.

Kazanjian: *It sounds like the book* In Search of Excellence *by Tom Peters.*

Bickerstaff: I haven't read that book, but I've heard a great deal about it. It's very similar. My understanding is that what Peters was after was these kinds of patterns of perfection, believing that success breeds success and really clever people generally don't lose that talent overnight. They figure out new ways to make their businesses grow and stay ahead of the competition. Ultimately that's the challenge— staying ahead of the competition. You hope those advantages are firmly entrenched. That is at the core of what I do. I want the business model to be superior, in an area that's growing rapidly, and where the market share is rising. There are many different data points to tell you that you have something different, unique, or special.

Kazanjian: *Break these down for us.*

Bickerstaff: A great business is one that has a readily identifiable business advantage, which is to say they do things systematically better than the competition and it shows up over and over again. Those kinds of advantages are usually in a couple of categories. One would be a product advantage because you have an offering that's different, unique, or proprietary. The company has developed a way to do something that's superior, whether it's patented or by process. Either way, it's extremely difficult to replicate. That's the foundation of a great business model. The other trait is that a company finds a more efficient way to do something, which I call a cost-structure advantage. You're the low cost producer, manufacturer, or distributor. If you are, those things tend to reinforce themselves as you add scale to the business. I think of it like this: Most businesses are extremely competitive. If you don't have the product advantage I described, if you don't have the best product, someone else does. If you don't have the lowest cost structure or aren't the lowest cost producer, someone else is. So if you're not enjoying one of those two advantages, at best you are likely to be a second-tier company. The leaders in most businesses or industries have those advantages. They have figured out how to develop and maintain them over time and have capitalized on them over and over again. That's at the core of, to me, what a great business is. The work I do is generally focused on identifying those advantages and discovering how they get perpetuated over time. What are the barriers to entry, and how difficult are they to replicate.

Kazanjian: *Are these great businesses almost always large companies?*

Bickerstaff: Not necessarily. I think the profile is usually reasonably big, in the sense that they're probably not micro-cap or small-cap. It takes a while for a business to establish the kind of enduring advantage I look for. It's probably from the midsized company up. There can be small companies that have created better business models and have a tremendous advantage, but the probability that it's enduring is lower for a small company than for one that's done it for many years. The ideal situation is a company going through the transition from small- and midsized to really large. Looking back at some of the great success stories out there, you could say they've been able to become really large because they have these inherent advantages that are multiplied manyfold and get better and bigger as the scale of the business grows.

Kazanjian: *Looking back over your career, give me a few examples of that.*

Bickerstaff: One would be Dell Computer, which was a reasonably small business when I first acquired it in February 1994. I thought Dell's business model was clearly superior. It was based on direct distribution, and it was the low-cost distributor. What's interesting is that that advantage actually widened over time because Dell got better and better at refining its own direct distribution model. Dell's advantage got wider because the competition couldn't catch up. If you sell indirect through a third-party distributor, in order to sell direct you have to compete with your own customer. That prevents people from moving quickly to this model. In the meantime Dell is refining its distribution model at a very rapid rate, continually finding lower

cost-distribution capabilities and managing working capital more efficiently. Dell's inventory turns have gone from six and seven times a
year to over 50 times a year.

Kazanjian: *How difficult is it for someone to overtake these companies. Don't they eventually lose their leadership position?*

Bickerstaff: It's so difficult to overtake or even catch up with those
businesses that they usually enjoy this extraordinary position for a
long time. Can they be overtaken? Sure, because things always
change. But you invest in them because they have that advantage in
their favor, and the probability of being surpassed is pretty low over a
relevant time horizon of a number of years. A decade from now, will
it still be the same? I don't know. But for the foreseeable investment
horizon, out several years, I think that's exactly why this is so appealing to me. You can have a high degree of confidence that it's not
likely to be surpassed in that time frame. In a way, that's the whole
point of my approach. I'm looking for those things that are very unlikely to get surpassed. Usually what happens is these businesses continue to take market share, have high and rising profit margins, and
it's just a manifestation of the advantages they enjoy. That's at the
core of what I emphasize in picking stocks.

Kazanjian: *Are there businesses like this in every industry?*

Bickerstaff: Generally speaking, yes. You can almost always identify
the best business in any area. There are certainly areas that are less interesting and where having the biggest advantage might not be that
meaningful. That's the other element of my philosophy. I look for an
industry where there are secular changes taking place that allow
someone with a better business model to have an open-ended opportunity for growth. The impact of that can be enormous on the company's financial structure. It's nice to be the best at something, but it's
really nice to be the best at something where dramatic changes are
taking place. In some industries, you find the best businesses are creating the change. Effectively they are capitalizing on the very changes
they are creating in their industries. An example of that in the financial services area is Charles Schwab. Schwab has dramatically
changed the way financial services are distributed to individuals.
Schwab is not only creating that change, but is also the biggest beneficiary of that change. They recognized early on that individuals

wanted more say about their own investment decisions, so they set out to provide the most information and easiest facility for individuals to transact business. That's been incredibly powerful. If you look at their asset growth in customer accounts and their market share, it's pretty significant how fast the company has grown. I think this reflects Schwab's creative product offerings and lower cost distribution model. By building this superior model, they're effectively creating change in their business. It's enormously powerful when you have the combination of those things.

Kazanjian: *Why is it so hard for the competition to overtake the leader? A lot of these little guys seem to come up with new, bright ideas but never can outfox the big guys. Is it because the large companies just adapt to them?*

Bickerstaff: That's one answer. Another is simply inertia. Inertia is one of the most powerful forces in the universe. Unseating customers is extremely difficult to begin with. As a business gets bigger, it does have the opportunity to copy, for lack of a better word, the advances its competitors make. If I am Schwab and someone improves upon my business model, there's no reason I can't incorporate that change into my offerings and still continue to enjoy competitive advantages.

The other thing happening now is we're in a period of very low inflation. In this environment, larger businesses generally have advantages because they are typically more efficient. I know it sounds silly because a lot of times large means bureaucracy and inefficiency, but large companies have the financial wherewithal to make major productivity investments in their own businesses, at least the clever ones do. As they do that in a period of little inflation or pricing power, there's no room for a smaller, less efficient company without these scale advantages to ever catch up. You're likely to see them attempt to raise prices enough to produce the kind of profitability that a larger business already has. I think this low inflation environment we've been in will continue for quite a while. It's very advantageous for large market share companies. People have talked about the performance divergence between small-cap and large-cap and why large-cap stocks have done so well. I think it's a reflection of how successful big businesses are at keeping and maintaining market share in a low inflation environment. I think a lot of this differentiation in the market has been a rational revaluation of these successful large businesses.

Kazanjian: *Say you've found a company, like Schwab or Dell, that you identify as being a leader with a great product. What other analysis do you do on the company to decide if it's a good stock to buy?*

Bickerstaff: I next look into the financial fundamentals of the business, to see if those advantages are being manifested in the financial results of the company. The most direct way you can identify that is by looking at market share. The business models we target typically grow revenues faster than their competitors, which is another way of saying they are taking market share. To me it's almost an airtight case that an advantage exists if you're showing significant growth in market share. It's very difficult to believe a company will be able to take market share for long unless it has something different or unique about its product offering. Rising market share is effectively proof that a business model advantage exists.

Then I look at profit margins and changes in profitability. Again, a company with sustainably high and rising profit margins is probably enjoying a business model advantage. The competition simply won't allow you to enjoy much higher margins unless you're offering something that's different or unique. We look at superior top-line growth, rising market share, and high and rising profitability as effective proof that a business advantage exists and that a company is clearly capitalizing on that advantage.

Kazanjian: *Just so I'm clear, you're comparing the profit margins from the company you're examining to those of its competitors?*

Bickerstaff: Definitely, and the fact that they are rising is important.

Kazanjian: *What about other items on the balance sheet, such as book value?*

Bickerstaff: Book value is generally pretty uninformative, because it often does not reflect the real value of the assets. Other balance sheet information, such as debt levels and what capital structure a business has, especially over the long term, can give you a good indication of whether the business consumes capital rapidly. Obviously, all things being equal, you'd much rather have a business that doesn't consume a lot of capital because the returns on that incremental capital would be very high. All businesses would like to generate very high returns on incremental capital. If a company requires a lot of leverage or debt in order to experience rapid growth, it's less valuable than a business that doesn't require external capital.

Kazanjian: *How does the role of management come into play?*

Bickerstaff: As we discussed, management is part of the initial analysis, in the sense that you want to see if the actions of management are proving their ability. Have they created and sustained a business model advantage? The other way to look at it is on a financial basis. What are the returns on capital on an incremental basis? After all, the principal role of management is to profitably redeploy capital in the business. I look at what management is able to do with this incremental capital and what kind of returns they generate.

Kazanjian: *Do you require meetings with management and onsite visits before investing?*

Bickerstaff: We typically have meetings with management face-to-face, but to literally be on-site with them is not a requirement. We need a good understanding about who's making the decisions and what they believe their competitive advantages are. You can't get away from the fact that these are the human beings making the most critical decisions, and we must evaluate their skills. Obviously access to them on an ongoing basis is helpful. We do that through face-to-face meetings, via teleconference, and electronically. There are many managements out there that can tell a wonderful story but can't ever bring it to the bottom line. We like to see proof in the financials.

Kazanjian: *What about the final step of your research process, which is valuation?*

Bickerstaff: Once I've found an attractive business, I must determine whether it's attractively valued. Is there incremental opportunity for me as an investor from here? It's nice to recognize that a business is superior, but you have to understand it's only going to give you a superior rate of return based on the price that you pay for it. How I examine valuation has evolved over time, but in essence it is an effort to determine the value of the entire business to an informed buyer. Valuations in the stock market, especially on a short-term basis, can be volatile and may not reflect the true value of a business. Over the long term, valuations in the stock market will gravitate toward a cash-flow-based value. We call our specific valuation metric "cap rate," or the rate at which a buyer would capitalize the ongoing cash flows of the business. This represents the pre-tax rate of return one will earn on the capital required to purchase the entire business. The actual calculation is pre-tax cash flow divided by enterprise value, or as I call it, the all-in cost of owning the business.

Kazanjian: *Define those two terms.*

Bickerstaff: Pre-tax cash flow starts with operating income. We add back noncash charges, such as depreciation and amortization, subtract maintenance level capital spending, or the capital requirement necessary to maintain the current level of operation. You don't include all capital spending because incremental invested capital is going to have some future return associated with it and it wouldn't make sense to count one without measuring the other. Since we don't necessarily have a real good feel for what that return is, we don't put it in the calculation. The denominator is enterprise value, which is typically the market cap of the equity plus any debt on the balance sheet, less any cash or marketable securities or things readily converted to cash on the balance sheet. If we were acquiring the whole business, it would effectively be our all-in cost.

Kazanjian: *What does that ratio tell you?*

Bickerstaff: It tells me on a pre-tax basis what the cash on cash return of the business is as it is currently structured. Why is that valuable? Because, one, it's pre-tax, so we can relate it to other potential investments, including real estate or fixed-income rates. It gives us some sense of the return we earn for an incremental investment dollar on a current operation basis. Typically the numerator of that equation grows, we hope rapidly. If it does, your cap rate is going up all the time, assuming the stock price stays the same. Let's say the numerator, pre-tax cash flow of the business, is $10; the total cost of the business is $100; and we're getting a 10 percent cash on cash return. In year two we still paid $100 for the business, but the cash flow grows to $12 and we'd now have a 12 percent return on our investment. If the numerator grows, we effectively earn a higher and higher rate of return. Think of a bond with a growing coupon. The bond has a price of par. If the coupon goes up the next year, the bond's probably worth more than par.

Kazanjian: *You're comparing the number you get from this exercise to the current market price?*

Bickerstaff: That's correct. The current market price in the sense of what the enterprise value is. The denominator gives me a price as if I were acquiring the whole business. The numerator tells me what pre-tax cash flow I effectively have discretion over or access to for owning the whole business.

Kazanjian: *Are you looking to buy the company at a certain minimum discount to what you think it's worth?*

Bickerstaff: That number moves around over time. The reason we invest in anything is to have more wealth tomorrow than we have today. The thing that erodes our wealth over time is inflation. Inflation is the ultimate arbiter of what rates we should be willing to accept as our investment return. As inflation and interest rates come down, valuations should go up because the cap rate on a business is nothing more than the rate of return we're earning, just the same way the current yield is on a debt instrument. With inflation low, and moving lower in my estimation, valuations should be moving higher. With inflation at zero or one percent, the cap rate on businesses that trade in the public market should and have been coming down pretty meaningfully over the last few years. Five-plus years ago, average cap rates were in the 8 to 10 percent range. Now they're around 5 or 6 percent. We've heard a lot in the last few years about valuations in the market being extreme, and they are higher than they used to be. But inflation is lower, and so are interest rates. Why would anybody pay us a 10 percent rate of return when inflation is only 2 percent? The answer is they wouldn't, at least not for long. So we should't expect 10 percent cap rates on the best businesses in America. You've seen a precipitous decline in interest rates and should see a further decline in the rates of return that all financial investments give, including stocks.

Kazanjian: *Yet stock prices have been going up in this low inflation environment.*

Bickerstaff: Right. The valuations are moving up because we'll accept higher valuations or lower rates of return because inflation is going down. Remember that earnings power has also been going up dramatically because the economy has been strong. The valuation shift in the market, in my opinion, has been rational.

Kazanjian: *Going forward do you think we can continue to enjoy great returns in the market?*

Bickerstaff: I wouldn't expect to have the same returns in the next five years that we've had in the last five. I think that expectation would be too high. By the same token, I think that the outlook for equity returns remains favorable. We have sustainably low inflation and strong economic growth. That's another way of saying that productivity in the economy has been exploding. I think that's been generally undermeasured and underappreciated. I do believe that we can have good stock market returns for the foreseeable future. Obviously there will be periods when the market goes down. We'll always have those short-term fluctuations. But I think the basis you start from is if the market is reasonably priced right now, going forward you should expect the returns from stocks to continue to be very good. What could go wrong is that, for whatever reason, inflation becomes a meaningful problem again, pushing interest rates higher and valuations down, or earnings are disappointing because economic growth shows dramatically. We had a tremendous valuation catch-up take place because businesses were extremely undervalued going back five years since the fear of inflation was much greater than what materialized. I think the realization that inflation isn't going to be a problem for the economy will allow us to see decent stock market returns for the foreseeable future.

Kazanjian: *I'm sure some of your companies have disappointed you. What's the main reason a company you think is great turns out not to be?*

Bickerstaff: There are two reasons. One, I'm simply wrong in my analysis and the advantages I thought were there aren't enduring. Two, the advantages I thought were there never existed. In other words, the company was successful for all the wrong reasons as opposed to being successful for repeatable good reasons.

Kazanjian: *What's the main reason a company loses its competitive advantage?*

Bickerstaff: It simply doesn't see change coming and fails to adapt quickly enough to whatever is changing about the marketplace. Again, let's say I'm the leading company in a given area. I should, if I'm paying attention, be able to see what's changing and come up with better solutions than a business without those advantages. In fact, I should constantly be looking for ways to improve my own business. I should consistently be reinvesting to sustain and expand my competitive advantages.

Kazanjian: *What makes you sell a stock?*

Bickerstaff: There are three reasons to sell a stock. One, the stock price goes up so much that it fully reflects my most optimistic view of the future financial results. In most cases like that I usually trim the stock back as a percentage of the portfolio but don't necessarily eliminate it. That is a function of my belief that these high-quality businesses tend to constantly outperform even my expectations. It's also a reflection of experience. Why would I give up my position in a company like Schwab simply because the stock price goes up a lot? Often, business fundamentals are improving even faster. Maybe what I should do is reduce my position, so if it has a valuation change on the downside it won't impact the portfolio as greatly.

Still, I likely would maintain a position as long as the business model advantages persist, being open to the possibility that investors are being overly conservative in their outlook for the company. The second reason to sell is in order to finance the purchase of a new stock. I always stay fully invested. This technique effectively becomes my optimization strategy, because it forces me to look at other companies already in the portfolio, identify the weak link in the chain, and sell it before making the new purchase.

The third reason to sell, which is by far my least favorite, is that everything goes wrong. Another way to say it is my fundamental analysis of the business turns out to be incorrect. The advantages don't exist, management hasn't been able to sustain or capitalize on them, the financial fundamentals that I expected don't materialize, there are persistent revenue and earnings disappointments, etc. It all falls in the same category, which is simply that the fundamental prospects of the business deteriorate. When that happens, whether the stock price has gone up or down, you should sell because the reasons you bought it to begin with aren't true. Those are the three reasons to ever take a stock out of the portfolio.

Kazanjian: *Your turnover is pretty low.*

Bickerstaff: Yes. Turnover since my days at Transamerica has averaged about 25 percent a year. I typically own about 30 stocks, so you're talking about selling on average six to eight stocks a year. Some of that turnover is caused by taking positions down as a percentage of the portfolio.

Kazanjian: *Do you try to be tax efficient?*

Bickerstaff: I think the way I invest is inherently tax efficient. I have low turnover and tend to stay with my gains for as long as the business fundamentals warrant it. Having said that, I believe I should make decisions for investment reasons, not tax reasons. I wouldn't force a decision in the portfolio based on tax considerations, because that will yield less efficient long-term investment decisions even though it might be more tax efficient in the short-term.

Kazanjian: *Why do you hold such a concentrated portfolio?*

Bickerstaff: I want my best ideas to have a big impact on the portfolio. I need to be willing to make a 5 percent or greater commitment to an individual business in the portfolio and then live with the results. I'm supposed to differentiate myself from the index. In order to be different from the index I literally have to be willing to have my portfolio look significantly different. One of the ways you do that is by concentrating it. If you have 100 or 200 stocks in the portfolio, it's very difficult to differentiate yourself versus an index. I think I'm likely to have an opportunity to generate extraordinary returns if my portfolio looks significantly different from the index. The other reason I concentrate is there simply aren't that many great businesses. Obviously it's a double-edged sword because if I'm wrong it's going to have a negative impact on the portfolio. I think over a long period my batting average has been sufficiently high that a concentrated approach is very much warranted. From a philosophical point of view I want the companies in which I have a great degree of confidence to have a big impact on the portfolio. I don't believe I can effectively differentiate what I do if I'm not willing to make significant investments in relatively fewer companies.

Kazanjian: *Do you focus on certain sectors?*

Bickerstaff: Not inherently, but in fact there have been areas of concentration in the portfolio where I find the greatest number of companies experiencing the kinds of business advantages and growth characteristics I target.

Kazanjian: *Where would those areas be right now?*

Bickerstaff: Technology is about a third of the portfolio. Financial services and health care are other areas of emphasis.

Kazanjian: *What about the Internet?*

Bickerstaff: If you mean direct investment in companies that make the Internet their only business, I haven't invested there. The business models of those companies are relatively untested. But I do believe the Internet is one of the most powerful changes in business in my investment experience. My portfolio has capitalized on the Internet through companies with great business models and smart management who are using the Internet as a way to change their own business model. Dell and Schwab are classic examples of that. Virtually every business you look at these days is utilizing the Internet in one way or another to capitalize on lowering its own cost structure.

Kazanjian: *You have an incredibly long record of outperforming the S&P 500. Most active managers have not been able to do that, or even come close. Why is that?*

Bickerstaff: I think there are a lot of reasons most managers underperform. I've worked with and around enough portfolio managers to have seen some good ones and some bad ones. I think the most common trait of people who underperform is that they don't have any particular discipline that gives them a systematic way to make decisions more or less the same over time. They get whipped around by changes in psychology. That is a recipe for disaster. One of the strengths of what I do is that I am pretty unyielding in looking for great businesses and figuring out what their characteristics are. Otherwise I feel as if I'm hoping they'll do well as opposed to being confident that they will. If I have a rule in investing it's don't hope. Have as much evidence going in your favor as possible. That's why I like business models with proprietary characteristics, since you generally have things going in your direction. That's a discipline I tend to be very strict about. I think many managers view investing as participating in the stock market as opposed to investing in real businesses. What happens if you focus on the stock market is you get bombarded with a lot of different information and have analysts in every industry telling you what's right and wrong. If you don't have a firm footing in your own philosophy you're likely to be unduly influenced by those opinions. From a psychological point of view, I think most investment managers fail to beat the index because they force themselves to make a lot of decisions. If I make a few decisions a year about businesses that I'm really confident in, I can have a pretty high batting average.

Kazanjian: *What you do sounds so simple, in terms of just looking for these great businesses. You'd think everybody would be doing this.*

Bickerstaff: I believe one of the strengths of what I do is its simplicity. Obviously, the devil's in the details in deciding and figuring out what great businesses are. It requires a lot of research and judgment. But at least I'm structuring the endeavor to give myself the highest chance to succeed. This is a common-sense, logical, disciplined approach. I can't imagine another way I would invest. I know many managers have different styles, but to me identifying great companies and participating in their success over a long period of time is what investing is all about. If you go back hundreds of years it's what merchant bankers did. They went around and found really clever entrepreneurs, gave them some capital, and participated in their success. That's all the stock market allows us to do. The beauty of it is we don't have to run the business or manage the minutia and the detail. We just have to identify which people are going to be successful.

Kazanjian: *Where do you find most of your ideas?*

Bickerstaff: The only accurate answer is everywhere. There are thousands of stocks out there. It can be from my own empirical observation about what's happening in the economy, or from the input of people I work with. It can be from company managements, Wall Street research firms, or many of other potential sources. But that's where the process only starts. It takes a while for me to get comfortable with a business, and I'm not going to buy a business the first time I hear about it. It takes time to look at its history, understand how it has changed, and figure out whether the people making decisions today are the same people who made decisions before. The process isn't any different from someone selecting an investment manager. You want to look at the results the manager has achieved. Is there a pattern of success? Are the same people making the decisions who used to make the decisions? Where you initially hear about an idea is a lot less important than what you do with a great idea once you find it.

Kazanjian: *Do you ever buy foreign companies?*

Bickerstaff: Very rarely. Generally, they're outside of what I consider to be my area of expertise, which is domestic businesses. I find plenty of opportunities in U.S. companies, and it's rare that I venture much outside that.

Kazanjian: *Would you be comfortable with someone owning your fund alone for their entire portfolio?*

Bickerstaff: As long as the person's investment horizon were sufficiently long. If it's someone who's a year from retirement with no future income stream, he or she should probably have no money in my discipline. If it's someone who is 30 years old with 30 years plus to go before retirement, from my point of view this is the way that makes sense to me to invest and therefore it's the way I would invest all of their long-term assets.

Kazanjian: *You manage about $8 billion, between your fund and private accounts. That's an awful lot of money for such a small number of stocks. Is there a point where you won't be able to be as effective because you have to put so much money to work?*

Bickerstaff: I don't think I'm anywhere near that point, but I do believe there's a practical limit to this. Since I typically buy larger businesses, I feel I can manage substantially more than I do now and still be equally effective. The obvious answer is that at some point there's a practical limit to the assets we can manage. I don't know if it's $10 billion, $15 billion or $20 billion, but we are monitoring that very closely.

Kazanjian: *In fact, you have a clause in your employment contract that states you can close your fund at any time.*

Bickerstaff: That's correct. I have discretion over when the growth stops. It isn't just the amount of assets, it's also the number of account relationships. I do have large institutional clients in addition to the fund, and they require service. I don't want to be taken away from what I enjoy, which is analyzing and making investment decisions. If assets somehow were to grow to a size that would impair that, our performance would suffer. Then our clients would grow tired of the fact that we couldn't provide performance anymore and would find someone else to run their money. I'm very interested in having a continued successful track record, so I'm not going to compromise my ability to do this with the same quality I think I've done it in the past for any reason.

Kazanjian: *Does the overall market factor much into how you put your portfolio together?*

Bickerstaff: It's almost exclusively done on a company-by-company basis. The one thing the market contributes is opportunity. Sometimes in market declines you get the chance to buy a business at a price you think is extremely attractive. Paying attention to what's going on in the market is helpful in identifying opportunities that you might have one day versus another day. But the market itself is significantly less interesting to me than individual companies.

I think you'll be hearing a lot more about this soft-spoken investment pro in the years to come. As I mentioned in the introduction, Glen has the best long-term record of consistently outperforming the S&P 500 of any manager that I know of. Glen's formula seems so simple: Look for companies with a history of success and good management. It's what he calls "patterns of perfection." But, as he points out, the devil is in the details. It takes a great deal of skill to separate the really great businesses from those that are just enjoying spurts of short-term success.

Glen is definitely a manager to keep your eyes on. He's young, committed, and competitive. He has also vowed not to take on more money than he can handle, an important consideration should the public start catching on to his great record and flooding him with new cash. ■

JAMES CALLINAN

RS INVESTMENT MANAGEMENT

Jim Callinan has always been a pretty aggressive guy. He played on the football team at Harvard and became one of the school's all-time leading rushers. He then went into accounting and dug deep into companies looking for potential fraud. In one case, he found it at his future employer, the parent company of the Putnam Funds, where he eventually landed a job following small, aggressive companies. (More on that in the interview.)

Jim's public mutual fund record goes back to 1994, when he took over Putnam OTC Emerging Growth. He immediately led the fund to market-beating returns, trouncing the S&P 500 by 18 percentage points in 1995. That strong performance caught the eye of Robertson Stephens Investment Management, which was looking for someone to take over its flagship Emerging Growth Fund. The fund had begun to struggle, after its long-time manager began to stray into larger companies. After a series of interviews, Robertson Stephens' management decided Jim was their man to save the struggling fund. Despite a difficult start, Jim has done exactly that, growing the fund's assets from $210 million in 1996 to more than $3.5 billion today. In the process, he has left his small-cap competitors in the dust, by beating just about every benchmark in sight, despite the fact that this area of the market was out of favor for many years.

Jim has some impressive academic credentials to back up his performance. He earned both a bachelor's degree in economics and an MBA from Harvard, along with a master's in accounting from New York University. In 1999, Jim and three of his fellow Robertson Stephens managers bought the firm from Nation's Bank and renamed it RS Investment Management. It was a fitting move, considering that this 38-year-old has dreamed of one day owning his own business from the time he was a little boy. Jim demands strong growth from the companies he buys, often in the range of 30 to 50 percent, and doesn't have much patience for underperformance. The turnover in his fund was around 120 percent last year, but being picky has definitely paid off.

Kazanjian: *You must be a pretty smart guy since you have three degrees, including two from Harvard. All of your degrees are in either accounting or economics, so I take it you have a keen interest in numbers.*

Callinan: I always wanted to get into business. My father and grandfather were both doctors. What I liked about their careers was that they were self-employed. I wanted to do something where I could have my own business, be a decision maker, and employ lots of people at some point.

Kazanjian: *Were you an entrepreneur as a kid?*

Callinan: No. I hated my paper route. I didn't mind physical labor but disliked mundane jobs.

Kazanjian: *Did you have any idea of the kind of business you wanted to start?*

Callinan: I just knew I wanted to be in business. I didn't like medicine and hated the sight of blood. My father kept me out of medicine and drilled into me early on that there were too many lawyers.

Kazanjian: *So you wound up at Harvard as an economics major instead?*

Callinan: Yes. You can do one of two things with an economics degree: go into sales or get more education. I went to New York and did a hybrid. I worked at Arthur Andersen during the day on the accounting side and then went to New York University business school at night. I took accounting and finance classes and graduated with a masters in accounting. At the time, the NYU business school was at Trinity Place, which is right across street from the old Trinity Church at the foot of Wall Street. I used to walk through the churchyard and on to Wall Street. It was extremely exciting to see traders from the floor out smoking cigarettes or talking. The bankers would be in their suits discussing stocks. I'd walk out there at night on my way to class and think about what a great place it was. That August, in 1982, the market went through 1,000 for the first time in a decade. My father was running his own pension plan for his employees. He had four offices around Cleveland. He would call me up and talk stocks every night until I started really liking stocks. I had a lot of friends from Harvard who were in investment banking. They talked about mergers, acquisitions, and doing LBOs in the early 1980s. It was a stimulating environment that was very much focused on the stock market. Even though the general public was not interested in the stock market, I was exposed to it very early in the bull run.

Kazanjian: *Yes, it certainly wasn't like today where everybody, including the butcher and beautician, is involved in the market.*

Callinan: There was no CNBC. I guess there was a *Wall $treet Week* at the time, but that seemed pretty new, too.

Kazanjian: *When did you buy your first stock?*

Callinan: In the fall of 1982. I bought Mylan Labs based on a tip from my father. This was an early generic drug company. Dad was buying it for his pension fund. The stock went up eightfold. I was bitten.

Kazanjian: *You then went on to Harvard for an MBA?*

Callinan: Yes. Something happened that propelled me to change careers when I was working on a Marsh & McLennan audit at Arthur Andersen. We actually found alleged fraud in the treasury department. The company has certain accounts where you own cash for 60 days, but at the end of that time have to pay it out to somebody as a fiduciary. The head of the department was investing in the "when-issued" repo market with this money. ["When-issued repos" are derivative securities of the U.S. government that have not yet been issued. Traders speculate beforehand on what the pricing will be "when (they are) issued."] Unfortunately, she was betting wrong, as interest rates rose, causing her prices to fall. She was getting margin calls and stuffing the trade tickets under the floor, into shoeboxes, under her desk, anywhere but in the files. She was hiding the issues in an asset account. We accountants couldn't reconcile where the assets were coming from or where they were. We knew she was sending cash to the brokerage firms, buying these when-issued securities, but they were really margin calls. No one could figure this out because the accounting system controls were so poor.

Finally, it was rumored that the day after the audit ended, a top official of Marsh & McLennan was having dinner at the Harvard Club of New York. One of the top salesmen at a brokerage firm said, "Do you know you have a $2.5 billion repo position, and are losing $25 million a day because interest rates are going against you?" It turns out they had an unrecognized $265 million loss as a result of that position. The more salient feature of the story for me was the fact that Marsh & McLennan hired traders from Morgan Stanley to outsource the portfolio and liquidate it without serious price impact. I had to work with them because they didn't really know where all the bonds were and I was one of the auditors on the account. As I found a bond by working backward through the margin calls, they would hedge it and then sell it out over the following weeks. It was really fascinating. They ended up making back something like $80–$100 million by just trading these bonds. At that point I told myself I had to go back to business school and get out of this accounting game and into the investment business.

Kazanjian: *Marsh & McLennan owns the Putnam Funds, which ironically became your next employer [as I alluded to in the introduction].*

Callinan: I remember looking at Putnam when I was an auditor and thinking what a great business it was. At that time I think it had only $13 billion under management. By the time I got a summer job there the next year, it was up to $20 billion.

Kazanjian: *You worked at Putnam in the summer while you were at Harvard?*

Callinan: Right. I worked for Larry Lasser for half the summer. He was the CEO. I did a study on performance fees for him, looking at whether they were good, bad, or indifferent. That report was delivered to the trustees.

Kazanjian: *What was your conclusion?*

Callinan: If you really had a lot of confidence in your portfolio manager, performance fees would be great for the business because you could earn higher fees, especially if you did it on a rolling basis. But I cautioned that they were not good for the overall shareholder base if you underperform the market for any period of time. If you start with performance fees and underperform, the revenues of the firm could be severely impacted, along with the service clients get. The ability to hire could then be impaired for other funds. My report was filled with equivocations.

Kazanjian: *Did Putnam ever implement performance fees?*

Callinan: No. I think Fidelity Magellan has proven it's a questionable strategy. I think they lost out on revenue of $20–$30 million a month during the long stretch when the fund underperformed, but during Peter Lynch's reign they earned huge excess fees.

Kazanjian: *What did you do during the rest of that summer?*

Callinan: Research on the investment management industry. It was great because I saw both the management and investment side of the business. I fell in love with the investment side.

Kazanjian: *After graduating from Harvard in 1987, you went right to Putnam?*

Callinan: Yes, after interviewing at Fidelity and Alliance.

Kazanjian: *Great timing. That was months before the crash. Did all of your classmates want to get into investment management the way MBAs seem to now?*

Callinan: I think there were only eight of us. We had been in a bull market for only about five years, and investment management just didn't pay anywhere near consulting and investment banking.

Kazanjian: *Has that changed?*

Callinan: Oh, yes. The huge institutional acceptance of hedge funds has really changed the whole dynamic of the industry. You made less than a good corporate lawyer if you were a senior portfolio manager at Putnam.

Kazanjian: *Are the opportunities still good for people now?*

Callinan: I think the investment management industry remains understaffed when it comes to research on the buy side. I think the sell side is overstaffed.

Kazanjian: *Is that going to change when the market falls?*

Callinan: When Internet stocks fall, the investment banks will see a huge purging of personnel. When I got out of school, no one was doing IPOs. Everyone was doing mergers and acquisition deals on the

investment banking side. Now the best banking jobs are working on
IPOs and technology mergers. We are in a bull market now, so even
the sales, trading, and equity trading jobs are very lucrative on the sell
side. On the buy side, I knew only one hedge fund manager. Now I
must know 20 or 30. They were always bears, shorting everything.
They were a little iconoclastic. Now hedge fund managers are more
mainstream and make as much as venture capitalists and investment
bankers.

Kazanjian: *Did you start out doing analysis at Putnam?*

Callinan: My first few years were very boring, but a great learning
process. I covered financial services, foods, beverages, electrical
equipment, and capital goods. Luckily I started covering Fannie Mae
during that time. At one of my first analyst meetings in 1987, I went
to a lunch at the Meridian Hotel for Bankers Trust. At my table were
Peter Lynch and Bruce Johnstone of Fidelity, plus Jerry Jordan of
Hellman Jordan. Bankers Trust would not go to visit Fidelity. That
shows you how far things have come since 1987. Jerry knew me because I played varsity football at Harvard for four years. He was a
Harvard alum and ex-football player himself. Jerry introduced me to
Peter Lynch. Peter was this nice, regular person. I was in awe of him
because he was a superstar at the time. He's in the prime of his career
and says, "Jim, what do you like?" I said, "I own this Fannie Mae,
but don't know much about it. I'm just picking it up." He says, "Fannie Mae! I own a ton of Fannie Mae. That thing's the biggest future
on the bond market you could ever buy. Stick with it." He told me he
also owned it personally. It was the biggest position in Magellan and
he even owned the warrants. It was like God blessed me because my
first stock selection at Putnam was Fannie Mae, which has gone up
from 50 cents to $70.

Kazanjian: *How did you find Fannie Mae?*

Callinan: I didn't find it. It was already in the fund, but many Wall
Street analysts were very bearish on the stock. Interest rates were rising. Fannie Mae fell 50 percent during the crash. But I liked it because
the company had and still has a monopoly on guaranteeing home
loans. Mortgage loans are also the last tax haven because interest in
deductible. For 90 years, this market has grown consistently at 10 to
11 percent per annum. That's an amazingly durable growth market.
Putnam went from 2 million shares to 6 million in Fannie Mae at the
time.

Kazanjian: *When did you move into following smaller stocks?*

Callinan: In 1990, I was selected to join the small-cap growth group at Putnam called Specialty Growth. My first industries were computer service, consumer products, retail, and health-care stocks. I started following Lincare, Bed Bath & Beyond, Paychex, and America Online when they were still small-cap names.

Kazanjian: *Are smaller companies more fun to follow than the bigger ones?*

Callinan: They are so much more fun. I really had a growth bias. I was always doing models three or four years out (which many at Putnam would ignore). If a company can sustain growth at this rate, it always turns out to be undervalued. I am an optimist and feel the market is smart. Many value-oriented buyers assume that the market is dumb. There's a certain mentality, a certain optimism you must have to be a growth investor. I always had that optimism about good companies and emerging growth industries with high rates of revenue growth. I believed the power of compounding would always bail me out. I really liked discovering and investigating exciting new things. I didn't like to buy something because it was selling for a low relative PE. I wanted to hit homeruns, and triples. I wanted multiple bag winners in new industries that Wall Street didn't quite understand yet. Those home runs would be 70 percent of the alpha (excess performance beyond the benchmark), the singles would be 20 to 25 percent, and the rest would be market performance. That was what I spent all my time on, trying to find great companies that would compound and that I could own for long periods of time.

Kazanjian: *Eventually you got recognized and became a portfolio manager yourself.*

Callinan: In the summer of 1994, I was selected to run the Putnam OTC Emerging Growth Fund.

Kazanjian: *How did you do?*

Callinan: I was up 20 percent during the second half of 1994, 56 percent in 1995, and 19 percent in the first half of 1996. We were in the top one percent decile and had a five-star Morningstar rating.

Kazanjian: *You said in the beginning you wanted to run your own business. So far it sounds as if you just worked at a couple of large, and presumably bureaucratic companies.*

Callinan: Putnam was incredibly frustrating. They had their strategy for fund management. It was to be in a style box. It was a great workable strategy for a very large organization. While I was there, Putnam went from 200 employees to 5,000. Our assets grew from $16 billion to $210 billion. The firm was incredibly successful, but I wasn't building any equity. I really couldn't be creative. I took the fund from $200 million in assets to $2.6 billion, which was a 13-fold increase. However, it was a 40-fold increase in the job requirement, in terms of time and effort. Where was the payoff, especially when I was rewarded based only upon my relative performance against the competitive universe?

Kazanjian: *You didn't get paid more as the assets grew?*

Callinan: I got paid more, but it was more of an incremental increase in compensation, not commensurate with the amount of effort I had to put in to outperform. I wanted to find a better venue where I could take a fund, turn it around, and make it a really big fund, just as I had at Putnam.

Kazanjian: *How did you wind up at Robertson Stephens?*

Callinan: Everything's sort of serendipitous. I was friendly with a lot of Boston managers. I'd see them at conferences. A fellow portfolio manager from another Boston firm heard that Robertson Stephens's portfolio manager for the Emerging Growth fund, their flagship fund, was retiring. He asked if I was interested in interviewing for the job. I called my institutional salesman at Robertson Stephens, who happened to be a managing director of the firm. He got me an interview in San Francisco with the head of the investment management division, Randy Hecht, who is still our CEO. We really hit it off. The job met my primary requirement, which was to get a small fund (it had $200 million in it at the time) with a really lousy one-year record but a great brand name. It had a great longer-term record, but had become a one-star Morningstar rated fund. We first met in December 1995, but they did not make an offer. I think they wanted to see how I did with a big fund [Putnam OTC had grown to $2.6 billion] for the first six months of 1996. They had other offers out and were pretty far along with some other candidates. I had a really good first half of 1996 and at the end of May, they offered me a great deal. They also sweetened it with a partnership interest. To become a partner of this emerging growth investment bank, in addition to getting my own fund and a certain percentage of the fund's revenues, was too good to pass up.

Kazanjian: *You finally had ownership!*

Callinan: I told my wife they hit eight or nine hot buttons. First, my wife and I always wanted to live in a warmer place. San Francisco was better than Boston in that regard. Second, I had a private equity ownership of something. Third, I had carte blanche to start an emerging growth group and build a team of dedicated analysts, just as we had at Putnam.

Kazanjian: *Did you overhaul the whole portfolio when you got there?*

Callinan: On day one. Two weeks into it, it was brand new. Still, it went down. During the four weeks after I started, it went from being up 17 percent for the year to minus 4 percent. It completely crapped out. Soon thereafter, my boss said, "When are you going to perform? I thought you were a superstar." He was not joking. I was upset. I screened for the best positioned companies, which had been radically sold off by many other fund managers. I bought the fastest growing of these companies that had the biggest chance for an up-side surprise. For three weeks in a row after his comment, we were the top-performing fund. It was my first lesson in how to profit from the extreme volatility in any equity category.

Kazanjian: *It sounds as if you were just playing a game to make the numbers look good, as opposed to really digging deep into the companies that you had the most conviction in.*

Callinan: In the small-cap area, you have to follow a very disciplined investment strategy. However, you must remain flexible enough to take what the market gives you because it will offer tremendous bargains in great companies and industry groups each year. You must purge out the companies that don't perform. It's not a category where you can buy and hold unless you're running an incredibly small portfolio and have the luxury of buying 25 to 30 names that you can do in-depth research on. Even then you're going to be wrong. You have to really turn over, as Peter Lynch said, a lot of rocks.

Kazanjian: *At this point did your performance turn around for good?*

Callinan: No. It turned around for those few weeks. Then small-caps, in the fourth quarter of 1996, went out of favor again.

Kazanjian: *So it was not a good start.*

Callinan: It was a really rocky start, although we did well on a relative basis. We borrowed some things I learned from Putnam to help us market. We said, "If small-caps are going to be out of favor, let's try to beat our competitive universe, so that we'll have something to crow about, at least to the small-cap consultants."

Kazanjian: *When did things turn around for you?*

Callinan: In April 1997. I had the worst feeling because that quarter I was down 14 percent and the Russell 2000 growth index was down 7 percent. The relative PE of the small-cap growth market got down to 1.15 times the market multiple, which was a historically low number. It matched the 1990 lows and the 1987 crash lows.

Kazanjian: *Most of your peers have performed poorly since 1997. What have you done that's different?*

Callinan: You criticized me last time I said it, but I think the correct strategy when small-caps are acting so badly relative to larger companies on a price basis is to buy the fastest growing companies, the best companies, no matter what their price because the group is extremely inexpensive.

Kazanjian: *I wasn't criticizing you, just observing that there's such a drive for performance in the fund industry. You sometimes wonder whether managers are willing to abandon their true discipline to buy stocks they would normally avoid just to pump up performance.*

Callinan: My true discipline is to take advantage of volatility. I tell shareholders they are paying me to take advantage of momentum sellers in my space. They're also paying me to have better information than 75 percent of my competitors.

Kazanjian: *How do you go about putting a portfolio together?*

Callinan: We start with the team. I have three analysts who report directly to me. They focus on broad areas of concentration in the emerging growth areas. We have a hardware person who does just technology hardware, from semiconductors all the way to telecom equipment. That's a huge focus of the growth economy. Then we have somebody who does software, the Internet, and computer services. I do business services as well as biotech and finance. Someone else does consumer products and medical devices.

Kazanjian: *How do you define an emerging growth company?*

Callinan: A company that grows revenues more than 20 percent a year. Our typical revenue growth company historically has averaged 31 percent.

Kazanjian: *Is there a certain market capitalization that you look for?*

Callinan: Yes. When I first started as a portfolio manager the upper limit was about $500 million. When I began at Robertson Stephens it was around $1 billion. Right now, we limit our initial position purchases to about $1.5 billion. We match whatever the Russell 2000 growth index or the consulting public considers to be the upper limit of small-cap.

There are four more criteria I use to evaluate stocks and construct a portfolio. For starters, they must have a proprietary advantage that allows them to gain a foothold in these new emerging industries. This may be as tangible as a patent or an FDA approval, which everyone can see and understand. Obviously, there are varying degrees of that protection because bad management can possess a great patent and couple it with a lousy distribution strategy. A lot of medical device companies have shown this latter trait. At the other end of the spectrum, this advantage can be something as intangible as a unique marketing strategy or relationship. The example I always use is Excite versus Yahoo!. Yahoo! was the established competitor with the first money advantage. Many look-alikes claimed "number two" status, but Excite had a unique marketing strategy which many on Wall Street did not understand. Excite had embedded its search engine inside AOL. When AOL announced and promoted its Internet gateway, Excite was the search engine you used to surf the web. It wasn't that Excite's proprietary advantage lasted forever, it just allowed it to gain a foothold and prosper. The third thing I look for is firms gaining market share. The stocks of companies that are not gaining market share in emerging growth markets, even if they're growing 30 percent, will not do well if the market's growing at 50 percent. Fourth, I need to see high margins or high returns on equity that confirm for me the degree of proprietary advantage.

Kazanjian: *How do you define that? What's high to you?*

Callinan: Over 10 percent operating margins, or over 17 percent return on equity.

Kazanjian: *If it doesn't meet that requirement you won't buy it?*

Callinan: It's not dyed in the wool. There are a lot of Internet companies with proprietary advantages that are growing revenues at 60 to 120 percent per year. They're gaining market share in their new space but don't have earnings. It's an evolutionary process and earnings can gush in future years. AOL is now gushing cash flow and earnings, but the years of its greatest relative performance were the "losing money years."

The fifth thing is management. We actually visit a company's place of business 80 percent of the time.

Kazanjian: *What do you get from visiting a company in person?*

Callinan: Three things. I have a three-hour rule. The first hour you get the canned presentation, which includes strategies, tactics, industry projections, etc. The second hour, if you press, the financial budget and how they're doing against it, and in the third hour you get the nonverbal clues and what I call the golden nuggets. Nonverbal clues are things like how the CEO treats the CFO or Chief Technology Officer, the way he looks at a secretary, or the way he treats you. Does he want to get you out of there after two hours or after 10 minutes? Does he really want to talk about his company? Does he love his company? Is this the beginning of the company or the end? Was "going public" the end of its existence or the beginning? I find that meeting with CEOs is incredibly fascinating because most of them are probably terrible. If you think about the odds of success for a small-growth company, with the relentless venture machinery of Silicon Valley, which invents a new competitor each week it seems, and the fraudulent abuse that managements and their sponsors try to pull over on public shareholders, you have really to be on your toes.

It's an incredibly labor-intensive process, and it'll never be indexed. You must do these management visits. You can't let Wall Street set your agenda. The other golden nuggets are off-hand comments about competitors and industry trends that give you extra confidence in the story. These comments may provide more information to build your mosaic about a new industry. A mosaic is an investment team, derived from gathering tiny bits of critical information from primary industry contacts to build an investment thesis. The difference between a good manager and a bad manager is confidence. By the same token, the difference between a portfolio manager who underperforms the market and a manager who outperforms the market is often confidence in the issues he or she owns. Warren Buffett says the biggest risk measurement in any portfolio is the amount of ignorance that the portfolio manager has over his or her names.

Kazanjian: *You talked about how you have analysts in specialized areas. Where do you get most of your ideas from? A lot of these smaller companies are so obscure that no one has ever heard of them before.*

Callinan: Seventy percent of our ideas come from IPOs that have been brought to market in the last three years.

Kazanjian: *So you buy a lot of IPOs?*

Callinan: Wait a minute. Let's define that. No one gets any good IPO allocations anymore. Too many people are playing that game. If you get an allocation of 60,000 shares, it doesn't do anything for a $1 billion portfolio. Basically, all of our major buy decisions are made on IPOs that have been trading in the after market for a period of time. We try to know more about a majority of these companies than the Street does once they start aging. That's where the buy side can add a lot of value for their shareholders. The Street, meaning investment bankers, is most interested in a company the day before the deal is priced. Once it's priced and trading, they're out pitching new business. They have to keep the pipeline filled with new deals. When an IPO goes down, the salesmen at that brokerage firm want to disassociate themselves from that name, lest investors blame them for buying a lousy IPO. They don't even want to talk to customers about why it went down. That's where the buy side can really make a ton of money. And because the issue is so new, no one really understands it. It's not like Johnny value manager is saying, "This is a great price for this new company." He doesn't even know the company. So you're not going to get a lot of value managers out there buying the stocks.

Kazanjian: *How long after it's public do you normally go in?*

Callinan: Who knows? It could be three years. In August 1998, I was buying Transwitch, which went public in 1995. It was trading for a low price. Finally, the business ignited because it landed a big contract to sell a lot of semiconductors to Tellabs. Every quarter since, the company has had great numbers. But it went public in the fall of 1995, and I bought it in the summer of 1998, nearly three years later. We also bought Knight/Trimark three months after its IPO because it had fallen 75 percent despite excellent fundamentals. We made two separate visits to their headquarters in New Jersey, and felt very comfortable buying about 1 million shares at $3.50. It now trades at around $40.

Kazanjian: *Do you get pitches from these upstart companies all the time?*

Callinan: We do, and we like that. It's our first introduction. We can then refer to our previous notes and either call them up or go visit their place of business if we're interested. I like to go visit because that's where we really spend quality time with the management team.

Kazanjian: *You're open to companies calling and trying to pitch you?*

Callinan: Yes, but they rarely do. They always have a banker or investor relations firm representing them. We're usually doing the calling. We have a universe of about 450 stocks that we constantly cull and reevaluate each quarter. If it looks as if they're failing two or more of our five qualification criteria, we'll take them out of our universe.

Kazanjian: *Do you read Wall Street research and talk to analysts from other firms, or is all your work done in-house?*

Callinan: I try to talk to analysts and equity salespeople. I don't really like to read a report unless I specifically ask for it. I don't like a lot of paper. I'm not a reader of Street research because the reports are usually poorly written.

Kazanjian: *In the final analysis, after doing your due diligence, what makes you decide whether or not to actually buy a stock.*

Callinan: First, I make sure it meets four to five of those criteria, the most important being proprietary advantage, top line growth, and gaining market share. If it has those three things, and a good business model or great management, I'm probably going to buy it. Trouble is there aren't many companies with all of those things. That's why they're cheap. I don't really look at valuation going in.

Kazanjian: *You said you sit back and wait until these IPOs come down. If valuation isn't a concern, why not just buy them right away?*

Callinan: I'm actually overstating the process. I do look at valuation. A lot of times I'll compare price to sales of different companies, especially within an industry group. I like companies that have gone down significantly in price so that I feel as if I'm getting a pretty good entry price. But I'm not really looking at valuation. Oftentimes, I'll look one or two years beyond the Street estimate and do a PE analysis on that number. You would think a lot of small-cap companies meet these rigorous criteria, but few do.

Kazanjian: *Do you set price targets?*

Callinan: On every company.

Kazanjian: *How do you determine what your target's going to be?*

Callinan: First our in-house analysts do it based upon comparable companies in the industry segment. We do it more as a check to make sure we periodically keep an eye on the five things we look for. If it hits our price target, that's usually because the company is doing better, so we may or may not raise the target, depending on what is driving the fundamentals. It's a discipline to make sure we periodically check our research on these companies.

Kazanjian: *How much patience do you have with a company if growth slows for a quarter or two?*

Callinan: If it stays above 20 percent growth, it's usually there for the duration. If we feel it has become noncompetitive because of industry dynamics, it will be gone. There are too many new things to look at and check out.

Kazanjian: *It's pretty hard for most companies to maintain 20 percent growth for long.*

Callinan: It is. The average small-growth company does it for less than two years. This is another reason why turnover makes sense in this asset class.

Kazanjian: *So you're looking to own a company in its sweet spot of growth and get rid of it when that ends.*

Callinan: I try not to think of it that way. Most companies aren't that good, and we know there's an 80–20 rule in stocks. Less than 20 percent of your portfolio will create 80 percent of your outperformance. In order to find that 20 percent you have to go through a lot of pain, turning over rocks, looking at stories, and talking to management.

Kazanjian: *Is that why you have so many stocks? You keep a pretty diversified portfolio of more than 100 names.*

Callinan: Yes, and I don't want to kill my shareholder base by forcing them to own large, concentrated positions in relatively illiquid and unproven companies.

Kazanjian: *When do you sell a stock?*

Callinan: Seventy-five percent of our sales are because of several of those five fundamental criteria being violated. Twenty-five percent of our sales are due to what I call a climactic price move, where the valuation is just so astronomical you could never justify the company growing into its PE. In some cases, you see a fantastically fast, explosive upward move in price.

Kazanjian: *What kind of turnover do you have?*

Callinan: High. Throughout my portfolio management career, I've averaged between 150 to 200 percent. I have been below the range (70 percent in 1995) and above (300 percent-plus in 1997 and 1998).

Kazanjian: *That means you're holding the average stock for only a few months.*

Callinan: Yes. But we really do try to get to know the companies. We're not buying charts, earnings momentum, or upside surprises. We're trying to buy great fundamental stories. We've added one dimension in that we want to buy explosive companies at really attractive prices. We spend a lot of time looking at companies that are really down and out in price only. I think that's one critical advantage over our competitors. But it's a subtle thing. It's not as if we have this magic black box.

Kazanjian: *Do you think having so many names in the portfolio dilutes your best ideas?*

Callinan: Yes. That's the price we pay to dampen volatility.

Kazanjian: *Not surprisingly, you own a lot of technology companies.*

Callinan: Technology is a misnomer. There's what I call the technology product, then there are services that exploit technology. There's a difference. The Internet exploits the existence of technology. Think about the capability of a router. It routes packets through a telephone network that was designed 70 or 80 years ago. E-commerce companies such as Amazon or Yahoo!, or information services such as MarketWatch or Multex, exploit the existence of those routers and have businesses that run on top of it.

Kazanjian: *To you the Internet isn't technology, then?*

Callinan: It's a multitude of services that run on the technology products made possible by the microprocessor, integrated circuit, software languages, and telephone switching and routing tables. I think I have a lot of technology, but if you backed out the Internet side of it, I have a reasonable amount of tech, probably a market-based weighting. We are very good at selecting individual technology issues. This is an important goal of mine—to outperform the industry segment. Now, Internet to me is an exciting emerging growth area. If I were called the small-cap value fund it would be different. I wouldn't feel so compelled to be in these emerging spaces. I'm an emerging growth fund. I want to be in exciting new areas. I want the fund to denote fun and exciting new growth industries that people want to work for, that are producing new revenue streams and supplanting old industries.

Kazanjian: *How much do you have in these areas?*

Callinan: If you combine Internet software with the Internet and computer services, it's about 40 percent of the fund.

Kazanjian: *Any other areas you're emphasizing right now?*

Callinan: I've always liked media. I tend to emphasize areas I've covered before, such as retail and consumer goods. I have a lot of biotech and am covering that myself now.

Kazanjian: *Would you expect to do more trading in the Internet area because the barrier to entry is so low, especially in the area of e-commerce, and today's leaders could easily get blindsided?*

Callinan: No It's no different from the way venture capitalists eat their young, or the way the networking industry has consolidated down into Cisco and Lucent. Yes, I've got to follow the winners and look for new emerging segments in the Internet. The Internet will be the Internet in three years, but there will be mature segments, just like in technology. That's certainly true for how Internet access will shape up in the next two years. Cable will have its share, and phone companies their share. They'll be fighting it out on the margin for a share of the time online. The growth area will be where people are spending their time on the Internet, not just access. You'll also have differences in targeting and in business access. There'll be more and more business applications taking place and a lot of little growth niches developing.

Kazanjian: *Small-company stocks have done poorly over the past few years. You've managed to stand far above that crowd. What has driven your performance?*

Callinan: My willingness to ignore the charts and to buy companies when they're down and out, yet still in an emerging growth phase with great top-line revenue growth. There's a whole camp in our business that buys and sells charts.

Kazanjian: *You mean the momentum investors?*

Callinan: Exactly. In fact, I think some fund companies are too big to really do any fundamental research on these smaller companies.

Kazanjian: *Do you think small-company stocks will do well going forward?*

Callinan: I actually have done better when small-caps underperform. I don't know why, because I don't go into large-caps. I just focus on small-cap hyper growth.

Kazanjian: *If you have a 100 percent equity portfolio, what percentage do you need in small-caps?*

Callinan: It depends on how old you are. If you're in your fifties, you probably need 15 to 20 percent. If you're in your twenties, just starting your portfolio, I'd say 80 percent.

Kazanjian: *Ouch! Why so much?*

Callinan: Because I think it's the fastest growing segment. Historically, it's always grown at an annual rate of 14 percent. Right now there's no better time to invest in small-cap growth stocks, especially emerging growth stocks. You're at a 25-year historical relative low valuation.

Kazanjian: *But if the market doesn't care, as it hasn't in recent years, these stocks won't move.*

Callinan: At some point it's going to care. When Coke starts to see its growth decline, investors will care. They'll say, "Where do I go for growth? *Voilà*, small-cap stocks."

Kazanjian: *Indexing has become big lately, partly because active managers as a group have done so poorly compared to the indexes and partly because small-caps have been out of favor and look so bad compared to the S&P 500. Do you think there's an even more compelling case to go with active management for small-caps?*

Callinan: If you look at the historical data, the Russell 2000 has been an easy index to beat. I think something like 70 percent of active managers outperform the Russell 2000. That tells you something there. Either the Russell is picked by brain-dead people and the way they construct indexes is wrong, or it pays to have an active manager. I think it's the latter. Russell rebalances 50 percent of the index every year. If they're not rebalancing it 150 percent a year, they're not reviewing it enough.

Kazanjian: *How do you invest your own money?*

Callinan: All of my money is in the fund.

Kazanjian: *Should investors stick with funds in this part of the market, or is it okay to buy individual small-cap stocks?*

Callinan: I go back to the Peter Lynch method. If you have time to do in-depth research on a company you happen to know well and you ask the right questions, you can buy the stock without much risk. Small-cap growth investing is far too labor intensive for most individual investors. They can succeed for awhile buying momentum or nice-looking charts. But, at some point, panic will set in as prices fall and the "magical black box" the individual has created will fail him or her. The great thing about a small-cap growth fund is that if you really trust the managers, you can take advantage of corrections in the market to buy more of a broad basket of companies. The manager does all the work for you and knows those companies extremely well. If I were going to devote 80 percent to the small-cap area, I'd put 70 percent in a fund and 10 percent in individual stocks that I knew well.

Kazanjian: *Based on what you've said, I assume you have to follow your smaller companies a lot closer than your bigger companies.*

Callinan: Yes. It's a very labor-intensive research process, and the road is fraught with peril. It's all a probabilities game, just like venture capital is. One out of ten venture capital firms hits a home run. Seventy percent of my holdings have come public in the last three years.

Kazanjian: *Small-cap funds in general do so much trading. Most of them are not very tax efficient. Are you better off keeping these funds in a tax-deferred account?*

Callinan: Yes. If you have a portfolio where 50 percent of your investable assets are tax-exempt, you should do all of your tax-exempt investing in small-cap stocks.

Kazanjian: *I assume you don't pay much attention to taxes.*

Callinan: None.

Kazanjian: *As a result do you normally pay out a big year-end gain?*

Callinan: It depends. We try to manage that, although if we've taken a lot of profits, there's no way to avoid it. But in large asset growth years, such as 1999, large gains are spread over a much larger denominator.

Kazanjian: *You've alluded to size before. Your fund has quickly grown past the $3.5 billion mark. When will size be a problem for you?*

Callinan: I think we've got a way to go. The better question is how many analysts and resources can you tap into and are you turning over enough new companies and buying stocks when they're down. Those are all the good things we try to do here.

Kazanjian: *Do you ever plan to close the fund?*

Callinan: No. We will expand research capacity first.

Kazanjian: *There have been a lot of changes at Robertson Stephens. A few months after you started there, the firm was bought out by BankAmerica, and then BankAmerica was bought out by Nations Bank.*

Callinan: It was a pretty turbulent time. Nations Bank's philosophy was to centralize the money management operations in Charlotte. Fortunately, the portfolio managers here had escape clauses that allowed us to walk away with all our money if they tried to move us more than 50 miles. We told them to put us up for sale. They said fine, but we couldn't find a buyer. This all happened in October 1998, when the market went down 40 percent, peak to trough. No one wanted to buy anything. Potential clients criticized us for not being able to sell ourselves. We'd been in the penalty box, in terms of marketing, ever since we announced we were for sale last summer. Finally, the management team here put together a bid to buy the firm out. On March 1, 1999, we consummated the sale.

Kazanjian: *So the firm is now owned by your top managers, including yourself.*

Callinan: Yes.

Kazanjian: *Robertson Stephens is a well-known emerging growth investment bank. But you just bought out the mutual funds operation, right?*

Callinan: Yes. The investment bank was sold to Bank Boston. We run mutual funds, hedge funds, and separate accounts. It's $8 billion altogether.

Kazanjian: *You also changed your name to RS Funds. Why?*

Callinan: RS was easier to spell. We wanted an easier tag: RS Investment Management. We thought we'd still get the halo effect of the

Robertson Stephens. If someone asked what RS stands for, you could say it formerly stood for Robertson Stephens. But as a part of the sale agreement, we had to change the name.

Kazanjian: *You finally own your own business.*

Callinan: I finally own it and employ some 60 people.

Kazanjian: *Is that exciting or scary?*

Callinan: It's exciting. The actual day we closed the sale the Internet stocks went absolutely crazy on the up-side, and we ended up with the second-best quarter we ever had.

Jim has most recently been making a name for himself as an expert on Internet companies. It started with a guest appearance on *Wall Street Week With Louis Rukeyser,* which for whatever reason decided Jim was a better expert on Internet stocks than any of the dot.com analysts on Wall Street. Now Jim has started a new fund entirely devoted to this sector of the market. I suppose that's really no surprise, since Internet-related stocks have fueled much of his incredible performance over the past few years. Thanks in large part to winning Internet investments, RS Emerging Growth was up 182 percent in 1999 alone! In turn, Morningstar crowned Jim as its domestic fund manager of the year.

When it comes to investing in small-cap funds, having a good manager is crucial. Performance in this area of the market varies more broadly than any other. Unless a manager makes some really bad moves, all large-company growth funds pretty much perform alike. But the disparities among small-cap managers can be huge. Jim has demonstrated he truly knows how to navigate these often dangerous waters.

The real test for Jim will be seeing if he can continue with this awesome performance as his fund balloons in size. But so far, so good. One caveat: If you decide to invest in Jim's fund, I recommend you do so in a tax-deferred account. His high turnover tends to generate large year-end distributions. ∎

RONALD CANAKARIS

MONTAG & CALDWELL

If you need one word to describe Ron Canakaris, it would have to be "disciplined." As we talked, Ron continually repeated how he and his investment team never stray from their style or process, which is why he believes he's been so successful for so long. What is his style? Combining earnings momentum and valuation, plus concentrating exclusively on a handful of large-company growth stocks. It's a formula that places Ron among the best growth fund managers of all time. Enterprise Growth, which he has run since 1980, has consistently outperformed the S&P 500 during his tenure. Ron's skills can also be accessed through an almost identical no-load fund, Alleghany Montag & Caldwell Growth, which was launched in 1994.

Ron joined Montag & Caldwell, one of the southeast's oldest investment firms, in 1972 as a portfolio manager and research analyst. A year after coming on board, Ron was named director of research. In 1984, he was promoted to his current post of president and chief investment officer. In addition to the fund, Montag & Caldwell manages money for many wealthy individuals and institutions and now runs more than $32 billion.

Even though Ron has a nearly unmatched record for excellent performance, there's a good chance you've never heard of him before. That's because the 55-year-old tends to shy away from the media. He's never been on CNBC, although he made an appearance on *Wall $treet Week With Louis Rukeyser* in 1998. He also avoids most press interviews, claiming his clients expect him to make money for them, not become a famous talking head.

The Atlanta-based manager remains optimistic about the outlook for U.S.-based multinational companies. And, despite his reputation as a growth stock investor, he explains in the interview why paying attention to value is such an important part of his process.

Kazanjian: *If things had gone a bit differently, you might have been known as Dr. Canakaris today.*

Canakaris: You got it. My father was a physician. He had aspirations of me going to medical school and eventually taking over his practice. I worked at hospitals in the summer, but really wasn't that interested in medicine, although I did start out as a pre-med major at the University of Florida.

Kazanjian: *How did you make the transition into finance?*

Canakaris: There was a finance professor, Jim Richardson, who took an interest in me. He taught me security analysis. He's since passed away, but Jim was really kind of an institution at the university. He was actually mayor of Gainesville for a long time. He had a big influence on the lives of many students. He worked with the Elks organization in Florida and helped them build an investment portfolio. He literally took it from a few dollars to around $30 million. At one point he decided it was time to hire outside managers for these funds. He interviewed a bunch of managers, including me and several other former students. He wound up hiring several of us. He started each of us out with $1 million and gradually built us up to the full allocation.

Kazanjian: *You were still a student at that point?*

Canakaris: That's right. It was a neat experience. I was very interested in sports and attended college on a football scholarship but I was always interested in math and statistics, so I eventually changed my major to banking and finance. I was certainly better at investing than football. I went to practice every day, but never played. I always say my contribution to University of Florida football was that I brought up the team's grade-point average.

Kazanjian: *What happened after graduation?*

Canakaris: I went into the Atlantic National Bank of Jacksonville's management training program. At that time the bank was very large and eventually became First Union Bank. We had a good group. When I got to the bank, I wasn't really quite sure whether I wanted to do commercial lending or investments. I knew after I got there that I definitely wanted to get into the trust department. I wound up in the investment department, but we worked with the trust department. I was with the bank from 1966 to 1972.

Kazanjian: *That was a great time for the market, wasn't it?*

Canakaris: Yes, it was. I worked with Mason Hawkins.

Kazanjian: *Who now runs Longleaf Partners.*

Canakaris: For a bunch of young guys, we had an unbelievable record. It was just incredible.

Kazanjian: *Were you learning how to pick stocks on the job? What was your strategy?*

Canakaris: When I got into the investment department, I did a lot of number crunching. I had tremendous flexibility to assume a lot of responsibility right away. During that period, I knew that for me to advance at the bank I had to be in commercial lending. Thirty years ago, investing was not the major function of the bank. You weren't going to get ahead in the investment department. The closest financial center was Atlanta, so I came up and interviewed with several investment firms. I knew this was what I wanted to do forever and that I needed to be at a firm where I could really make a career out of it. I joined Montag & Caldwell in 1972 and have been here ever since.

Kazanjian: *When you came to Montag, which has been around since 1945, the firm was going through some turbulent times.*

Canakaris: It really was, and had been for quite a while. I was one of the people they hired in building a new management group. The firm didn't grow that much from 1972 to 1985.

Kazanjian: *How much was the firm managing when you arrived?*

Canakaris: About $400–$500 million. It didn't change a whole lot for years.

Kazanjian: *Was that because of performance?*

Canakaris: The performance was okay. There was a lot of turnover and I think that held us back. We always had a good investment product. After I got here I became director of research, then president in 1983. We put together the current leadership team in 1984–85. The rest is history. From then on, personnel turnover was dramatically reduced. I think we hit $1.2 billion in assets in 1991 and $3 billion five years ago. Now we're at $32 billion.

Kazanjian: *That's incredible growth. How have you been able to bring in so much money that quickly?*

Canakaris: By staying focused on large-cap growth, which we do best. We have a very disciplined investment process that has met the test of time. And we have a very strong team that I wouldn't want to compete against. Years ago, we put together a strategic mission statement that said we were going to add value in client service, generate superior investment results, maintain high ethical standards, and grow the firm in a managed way. We've lived by that mission statement every day since. We've also eliminated the politics common in many firms.

Kazanjian: *Despite the incredible bull market, it's amazing how many investment firms really haven't grown that much. Those that have grown have often run into trouble.*

Canakaris: A lot of firms make mistakes because they don't organize the investment process properly. They send the guys who have established the performance record out to make presentations and develop new relationships, and the investment process gets diluted. They take their eye off the ball. What we've done is kept our team focused on manufacturing the product. The group of analysts I lead is responsible for manufacturing the product. Our portfolio managers approve all the recommendations because they're out there working with the clients and must have confidence in what's in the portfolios. We have marketing people who bring in business, traders who execute, and operations people. If you're organized along those lines, and you're a large-cap growth manager, there really isn't anything to hold you back. There's the potential to become of infinite size, really. Then, as I said, in terms of growing the business, we have stayed focused on large-cap growth. We haven't become distracted by other products.

Kazanjian: *How many people do you have now?*

Canakaris: Fifty-seven people managing $32 billion. That kind of streamlined organization was the vision all along.

Kazanjian: *The firm now has an outside owner. Why was it sold?*

Canakaris: We wanted to make it possible for some of our younger people to afford to have ownership in the firm. We wound up becoming a subsidiary of Alleghany Corporation, which is a financial holding company. It's been a good relationship because we have plenty of incentive, in terms of profit sharing. They give us total autonomy and independence.

Kazanjian: *Do you try to hire managers who are more experienced, or do you prefer to cultivate younger people into your way of thinking?*

Canakaris: Both. The main thing is we want them to have a growth philosophy. If they don't have that, then it's not fair to them. We don't want to hire value investors. We have tremendous discipline, in terms of our whole investment process and its implementation. All our equity portfolios look exactly alike, except for rare client exceptions. When we come together and vote on a stock, it goes into all of the portfolios. Regardless of whether you're Cornell University, UPS, or the Montag & Caldwell Growth Fund, your portfolio is going to look the same.

Kazanjian: *You manage three mutual funds now?*

Canakaris: Right. I run the Montag and Caldwell Growth and Balanced Funds, plus the Enterprise Growth Fund. [Montag and Caldwell and Enterprise are almost identical large-company stock funds. The only difference is that Enterprise Growth charges a sales load, while Montag and Caldwell is a no-load fund. The Montag and Caldwell Balanced Fund holds a combination of stocks and bonds.]

Kazanjian: *How long have you been managing Enterprise Growth?*

Canakaris: That fund goes back 30 years to when it was the Alpha Fund. I've personally managed it since 1980. *USA Today* screened for mutual funds that had outperformed the market going back to 1982, and Enterprise Growth was one of them. The reporter told me the common characteristic of diversified mutual funds that outperformed the market over a long period of time was that their investment process combined earnings growth with value. That's exactly how we do it around here.

Kazanjian: *So you're a growth manager that combines elements of value. As I understand it, you actually changed your valuation process in 1975.*

Canakaris: We used to combine growth and value using relative PEs. When I came up here to interview, Gene Caldwell asked me two questions toward the end. He asked, "Ron, what makes the market go up and down?" I thought and said, "Mr. Caldwell, I think money makes the market go up and down." I got that right. Then he said, "Ron, how many mistakes have you made?" I sat there, and this is the honest truth. I replied as sincerely as I could, "Mr. Caldwell, I don't think I've made any mistakes." In later years, Gene used to say I was the only guy he ever interviewed in his life who had never made a mistake. It was true during that time. Everything we recommended went up.

Kazanjian: *Then came 1973. The mistakes must have been plentiful that year.*

Canakaris: I got promoted to research director in 1973. That was a great learning experience. I really did grow up in a bear market.

Kazanjian: *Does it concern you that there are so many young managers today running funds that have never experienced a long-lasting bear market?*

Canakaris: Yes. The other thing that concerns me is that a lot of the young people have grown up on computer screens and just look at data. They don't dig enough in terms of really understanding companies and what makes them click.

Kazanjian: *Let's talk about your investment process. When you begin putting your portfolio together, what are you looking for?*

Canakaris: Initially we screen for companies with 10-plus percent growth. Then we combine earnings growth with value. We want stocks to be attractively priced in relationship to the level of bond yields and to show strong earnings growth over the intermediate term in relationship to the earnings growth of other companies. That's the timing device. We believe the best measure of value is the present worth of a future stream of income. As I mentioned, back in the late 1960s, early 1970s, we used relative PEs. Then, we developed this present value approach and have used it ever since.

Kazanjian: *What goes into the present value model?*

Canakaris: The present worth of a future stream of income: The present value of each year's dividend, if there is a dividend, and the present value of the projected price we hope to receive 10 years out. That projected price would be the tenth year's earnings times the reciprocal of the discount rate. If the hurdle rate is 10 percent, we put a ten multiple on earnings ten years out and then discount it back to the present if the hurdle rate was 6 percent, we'd use a 16.7 multiple [10 ÷ 6 percent]. Remember, you have two income streams for all dividend-paying stocks—dividends and the projected price. The hurdle rate is related to the level of bond yields and the financial characteristics of the company. Because stocks have a higher standard deviation in relationship to bonds, they always require a higher rate of return. A company whose earnings variability is low, whose financial characteristics are very attractive, and whose stock trades well will have a lower hurdle rate than a company whose earnings are more variable or whose financial strength and financial profitability ratios are less favorable. We have an array of discount rates for different companies.

Kazanjian: *It sounds as if in the beginning it's a purely quantitative process.*

Canakaris: We use quantitative tools to our advantage. It's just a way of being more efficient. But then you've got to dig.

Kazanjian: *How many companies do you have in your initial screening database?*

Canakaris: We start out with the Compustat database and come out with about 300 or 400 companies.

Kazanjian: *Do you screen just for large-company stocks?*

Canakaris: The minimum market cap is $3 billion. When our firm was smaller we included smaller companies that we thought could eventually become big. I don't believe our performance ever benefited particularly from having the smaller stocks.

Kazanjian: *From there, what additional digging do you do?*

Canakaris: We get down into analyzing the fundamentals, to come up with a portfolio of stocks for our clients that offers the best combination of earnings growth and value. Typically we hold 30 to 40 stocks. We don't feel you need more than 40 stocks to have plenty of diversification.

Kazanjian: *Is this purely a stock-by-stock process, or do you concentrate on certain sectors?*

Canakaris: It's mainly a bottom-up process. It starts with identifying the most attractive individual stocks, on the basis of fundamental analysis. Although it can incorporate good top-down thinking, we don't get caught up in concepts. [A bottom-up manager searches for stocks on a company-by-company basis, paying little attention to outside general economic forces and trends. A top-down manager begins by analyzing the overall economic landscape in search of potentially profitable industries or themes. Then, he or she begins looking for stocks that could profit from these themes.] Concepts don't put dinner on the table at night. You must have good earnings growth and value. But focus on key concepts shapes the analysis. We really understood, for example, what the triumph of capitalism meant. We understood what the transition to client server management information systems meant. That helped us to capitalize on stocks that were attractive based on our bottom-up work.

For example, let's take the triumph of capitalism. You have a $30 trillion global market opportunity now, So we've been adding to positions in multinationals such as Coke, Gillette, Procter & Gamble, and McDonald's. The same thing is true for technology. We understood the transition to client server management information systems and distributed computing. Back in the early 1990s, when growth managers had such an awful period, we beat the market because we made a transition from drug stocks into cyclical growth names, which were primarily technology companies. That shift was all bottom-up driven because we saw earnings momentum developing for these technology companies, and they were very attractively priced. Going into 1992, everybody was worn out with the weakness of corporate profit growth and the economy. We knew on a top-down basis that corporate profit growth would have to be stronger, and we had all these technology companies from our bottom-up work that were showing accelerated earnings growth. We knew they would be competitive holdings in this environment. At the same time we were concerned the drug stocks were fully priced and saw these companies being attacked from all different directions, clouding both near-term and long-term earnings growth potential. Our process is very conducive to interrelating good top-down thinking with our bottom-up work.

Kazanjian: *From a top-down perspective, what areas do you like?*

Canakaris: The consumer global growth companies are very attractive. You have global economies beginning to improve, and the competitive positions of these companies is as strong as ever. Research-driven pharmaceutical stocks, such as Pfizer, offer good value and earnings growth. Beyond that you have some powerful demographics in place. The baby boomers are in their peak earning, spending, and savings periods. That benefits a lot of different consumer-product and research-driven health-care companies. Finally, the build-out of the Internet is creating tremendous demand for technology products and services. You're into a rapid acceleration of adoption of the Internet, PCs, and cell phones. That's going to be good for a lot of different companies.

Kazanjian: *What percentage of your portfolio is in the tech area?*

Canakaris: Twenty-five percent.

Kazanjian: *I know you focus on large-caps, but do you think people need to own some small-caps as well?*

Canakaris: I'm sure there's a place for small-cap, but that's not something we're going to do. We want to stay focused on what we do best. We're not going to do different things. We all know if you try to do a lot of different things, you never do anything real well. Firms often move into other areas because their main product isn't doing well.

Kazanjian: *Do you stick exclusively with U.S. companies?*

Canakaris: Yes. We figure 40 to 45 percent of their sales come from overseas. We don't feel a need to own international stocks.

Kazanjian: *What about the cross-correlation argument, which says you need some overseas exposure because international markets move in a different direction from the United States and add to diversification?*

Canakaris: That sure hasn't happened. Everybody says that, but it hasn't been true.

Kazanjian: *Assuming a company looks attractively priced, what else do you check before deciding whether to own it?*

Canakaris: We get down to the nitty gritty in terms of the industry trends, demand for the company's products, the company's market share position, and how much opportunity they have to increase market share. We go through the whole income statement and balance sheet analysis from top to bottom, looking at sales, the potential for sales growth, global opportunities, how well management controls costs, how much discipline they have, the nature of the accounting, whether it is conservative or liberal, the strength of the balance sheet, and the potential for financing.

Kazanjian: *You want companies growing by at least 10 percent. What if it gets higher, to say 20 or 25 percent? Do you get nervous?*

Canakaris: No. Ten percent is our minimum. In addition to superior long-term earnings growth potential, we want to see acceleration in earnings growth relative to other companies over the next six to twelve months. We rank stocks by their current earnings momentum. In a period of weak corporate profits or a recession, you don't need as much earnings growth to be attractive as you do when the economy's strong.

Kazanjian: *Do you do a lot of trading?*

Canakaris: No. We have 30 to 50 percent turnover, which is low for a growth manager.

Kazanjian: *But you do look to keep up with what's going on with the market, in terms of where the money's going, which areas look attractive, etc. Do you go out and visit companies?*

Canakaris: We don't do a lot of that. They come here a lot. We talk to them all the time, though.

Kazanjian: *Maybe it would help if you took us through a specific example of how you came to own and value a stock that's in your portfolio today.*

Canakaris: Let's take Hewlett Packard. When we first bought HP in 1998, the stock was weak because of disappointing sales and earnings. Costs were running ahead of sales. There are not a lot of technology companies that have met the test of time, but HP has. The company is constantly reinventing itself. It started out as a test and measurement company, then got into the computer business, then pioneered risk architecture, then the printer business. We were convinced that they were going to get costs under control. The stock really came down to a very attractive valuation area. It was selling at a significant discount to present value and we saw earnings accelerating.

Kazanjian: *How did you determine HP's present value?*

Canakaris: You have four ingredients to determine present value. The first is normalized earnings—earnings that can be earned in good and bad times.

Kazanjian: *How do you figure that out?*

Canakaris: We analyze historical return on equity relationships and historical profit margins and determine what a good mean relationship is. For cyclical companies you've got to be real careful. One year their return on equity could be 40 percent and the next year 5 percent, or earnings could grow 10 percent one year and 5 percent the next. You want to pick midcycle earnings, or the kind that are sustainable on the company's equity. For a drug company, Pfizer for example, actual earnings and normalized earnings are usually pretty consistent because earnings growth is consistent. A second element is the payout ratio needed to calculate the present value of the dividend stream.

Kazanjian: *How do you determine the payout ratio?*

Canakaris: We look at historical data and what management suggests the payout will be going forward. Then you add in your growth rate of dividends and earnings. In HP's case, we used 14 percent long-term growth. Fourth, you look at your hurdle rate, or required rate of return. That's related to the financial characteristics of the company and the stock, plus the level of bond yields.

Kazanjian: *In the end, what did the numbers look like for HP?*

Canakaris: We want to buy stocks at about a 20 percent discount to intrinsic value, or this present value that we're talking about. In other words, 80 percent of fair value. Number one, we determined HP's sustainable earnings growth rate was in excess of 10 percent. For valuation purposes we used 14 percent. The stock was selling at a discount to present value. Its earnings momentum numbers were above average looking out over the next six months. Thus, HP had strong secular growth, sold at a discount to present value, and enjoyed good intermediate term earnings acceleration. With the tech companies, the main thing you want to see is that costs are under control. Then you want good demand for the products. If the financials are strong and costs are under control, you have less risk. When we did the analysis on HP in March 1998, we put normal earnings at $3.25, used a 14 percent growth rate, and a 15 percent payout rate. At that time the hurdle rate was 7.75 percent. The present value came to $80, and the stock was $63. That means the stock sold at 78.8 percent of fair value.

Kazanjian: *Did you set a price target going in and say this is worth $80, so when it gets to $80 I'm selling out?*

Canakaris: No, because the value's going to change with growth in normal earnings. Unless you change your growth rate, given no change in interest rates over a 12-month period, your value will go up with growth in normal earnings. Given no change in interest rates, HP's normalized valuation would move up 14 percent. The other part is interest rates. If interest rates move up or down, that's going to impact the valuations.

Kazanjian: *What about the market overall? Does that work into your picture at all?*

Canakaris: No. I look only at the level of bond yields and the fundamentals of the company.

Kazanjian: *What is your sell discipline?*

Canakaris: It's twofold. When a stock gets to a 20 percent premium to fair value, we either cut back or sell. The other is, we have an add-or-delete rule. Our rule is that when a company has an earnings disappointment, we analyze the situation. If we're not willing to add to our position, we sell the stock. That's called add or delete.

Kazanjian: *So, you must be willing to buy more of every stock in your portfolio today?*

Canakaris: That's true. When we get a new account, we optimize it to exactly what our current model position is. The good part of these two rules is that when a company develops momentum in its core product line, that momentum is usually stronger than expected and lasts longer than investors expect. Having this 20 percent rule keeps us from selling too early. A very common mistake investors make is selling too early. The other part of the discipline, the add-or-delete rule, keeps us from freezing up. We use our time efficiently. What can often happen is that you keep hoping and praying things will get better and wind up spending much of your time in meetings discussing one stock that may be 2 percent of the portfolio. It drags everything down. If we're not willing to add to positions when a company has an earnings disappointment, we go on to something else.

Kazanjian: *Some managers hold on to companies they wouldn't buy more of at today's price but are willing to maintain their current position. You don't work like that?*

Canakaris: Absolutely not.

Kazanjian: *Do you limit the portfolio to 40 stocks, or do you just have a hard time finding more ideas than that?*

Canakaris: Right now, our policy is to hold no more than 40 names.

Kazanjian: *Why do you concentrate so much?*

Canakaris: Because we feel that you should emphasize those stocks you feel most strongly about and that you have the most conviction about.

Kazanjian: *Do you try to equally weight these positions?*

Canakaris: Not necessarily. The bigger, more attractive companies will have a larger position. When a position gets above 5 percent, that usually means the stock may be ahead of itself a little bit, and we'll cut back.

Kazanjian: *Going back to your sell discipline, you sold out of Cendant in 1998 before the word of accounting irregularities came out and the stock got pummeled. What made you get out of that stock? Did you see that coming, or was it just luck?*

Canakaris: First, we got concerned that Cendant was making too many acquisitions. We had cut it back initially in the low to mid-$30s because it had grown to 4 percent of the portfolio. We actually sold just because of valuation. Then, when it moved up even higher, we got concerned about all the acquisitions. There were some other things that bothered us, too, so we decided to sell.

Kazanjian: *Large-company stocks have done so well over the past few years. It's clearly been the place to be. Do you see that continuing into the new millennium?*

Canakaris: Yes. Again, we combine earnings growth with price. That means adjusting to different market conditions and not being out of phase for long periods of time. In terms of large-cap growth, I think the outlook is good because these companies have a tremendous global market opportunity, and it's likely the U.S. economy will do well over the next few years. Large companies, because they have the global market opportunity, are better able to cope with worldwide competition. I suspect they'll continue to do quite well.

Kazanjian: *As you know, all of the managers featured in this book have been able to beat the S&P 500 over the past several years. The traditional argument is that it's very difficult to beat the S&P as a large-cap manager. You've obviously done it. What makes you so different?*

Canakaris: It's the passion to add value. It's staying very focused on your product—large-cap growth—having a very disciplined process that's met the test of time, and having a strong team. Those are the three major reasons. I was thinking last night about the questions you might ask me. I'm in Rotary and have been for 15 years. I've got 15 years of perfect attendance. My wife said that kind of says it all, in terms of my commitment. By setting that pace and tone, it affects other people. I think we have a team with the passion to add value and do more than just profit financially. In looking back, I've always had this passion to put all my energy behind whatever I was doing, whether it was sports in high school, making good grades later on in college, or picking stocks today.

Kazanjian: *Do you think individual investors are better off putting together a concentrated stock portfolio, like you, or should they stick with mutual funds?*

Canakaris: I think they're better off in mutual funds, provided they do their research. You get professional management. It's like anything else. Doctors shouldn't be buying stocks. They don't have time to do it. By the same token, I don't have time to be installing sprinkler systems, or working on cars.

Kazanjian: *How do you find a good fund when there are so many to choose from?*

Canakaris: You have to do research, just as you do before buying a new car. There are hundreds of places you can do this now, especially on the Internet.

Kazanjian: *What is the biggest mistake individual investors make when it comes to investing?*

Canakaris: Getting caught up in the latest hot trends. It's the "What have you done for me lately" thing.

Kazanjian: *I wonder, now that your firm has grown and runs so much money, whether your size will hurt performance.*

Canakaris: I think it has helped. Again, if you're organized as we are and specialize in large companies, there is no reason you can't continue to add value and really become of infinite size.

Kazanjian: *What do you do away from the office?*

Canakaris: I enjoy sports, and I jog with our dog. Her name is Wall Street. My dog appeared with me in both *Money* magazine and *Wall Street Week With Louis Rukeyser*. She gets more press than I do.

Kazanjian: *That's true. You rarely do media interviews, unlike many fund managers. Why are you so media-shy?*

Canakaris: I just don't believe you should advertise your performance and how great you are. I think clients appreciate that. They would rather have a manager that's recognized as being a good manager, instead of a talking head on CNBC. When you do too much of that stuff, you become a commodity. It's a distraction. You should be spending that time working for your clients. But I've really enjoyed talking with you.

You can easily detect Ron's shy passion for this business in his voice. I say shy because Ron is very soft-spoken and clearly doesn't revel in the interview process as much as some of his more media hungry peers. In fact, it took some prodding to get Ron to agree to this interview in the first place. As I mentioned, he rarely talks with the press.

Ron is also clearly passionate about the people he works with and continually wanted to give them praise for contributing to his success.

Although large companies have enjoyed unprecedented growth in recent years, Ron sees no reason this trend has to change any time soon. He will continue to buy companies with growth in excess of 10 percent and reasonable PE ratios. Ron is perhaps the biggest large-cap "purist" among the Wizards, given that he never strays into smaller companies. He has also latched on to a trend that is becoming ever more prevalent on Wall Street—buying U.S.-based multinationals, instead of investing directly in foreign companies. In fact, a company's potential for global growth is one of his key requirements. He feels that gives it a unique competitive edge, which can sustain a trend of upward earnings for years down the line. ∎

CHRISTOPHER DAVIS

DAVIS SELECTED ADVISERS

It's certainly not surprising that Chris Davis wound up in the investment management business. After all, his dad and grandfather are both legends on Wall Street, and he was immersed in the industry from birth. What is unusual is that Chris initially had another career goal—becoming a priest. He earned a master's degree in philosophy and theology at St. Andrews University in Scotland. But after graduation and spending a year working for the church, he realized he did want to work in the financial world after all.

Chris's grandfather, Shelby, Sr., made a fortune investing in insurance stocks in the 1950s. He turned a $100,000 initial investment into a portfolio that was worth more than $800 million at the time of his death in 1994. Chris's dad, Shelby, Jr., began working for the Bank of New York in 1958 and became its youngest vice president since Alexander Hamilton. In the mid-1960s, Shelby, Jr. and two partners started their own investment firm and launched the New York Venture Fund in 1969.

Chris began his investment career at State Street Bank and spent several years as a financial services analyst at Tanaka Capital Management. He joined his dad's firm, Davis Selected Advisers, in 1991 and launched the Davis Financial Fund that same year. Chris quickly proved he inherited the investment skills passed down from the paternal side of his family. After establishing a consistent record of beating the S&P 500, at the age of 32 Chris was made the primary manager of his dad's two funds, New York Venture and its no-load sibling Selected American Shares. He comanaged the funds with his dad for a couple of years before that. Shelby remains the firm's chief investment officer, while Kenneth Feinberg was brought on board as a comanager to help Chris run the funds in 1998.

Chris manages money using the same style developed by his dad and grandfather. He looks for first-class management and views stocks as partial ownership in businesses, not pieces of paper. The Davis philosophy calls for buying companies with high returns on capital, strong balance sheets, low-cost operations relative to the competition, dominant market shares, successful international operations, and high-quality earnings.

Kazanjian: *Since both your dad and grandfather were in the business, you must have started speaking investment talk when you were born.*

Davis: Yes, but more important, dad taught us that stocks were businesses and these businesses were made up of people. He captured our imaginations early, showing us the big picture before worrying about the smaller stuff, like PE ratios and earnings per share.

Kazanjian: *Did you go out on company visits with your dad when you were a boy?*

Davis: I did from a pretty young age. I remember being at a conference for the New York Society of Securities Analysts. They stopped the presentation and said, "We have our youngest analyst ever here, could he stand up?" I was very embarrassed, but also sort of proud. I must have been only 12 or 13 years old.

Kazanjian: *You helped your grandfather, too, right?*

Davis: That was a little bit different. My first job with my grandfather was probably as his cook during the summer when I was 12 or 13. My first job at his office was working the teletype. Orders were placed over the teletype, in the days before faxes. He was terribly impressed that I could learn to operate the teletype. He was a very severe person. He was legendary for the holes in his shoes and his frayed collars, but also for more subtle things. For example, when I would go with him to a meeting, he would hold his jacket with one hand and jog. He was in his midseventies by this time. It was a shuffle jog. He said, "I work for people, and if a customer sees me on the street, it's good for him to know that I'm not lazing around."

Kazanjian: *Did your grandfather specialize exclusively in insurance stocks?*

Davis: Not by the time I started working with him. He began all his work with the central premise that you should adjust the accounting reported on Wall Street for what he would call owner earnings. That's a concept we still use today. In other words, look at what the business really earns, not just what the financial statements or accounting practices might indicate. In the 1950s, he discovered that life insurance companies were generating the greatest growth and greatest value, yet had the biggest reported losses of earnings. It makes sense, because every time a life insurance policy is sold, a big commission is paid. The marketing costs are recognized up front. That policy might be on your books receiving income for 20 or 30 years, but it goes in the first year as a loss. In those days, that was called statutory accounting, which is like cash accounting. Grandfather began in the life insurance area. It was obviously a wonderful time with the soldiers coming back, building their homes, starting families, and buying insurance. The revelation that came from this was recognizing that the market isn't efficient, that there are tremendous opportunities to be had from approaching the business as an owner rather than just processing the rehashed Wall Street information. He applied that in other areas too. By the time I got there, financial stocks were still 80 to 90 percent of his portfolio, but insurance stocks were less than 70 percent.

Kazanjian: *At one point you thought about becoming a priest.*

Davis: Yes. I went to St. Andrews University in Scotland. Ironically, it was while living in Europe that I got to know my grandfather the best. He wasn't the sort of man you approached much as a child. I was studying philosophy and theology, and he would come over to visit his Scottish clients. We'd go out to dinner and spend the night together. He was a very conservative Republican. Being a student at the time, I was at the other extreme. It was something that never fazed him in the least. He always quoted the French prime minister who said, "If you're young and conservative, you lack a heart, but if you're old and liberal, you lack a mind." We would call on his customers together. He would talk to them about how U.S. stocks were a good value, particularly financial stocks. The biggest magnet that both dad and grandpa held out was that when they got off the train at night they looked different from most of the other men. They looked happy. They seemed to have a spring in their step and were excited about what they did. They made investing so interesting by talking about the businesses they owned, instead of the pieces of paper that wiggled around in the newspaper every night.

In terms of the priesthood, I did my master's in philosophy and theology. I was considering the priesthood but wasn't far along in seminary. A family friend who was a priest suggested that I go and work in the church for a year before putting in all the time in seminary. I was a pastoral assistant at the American Cathedral in Paris. Although the experience was wonderful, it made me realize that being a priest wasn't my vocation.

Kazanjian: *Were you looking for the meaning of life, or why were you studying theology?*

Davis: I felt as if the church had the potential to be the best vehicle for social work in the world. The whole premise of the church is not that you're a victim. It's that you're a creation. I thought that was an empowering message. I wanted to possibly teach. I loved working with kids. That's what drew me into it.

Kazanjian: *With all of that exposure early on, it's interesting that you didn't always want to be an investor.*

Davis: It's funny, because I loved my summers working in the investment world. I never thought of the investment world as being glamorous. My grandfather and dad each lived in the same houses they bought when they first got married, their whole life. There were no limousines or jet planes. You never had a sense that this was a particularly glamorous profession.

Kazanjian: *Let's face it. Your grandpa was a cheapskate.*

Davis: Oh, of course. He was legendary for it. I think we all are. It's in the family gene.

Kazanjian: *After deciding against the priesthood, what happened next?*

Davis: I moved to Boston. There is a "Davis policy" that you can't go to work for the family business without first working somewhere else. The reason is that any family business runs the risk of becoming the employer of last resort for people with the same last name. The first step in running a meritocracy is making sure people can work somewhere else first. I was very interested in the research side of the investment business. It never occurred to me to look into trading, sales, or investment banking. The reason I loved studying in school was I enjoyed the research. I had never studied accounting, but there was a great opportunity at State Street Bank. Like any big bank, they're very generous in their training program about funding whatever classes you want to take. I decided to immerse myself in the investment business for five years on the theory that, at end of the day, I'd be 29. If it wasn't what I wanted it would be easy to go back to teaching or something else. I went to school at night, which they funded, to study everything I hadn't studied in college, including accounting. I worked in the mutual funds division as a fund accountant.

Kazanjian: *Were you working toward an MBA?*

Davis: No. My father and grandfather were always clear that they didn't feel an MBA was worth anything in the investment business. I just felt it was important to learn all the accounting I needed. This was right in the depth of the savings and loan crisis, and all good banks, savings and loans, and insurance companies were being tarred with the same brush. I began following financial stocks and found many selling for half of book value, or less. I went from State Street to work as an apprentice for Graham Tanaka, whom I had known from working with my dad in the summers at Fiduciary Trust. He also managed one of my dad's mutual funds. I did everything there. We worked six to seven days a week, and a number of times spent the night at the office. While working for Graham, I was also going to the College of Insurance.

Kazanjian: *When did you finally come to join your father?*

Davis: While working with Graham, I went to an analyst meeting for Chubb. I looked around, and there was my father furiously taking notes. I waved at him and he gestured across the table. There was my grandfather taking notes. That's when the seeds were planted. Dad and I had stayed close during this entire period. It was at about this time my grandfather's health was deteriorating. He came to work every day on the early train. By now he was in his early eighties. He asked if I would come in after work to check his books and keep an eye on things. Gradually my responsibilities there kept increasing. I started writing his insurance letter for him every week. I write the annual reports for our funds now. It's very important to have that connection with your customers. I gradually took on more responsibility and certainly worked very closely with my dad. My grandfather gradually determined the best strategy for him was to be invested in our funds. He wanted us to manage the portfolio but liked the idea of having independent directors for governance. All the dangers of a family business have to do with introversion. You lose the rigor that come from being under public scrutiny. When father and I started talking about my coming into the fund company, the first thing we agreed on was that I'd start my own fund so the business wouldn't be viewed as the employer of last resort. I needed my own record to stand on. I launched the Davis Financial Fund, since that was my area of expertise.

Kazanjian: *You wound up specializing in the same area as your father and grandfather had?*

Davis: It was partly a coincidence. If the real estate debacle hadn't happened when it did, I probably wouldn't have studied financial stocks. It seemed like such a huge secular opportunity. One of the things my grandfather and dad both emphasized is that the worst thing in the world is to think your circle of confidence is bigger than it is. The best thing about investing is you don't have to be the smartest. You just have to be able to identify people who are smart and invest with them. A lot of success in investing comes from humility. That's very different from investment banking or poker where it's about bluffing, aggressiveness, and arrogance. One thing I had the humility to recognize is that there are people getting out of college every day and coming to Wall Street who are smarter than I am. They are going to make their fortunes in the technology and biotech sectors. For me, the idea of insurance had a certain amount of appeal. Many people have become billionaires from insurance stocks, including Warren Buffett. There's something lucrative about insurance that is not widely understood. When's the last time the valedictorian of Harvard decided to go into insurance? I felt that was a great opportunity, one my grandfather and father certainly had helped to make clear.

Kazanjian: *It doesn't sound as if your father and grandfather were very trusting of you kids, since they were always making you prove yourself. Is that good or bad?*

Davis: Actually, they were trusting. They believed we could make it on our own. My grandfather felt it would be demeaning to his grandkids for them not to make it on their own. I don't think I could possibly have the relationship I have with my dad if I hadn't had the experience of working elsewhere.

Kazanjian: *You started the Financial Fund in 1992. What was your original mandate?*

Davis: I was allowed to be entirely in financials, but I wasn't restricted. The purpose was to take advantage of what I felt was this great opportunity in financial stocks. A general fund couldn't be 80 percent in financial stocks. I wanted to be able to really concentrate, without being limited. That makes it very difficult to market. One of the things I had in the back of my mind was that if I could build up my own record in a style of investing that was compatible with dad's flagship fund, New York Venture, that would be an important credential to present to the independent board when the time came to determine whether I would be able to run Venture.

Kazanjian: *Did you have the same investment philosophy as your father going into this?*

Davis: I think we overlapped a lot. My father is able to process so much information. Part of that's just from having been in the business a long time. He's seen it all. The Financial Fund, from the beginning, was likely going to have fewer stocks in it. That's a small style difference between us that comes from not having been around as long. I haven't seen as many companies as my father.

Kazanjian: *You took over both Davis New York Venture and its no-load sibling Selected American Shares from your dad in 1997. Is he still involved with the funds?*

Davis: Absolutely. He said if he could put anything on his business card, it would be "senior analyst." In our company, that's the highest title. He's our chief investment officer. We talk just about every day. He's always speaking with companies and looking at what we do. He's not putting in trades, and hasn't for a couple of years. My co-manager, Ken Feinberg, and I would never buy a new stock without talking to him about it. We'd be crazy. He's an incredible resource. One of the most valuable things he contributes is that he's known many of these companies for years. He's a tremendous filter. Also, we've built a culture that spends a lot of time studying our mistakes.

If something goes wrong in one of our companies, we are able to review that with him. It's not an environment of fear where you try to cover up your mistakes. It's a place where you can learn from them.

Kazanjian: *How much does the company manage now?*

Davis: We have about $20 billion in all of our funds.

Kazanjian: *How much of that is in the Financial Fund?*

Davis: About $2 billion.

Kazanjian: *What percentage of the New York Venture and Selected American portfolios are in financial services stocks?*

Davis: Probably 40 percent.

Kazanjian: *I profiled your dad in my book* Growing Rich with Growth Stocks. *Many people commented about how the Davis investment approach is so simple, which is really the point. Do you think that whole idea of common-sense investing has been completely lost in this day of online trading and the Internet?*

Davis: Yes. In a way people have made the business much more complex than it really is, yet they've also lost track of how difficult it is to execute. The structure of the business is very simple. The difficulty is in adhering to that. Everybody who is investing is doing the same thing. They are putting out money today with the hope or expectation of getting more money back in the future. That's all investing is. For us, the whole investment process boils down to two questions: What kind of businesses do you want to buy and how much do you pay for them? The first is the glamorous part of the business. You want to buy growing businesses with great management and sustainable competitive advantages. But the second part of the equation, how much you pay, gets lost in the shuffle. The first part is the art of the business, the second part is the science.

Kazanjian: *How do you go about valuing a business?*

Davis: First we ask what the owner earnings of the business are. If you owned the entire business, how much money would you be able to put in your pocket at end of the year after reinvesting enough to maintain the company's competitive position, but before reinvesting for growth? We call that owner earnings. In every industry the adjustments you make to get to owner earnings are different. You would make adjustments, for instance, if the company issued a tremendous amount of stock options. You'd figure out the value of those options and deduct that from current earnings. It's a compensation expense. You'd also make an adjustment if a company's depreciation rate were much higher or lower than the amount of capital it needs to spend and reinvest to maintain the business. In a number of railroad companies today, the number they have to spend just to keep the railroad running, not to buy capacity, is higher than the current depreciation. This means the owner earnings will be lower that the reported earnings. In other companies, depreciation is overstated. Another adjustment would be for noncash charges or deferred taxes. Those all will show you how much the business is earning today.

Kazanjian: *What's the next step?*

Davis: Next we ask how much do you pay for the business? Everybody talks about PE ratios, but we look deeper. We adjust the E to owner earnings from reported earnings, adjust the P to the price you pay for the business for debt, and other assets or liabilities that aren't integral to the business. For example, if you have two companies with a PE of 20, where one is leveraged with 50 percent debt to capitalization and the other has no debt, you come up with very different valuations. Superficially, people would say since they're both trading at a PE of 20, they are valued the same. What we're trying to get at is this: How much would we have to pay to buy this entire business, and how much would we earn the first year after buying it? All of that process is what we call the first-year coupon of the business. The earnings stream is fairly low in any company today relative to the risk free rate. Imagine if that number came out to an adjusted PE of 20. It would be a 5 percent coupon. You can buy a bond today and get 6 percent. So why would you buy the business? The only answer is because it must be able to reinvest that coupon at a higher rate of return. Otherwise, you'd be crazy not to buy the bond. In other words, the company is going to grow.

Kazanjian: *So for the second part of the equation, you're trying to figure out what the company is doing with the cash it generates each year?*

Davis: Precisely. McDonald's is opening new stores that are generating higher returns than their existing stores, which is very good. It's like buying a bond where instead of reinvesting the coupon at the risk free rate you're reinvesting it at the incremental return on equity of the business.

Kazanjian: *But what do you look at first, the good business or the valuation?*

Davis: The good business. The key factor that will ultimately determine the success of your investments is what they do with the cash they generate.

Kazanjian: *You prefer companies with relatively lower PE ratios and growth rates. Why is that?*

Davis: It's not that we're afraid of growth. We've certainly owned companies with no earnings and infinite PEs. The reason we tend toward lower PEs is when we do the analysis, if we have to get out to year eight or ten before we cross the line of the risk free rate, we have to make a lot of assumptions about how predictable that business is. You wouldn't want to make ten-year predictions for most technology companies. It happens that the technology companies we own, such as Hewlett-Packard, were bought at 15 PEs, the equivalent of the risk-free rate. We are very happy to do that. But if we paid a 50 PE for it, that would be different. If you start with a 50 PE, your coupon is 2 percent. Let's say it goes up 50 percent the next year. You're up to 3. Then 50 percent the year after puts you up to 4.5. You have to get out a bunch of years before you even cross the risk free rate. In businesses such as Coca-Cola and Gillette, that's not too risky. For a lot of banks it's not so risky. But the further out you get, the more secure the business has to be. There just aren't many businesses that are that secure. That's one of the things grandpa and dad really helped me with. Here's another great example. Every analyst report I get on my desk from the sell-side has an estimated long-term growth rate of the business in question of 15 percent. Some are higher. You don't see any lower. Let's go back to 1972 and look at the Nifty Fifty. Those companies were the best in America. Many still are. They were names such as Pfizer, Gillette, Coke, Disney, and Merck. How many of those do you think grew their earnings 15 percent a year from then until now?

Kazanjian: *Maybe five.*

Davis: Three. Philip Morris, McDonald's, and Merck. None of the rest. The point is that it's just about impossible to grow at 15 percent for a long period of time. Owning a 12 or 13 percent growth rate can be tremendously profitable provided you don't overpay for it. Similarly, owning that same 12 or 14 percent growth rate can be disastrous if you do overpay. How much you pay for the business is going to be a big determinant of the return.

Kazanjian: *What kind of growth rate are you looking for then?*

Davis: Eight to 12 percent. That's our happy zone. If the growth rate is lower, you need a higher coupon to start.

Kazanjian: *Do you care about the outlook for and valuation of the stock market overall?*

Davis: No. My grandfather was much more optimistic than my dad. My dad always said that was because my grandfather got in the business in 1950 when the market was at a low. He got out of the business in 1968, when he became an ambassador, with market at a high. At the end of his appointment in 1974, he got back in again at a dead low. By chance, he never experienced firsthand a bear market during his entire investment career. My dad, as he likes to say, got into the business in 1958 after a huge bull market, then started his own company in 1969 right at the top of the market. Twelve years later the market was at the same level. He's much more aware of things that can go wrong. He couldn't have timed it worse than starting New York Venture Fund in 1969, yet it came out okay.

Kazanjian: *What makes you sell a stock?*

Davis: One reason is if we discover the data we relied on to make our investment decision were unreliable. With few exceptions, if there were accounting problems, or fraud, we would sell immediately. We rely too much on those data. If they're in question, we aren't interested. The second reason to sell is when you are mistaken either about the economics of the business or in your assessment of the people running the business. It's not an emergency sale, just a gradual loss of conviction. We classify both these first two types of sales as mistakes. It's not a mistake to buy a stock that goes down. Every stock we buy statistically will likely trade below what we paid for it at some point in the future. That's not a mistake. A mistake is when it does go down and you want to sell it.

Kazanjian: *Given your investment approach, I assume you don't do much selling.*

Davis: The turnover in the Financial Fund was 9 percent last year. It's very low.

Kazanjian: *Are there any stocks you think you can buy and hold forever? Or is there always a time you're going to want to sell?*

Davis: There's always a time when the outlook for the business could deteriorate enough that you'd want to sell. I think we're less likely to sell because a stock's gone up than we used to be. We learned that from Bill Miller of the Legg Mason Value Trust [who is featured elsewhere in this book]. One reason the S&P 500 is hard to beat is because it never sells its winners. It never cuts the flowers to water the weeds. Our favorite holding period would be forever.

Kazanjian: *What are companies you have held forever so far?*

Davis: AIG, American Express, McDonald's, and Wells Fargo.

Kazanjian: *I heard an adviser the other day say he no longer buys small-cap funds because he doesn't like how they buy companies when they're starting out only to sell them as soon as they became successful.*

Davis: Buffett has talked about that. He said that's as if you were in the business of investing in college basketball players, where you've got Michael Jordan, and you're forced to sell him after his first year in the NBA just because he grew too big to be in your portfolio. It's crazy.

Kazanjian: *Having said that, do you buy both small- and large-stocks?*

Davis: Yes. We're totally size agnostic. We tend to gravitate toward mid- to large-size companies because there aren't a lot of small companies with proven management, strong balance sheets, and leading market shares.

Kazanjian: *Let's talk more about financial stocks, which are your specialty. What do you like most about the industry as a whole?*

Davis: A lot of the reasons I love it are the mirror image of why a lot of people hate it. Money never goes obsolete. People invert it and say we don't like it because it's a commodity. I like it because great management in a generally undermanaged industry is like a fox in a hen house. There's tremendous opportunity. That tends to be what happens in the financial services area. Great management drives a company to huge growth opportunities because the industry is vast and enormous. It's a business where everybody's a customer. Every month people do business with their banks and insurance companies. It's a growth business because of the demographics, and it's global. Plus, even industry leaders sell at steep discounts to the average company. One of the things we emphasize is that there's no such thing as the financial industry. There is such a thing as the life insurance industry, the property casualty insurance industry, the regional banking industry, and the investment banking industry. This is particularly true when you look back over 30 or 40 years. People say, "The year has been big in financial stocks and they've been hot right now, but what are you going to do if they go out of favor?" There are financial companies that will make more money if interest rates go up, there are others that will make more money if rates go down. It's a vast business that's not widely understood or followed. That's one of the reasons fortunes can be made in it.

Kazanjian: *Tell us how to make those fortunes.*

Davis: One thing financial businesses have in common is that a lot of the valuation and numbers on the balance sheet are based on estimates. The most important rule in investing in financial stocks is determining whether those estimates were made by credible people. Are they believable? The greatest danger in financial stocks comes from leverage and the fact that if you're right 80 percent of the time, you're out of business. Past performance is a pretty good indicator of future performance in many financial companies. The time for you to make a fortune in financial stocks is when there is a change, whereby a lousy past gives way to a potentially wonderful future that's not widely believed or understood. For example, a change in senior management at American Express. A recognition that regulators were forcing Wells Fargo to take reserves against loans that were actually performing loans and that their earnings power was much greater than what was being reported.

Kazanjian: *Do you evaluate all financial services companies the same way, or do you look at an insurance company differently from the way you look at a bank?*

Davis: They're all different. In commercial lines property casualty insurance the most important thing is your reserves. Are you underwriting the risks appropriately? Are you making the right guesses about future losses? In personal lines property casualty insurance I think more and more the story is about cost and distribution. So GEICO wins because it goes directly to the customer and is a low cost operator. Progressive wins because it has innovative distribution. In life insurance, it's increasingly going to be about branding and distribution. In banks, it's about expenses and how well you adapt to a changing environment. In credit cards, it's about pricing, marketing, and underwriting your risks. Everyone's different. What they all have in common, if there is one common variable in every financial company we own, is that we trust the people making the capital allocation decisions. That's much more important in a financial company than in most other industries.

Kazanjian: *Management is obviously very important to you. Do you have to visit and meet with them before you buy the stock?*

Davis: By and large, yes.

Kazanjian: *How do you know good management when you see it? Everyone says we want good management, but how can you know for sure they're not just good talkers?*

Davis: A recent *Fortune* article studied both successful CEOs and those who failed. They could find only one thing in common—all of the CEOs who failed didn't execute in the day-to-day operations. It wasn't about vision, it was about execution. That was the closest anyone has ever come to using my grandfather's phrase, which was "All you have to determine is whether they are doers or bluffers." That's a funny characteristic to look for. But you know it when you see it. Do they have a record of doing what they say they're going to do? Therefore, can you rely on them, and are they credible? We can analyze the quantitative side of the business, but we really have to know if the information that we're getting from management, our partners, is credible. That doesn't mean they don't make mistakes. There are different ways to get at that: Talking to competitors, customers, suppliers, and looking at the record helps. What's funny is everybody says they want good management, but I bet if you got 100 sell-side reports, only three would mention management. The other 97 would talk about performance in the quarter. People say it, but I don't know how much people mean it.

Kazanjian: *Are there any other major characteristics you look for in every company?*

Davis: We love insider ownership. We like financial companies with good returns on capital and high-quality earnings. In financial companies you have tremendous flexibility in how you report earnings. We like low cost structures, such as consolidators, and companies with dominant or growing market shares. We like companies with strong balance sheets. You have to make sure you understand the balance sheet because that's a key driver of a financial company. We love financial companies with great international operations. I think American financial companies have a huge lead. People always say they would rather buy a European financial company since there are only ten banks in Britain and 3,000 in the U.S. But the 3,000 in the U.S. are competing with 3,000 others. They're lean, focused, and cutthroat to survive in that kind of environment. What you've seen in banks in Europe is complacency that comes from being an oligopoly. That's another case where what people see as a weakness in the industry we see as a positive. Finally, it's vital that the companies we invest in understand technology and use it smartly. That doesn't mean they're technology companies themselves, but that they understand both the risks technology poses to their business and the opportunities to use technology to lower their costs and improve customer service or marketing. Think about how the credit card companies defeated the banks. Bank of America invented the credit card and had a big group of customers with credit cards. How did they lose all those customers? Companies that were technology driven specialists got into the credit card business, sliced and diced the data better, got the right card to the right customer, and took that business away. They used technology. They didn't have any other advantage. It's so important that companies at the senior level understand and use technology well, especially with the Internet.

Kazanjian: *Do you think most financial transactions will take place on the Internet going forward?*

Davis: Certain ones. How does the Internet differ from a mortgage banker? You go to a mortgage banker, and he says here are 40 different bids for your mortgage, let's take the lowest one. The Internet's going to do that same function. Is it going to change the mortgage banking business? You bet. But does it change the business of getting the mortgage and the nature of mortgages that go to Golden West or Fannie Mae, or the importance of credit quality and low costs? Probably not.

Kazanjian: *Where do you get your investment ideas from?*

Davis: We're deep enough into the financial services area after five to six decades that we have a great asset few portfolio managers my age could ever have developed on their own, which is the network of companies we have owned and followed over the years. They're often the best source of new ideas. One of Andy Grove's (the chairman of Intel) famous questions to ask a management is, "If you had a silver bullet, which of your competitors would you shoot?" That often leads you to good companies.

Kazanjian: *What is the single best lesson you've learned in your investment career so far?*

Davis: If you're in a great company run by a great manager, you can't imagine how far they can go. My grandfather bought AIG at their IPO in 1969. You just couldn't imagine where somebody like Hank Greenberg could take that business over 25 years. My dad has followed Morgan Stanley since graduating from Princeton. When you get a great management running a great business, you can't predict any static model with sales targets that will be absolutely accurate. Sun America was the best example in my investment tenure. I bought that company right after it split from Kaufman and Broad, the homebuilder. I never would have predicted where it has gone under Eli Broad's leadership.

Kazanjian: *Do you feel pressure to perform like your dad, now that you've stepped into his shoes?*

Davis: I do. One of the things my dad said to me early was, "Chris, if I thought about my father's record every day when I came into the office, I never could have gone into this business. You just are going to do it your own way, and you're going to build up your own record. It'll be something that you'll want to be able to look yourself in the mirror after 30 years and be proud of. But you can't be benchmarking yourself to people who operated in a different time and era and did it in a different way.

Kazanjian: *You now work in your grandfather's old office? That must be kind of surreal?*

Davis: I love it. He was a very reassuring person. My office is full of quotes that came from him. The famous Roosevelt quote about "It's not the critic who counts, not the one who points out how the strong man has fallen or how the doer of deeds might have done them better. But the credit belongs to the one who's in the arena." Another, "If you don't admit you make mistakes, you don't learn from them." He wasn't part of Wall Street, in the traditional sense and didn't deal with all the sell-side research and analyst reports. He was able to be an independent thinker. That's the other great lesson. It's important to think critically and independently in a business where you're inundated with information. The opportunity that my grandfather saw in life insurance stocks is still out there. It might not be in life insurance stocks specifically, but there are always opportunities present when a company is perceived poorly and valued mistakenly.

Kazanjian: *How do you know when that point is here?*

Davis: Of course, you don't. It's a batting average game. It gets clearer over time.

Kazanjian: *Given your pedigree, do you believe investment skills can be inherited?*

Davis: I don't think so. Success in investing is as much about disposition as it is about skills. People are constantly being judged by quarter-to-quarter numbers. It's a very irrational environment that forces people to do things they wouldn't normally do with their own money.

Kazanjian: *How do you invest your own personal money?*

Davis: Right in the fund. Our independent directors are our largest shareholders after our family. That keeps you from doing stupid things. A lot of portfolio managers I know, and I'm not kidding you, do window dressing. It's going to be the end of a quarter, so they kick out their losers because they don't want to show they owned a company that blew up. Instead, they buy some stock that had a great quarter so it's in the portfolio when the report goes to print for the quarter. That's irrational. You'd never do that for your own account. You're doing it because you're being judged in a very superficial, short-sighted way.

Kazanjian: *Given what you just said, should people just go out and build their own portfolios of individual stocks since they're the only ones truly interested in looking out for themselves?*

Davis: By and large, if people had the right temperament to buy their own stocks, they would do better than they would do in the average fund. A good friend's grandfather built one of best portfolios I've ever seen. He worked in a manufacturing company and every quarter took whatever money he had and bought one stock. He never sold. That portfolio not only beat the market but probably beat every money manager around, and probably still does. He had that Yankee temperament to buy good companies and didn't kid himself that he knew more than everyone else. He bought the local bank, the newspaper, Merck, Johnson & Johnson, things like that. If people would do that, buy ten great stocks and stop imagining that they're going to be the next Bill Gates or Warren Buffett, they'd probably do better than they will with a lot of funds.

Kazanjian: *Along those lines, should people plan on buying and holding forever, or do you always need to look for opportunities to sell?*

Davis: I think you should buy and hold forever unless something goes terribly wrong in the businesses you own. But you should absolutely forego trading. That's just nutty.

As I mentioned, I had a chance to interview Chris's dad, Shelby, a couple of years ago for my book *Growing Rich with Growth Stocks*. I asked Shelby whether he thought great investment genius was an inherited trait. He told me that was doubtful, but one wonders when looking at the Davis clan. Their stock-picking savvy seems to carry on from one generation to the next. What's more, Chris and Shelby even talk alike. I was on a conference call with both of them a few years ago, and one would finish the other's sentences. Before long, I almost forgot who was talking. Even now, my conversations with Chris sound a lot like my talks with his father. (Incidentally, Chris's older brother, Andrew, is also a fund manager with Davis Selected Advisers.)

Nevertheless, Chris seems determined to make a name for himself, outside of his father's shadow. Shelby remains part of the firm, although Chris is now responsible for all of the day-to-day investment decisions. Chris clearly has strong passion for this business, and I expect him to someday achieve the "investment legend" status that many have already placed on his famous dad.

One final note: Shelby's secretary once made a comment to me that I thought said a lot about Chris's character. She told me that despite all of his wealth and success, Chris was genuinely one of the nicest guys she knew. I thought that was a great compliment, especially in a business where big egos run rampant. ∎

AMY DOMINI

DOMINI SOCIAL INVESTMENTS

A my Domini never was much of an activist when it came to environmental or politically correct causes, even in her days as a liberal arts college student in Boston during the early 1970s. It wasn't until after several years as a stockbroker that she began to think it might be a good idea to avoid investing in companies with products or services she didn't believe in. After doing some research, she found others shared her interest in this discipline, which is now known as socially responsible investing. But back then it wasn't a formalized process, and only one mutual fund claimed to buy only socially responsible companies. Now, thanks in large part to Amy's efforts, socially responsible investing has become a significant force in the investment industry.

Amy launched the Domini 400 Social Index in 1990, along with her partners at Kinder, Lydenberg, Domini & Co., a corporate accountability research firm. The index has become a recognized benchmark for socially responsible investors. It contains 400 companies that have passed her many social screens. Amy had a tough time selling any of the major fund families on the idea of starting a portfolio to track the index, so she launched her own fund, Domini Social Equity, in 1992.

For years, people have argued that you shouldn't invest with your heart because your returns will suffer. Domini has proven that notion wrong. Domini Social Equity has managed to slightly outperform the S&P 500 index since inception, even after expenses. That, the 50-year-old manager says, proves you don't have to give up performance to own companies that do good. Amy serves as president of the fund and gets involved in all management decisions, including which stocks are in or out. She also oversees a number of private accounts for wealthy clients.

To pass Domini's social screens, companies must not be involved in the manufacture of alcohol, tobacco, nuclear power, or weapons. She also shuns gambling enterprises and looks for those businesses that are strong in such areas as the environment, hiring practices, community relations, and product development.

Kazanjian: *Tell me a little about your background.*

Domini: I started my professional life as a retail stock broker in 1975. I spent ten years at a firm in Boston's Harvard Square.

Kazanjian: *Did you grow up wanting to be in the investment business?*

Domini: Heavens, no. I grew up in Connecticut, and my formative years were all during the civil rights movement and the Vietnam War. After graduating from Boston University in 1973, I wound up as a broker by chance. Fortunately, my timing was very good. I was registered in January of 1975. The market bottomed in December, so I came in at a very opportune moment.

Kazanjian: *Being a broker primarily means being a salesperson. Were you good at the sales part of the business, or were you actually interested in the investment part?*

Domini: I was lucky. I worked in a small setting where you could do your own thing. This is when the brokerage industry, for better or for worse, was basically a gentlemen's club. It hadn't yet developed that sales mentality. That came about five years later. To give you an example, in the ten years I was a broker, I never sold a mutual fund. It wasn't something brokers did. The business changed pretty dramatically over a short period. At that time everybody listened intensely to the research their firm was doing. I got a lot of my clients through teaching adult education classes on investing.

Kazanjian: *Were you picking socially conscious stocks at that time?*

Domini: No. Over the course of my first five years I heard an occasional person say, "I wouldn't ever buy that stock because of this or that." One was a woman who was very upset because she owned a lot of Scott Paper Company and had read in *Audubon* magazine that the songbirds were dying due to the use of dioxins. Scott Paper was one of the companies the Audubon Society hoped would stop using dioxins. She got very upset because her deceased father had purchased the stock and she didn't want to sell a stock he had bought her. It was a pretty emotional thing for her. That got me focused on the issue. Another time, I was looking at a church portfolio. It owned companies that benefited from weapons. The church had a big peace program going on, so I was surprised by that. Those two things came together for me. I started thinking I really didn't want to be in the position of selling something I didn't believe in. My firm was very enthusiastic about Lockheed, which has since merged. I didn't want to be out recommending Lockheed to people. It was over the course of my first five years as a broker that my ideas began to gel on this. By 1980, I was interested enough in this subject that I thought I would try to do something about it.

Kazanjian: *Were you always one to take a stand and be socially aware growing up?*

Domini: No. I was totally oblivious as a kid. I guess it came from being your classic Eastern liberal.

Kazanjian: *Were you against the war?*

Domini: I was. At the time I was living in the greater Boston area. If you lived in Massachusetts, you didn't meet anybody who was for the war. I'm still always amazed at who wins national elections. In Reagan's first election, the only person I knew who was going to vote for Ronald Reagan was my secretary. That's Massachusetts.

What influenced me more at that time was that I couldn't see the logic of investing in something I didn't like. At the time, in order to do a search on a given topic, you didn't go to Yahoo! and type it in. I went to the Boston College library and paid them $183 to do a computer search on the words "ethics," "morals," "stocks," and "bonds." Three weeks later I got a list of articles like "The Ethics of Mother-Child Bonding." There was *one* article in all that about a mutual fund called Pax World, which was a socially conscious fund.

Kazanjian: *What were you hoping to uncover through this search?*

Domini: At that time I had to go to the American Friends or the Quakers to get lists of people making weapons. Harvard University maintained a list of companies doing business in South Africa. There were a whole series of things I just didn't know about, including alcohol, tobacco, and gambling. Those are all easy things to research now because the computer has changed everything. But this was in 1980. I was trying to make a list of who was in those businesses. When I found a mutual fund that made an effort to keep an eye on these things and realized it was actually a discipline, it really excited me. I was going to try and make this the way I ran my business. I told a friend this and he thought it was practically the funniest thing he ever heard. He almost jokingly told me I should write a book about it. He annoyed me so much I decided I would write a book and would learn more about the subject by teaching others about it. I offered a class at Cambridge Adult Education called "Ethical Investing."

Kazanjian: *Is that the name of the book, too?*

Domini: Yes. It was published in 1984 by Addison-Wesley. A woman from Addison-Wesley called and said an editor saw I was teaching a course on ethical investing and thought it would be a good book idea. She asked if I had ever thought about writing a book. I told her, "You're not going to believe this, but I have a book proposal."

Kazanjian: *How did the book do?*

Domini: Terribly by today's standards. It went into four printings and sold about 22,000 copies.

Kazanjian: *For an investment book, that's not too bad.*

Domini: Certainly it's the best seller I've ever had my name on the cover of.

Kazanjian: *Did you eventually leave the brokerage firm?*

Domini: The book came out in 1984. By then I had gotten to know all of the individuals and firms that specialized in this kind of investing. One individual I actually dedicated the book to was Joan Bavaria. Joan was president of the management firm Franklin Research and Development Corporation, which recently changed its name to Trilium Asset Management. I joined Franklin in 1985. That firm did nothing but work with clients who wanted to integrate social criteria into the investment process.

Kazanjian: *You started there as a portfolio manager?*

Domini: Yes. Franklin was a wonderful place to work nine days out of ten, but I had been a broker for too long and wasn't used to having a boss. I was used to completely controlling all of my work variables. I then found out about Loring, Wolcott & Coolidge, a firm with a 200-year history. It's an association of individuals who serve as professional fiduciaries. It is structured so that each individual trustee builds his or her own relationships, sharing the firm's common values. Their clients wanted my kind of investing, which by then was being called "socially responsible." Once I got there, I realized right away there was a need for research on these companies. After getting commitments from a few competitors to buy the research and some venture capital, I teamed up with Peter Kinder and Steve Lydenberg to launch Kinder, Lydenberg, Domini & Co. (KLD), which is a corporate accountability research firm based here in Boston. We sell information to all of the mutual funds and asset managers who want to apply social criteria. We research all the big companies. The person managing the portfolio uses this research to decide whether a company he or she is considering meets the portfolio guidelines.

Kazanjian: *How many stocks do you cover?*

Domini: About 850 companies. We put together full 15-page reports telling everything you ever wanted to know about a company. In addition, we offer lists of companies involved in alcohol, tobacco, weapons, gambling, and nuclear power globally.

Kazanjian: *What was KLD's original mission statement?*

Domini: We defined our corporate mission as removing the barrier that existed to socially responsible investing. The world had shifted as American corporations divested themselves from doing business in South Africa. The field had moved away from where I started. It was no longer about, "I don't feel like making money by buying weapons." It had moved to, "I'm going to use my investment dollars to make the world a better place."

Kazanjian: *Is that how socially responsible investing really began, with investors trying to stay away from companies doing business in South Africa?*

Domini: That's when you saw a shift in ethical and socially responsible investing. Before you had some other things going on. For instance, there was an early Earth Day in 1972, and four or five mutual funds started at that time as environmental funds. None of them survived. Their only screen was that they didn't invest in nuclear power. Then there were the church-based screens, which avoided alcohol, tobacco, gambling, and weapons. To be a Methodist, in the strictest sense, meant you didn't believe in making money from the manufacture of alcohol, tobacco, or gambling. The South Africa movement began in 1971, when the Episcopal church asked General Motors to get out of that country. The head of the South African portion of the Anglican church, Desmond Tutu, asked for their help. The resolution with GM didn't get enough votes to pass, but it prompted one of their board members, the Reverend Leon Sullivan, to create a code of conduct for GM that became a model for others. The goal was to bring about the gradual removal of apartheid. From 1971 until 1984, when the divestment movement in America really got underway, we saw the same kind of activism we see today around such issues as the sweatshops and diversity. Shareholder activism helps investors understand emerging issues and shape positions on them. It has always been very closely linked with socially responsible investing and is something we consider to be a twin or sister movement.

Kazanjian: *Are companies starting to pay more attention to this?*

Domini: About a third of the dialogues that go on every year don't actually come to a vote, because people take action before that. Socially responsible investors attempt to create an environment within which corporations and investors integrate long-term and ongoing corporate accountability.

Kazanjian: *When did you set up the Domini 400 Social Index?*

Domini: The index was the logical next step for us. Our goal with the index was to define the term "socially responsible investing." We also wanted to dispel the notion that you had to give up some financial gain when applying these kinds of criteria. We didn't know whether you did, but it didn't seem logical that avoiding trouble should cost you money. It hadn't been my experience managing assets, so I thought it was worth the chance and designed the index to reflect the market by using only companies that met the criteria a classic socially responsible investor wanted to find.

Kazanjian: *When did you start the index?*

Domini: It went live in May of 1990.

Kazanjian: *How did the fund come about?*

Domini: Once the index was launched and we had five years worth of back-tested performance, I went to Vanguard, Calvert, and other fund companies trying to get them to take this idea and make a mutual fund with it. Nobody would. We didn't feel this theoretical exercise would carry as much weight unless it were offered as an investment product. Also, as an index you're the owner of the company almost forever, so an index mutual fund was a perfect vehicle for shareholder activism and something we wanted to do. Since nobody wanted the idea, we naïvely decided to start the fund ourselves. I found a firm that would serve as our administrator, and we had various other outside vendors. About two years ago I got shareholders to approve the creation of an independent management company. We're now over $1.4 billion.

Kazanjian: *So you first created the index and then decided to start your own fund to track it. When was the fund launched?*

Domini: Domini Social Equity Fund went live in June 1991.

Kazanjian: *There are 400 companies in the index?*

Domini: Four hundred companies, market capitalization weighted. It fully replicates the Domini 400 Social Index, just as the Vanguard Index 500 Fund replicates the S&P 500 index.

Kazanjian: *Is it 400 of the 500 in the S&P?*

Domini: No. Two hundred and fifty are S&P companies. When we created the index we wanted to apply the social criteria a classic investor applies, and at that time South Africa was one of them. When you eliminated alcohol, tobacco, gambling, nuclear power, military weapons, and South Africa from companies in the S&P, you lost 200 companies right there. Then, when you collect data on the environment, employment practices, community, and product safety, another 50 of the remaining 300 fall off. We made it a policy to say we hold about 250 S&P companies and about 150 non-S&P companies. That allows the index to perform like the market does, at least generally speaking.

Kazanjian: *What screens must a company pass to be included?*

Domini: First there are some of the older avoidance screens. For instance, there's alcohol, although we still have to define what alcohol is. It's the liquid. We don't define it as the supermarket that sells it or the newspaper that advertises it.

Kazanjian: *So alcohol is one. What else?*

Domini: Tobacco, gambling, nuclear power, military weapons. Once you define the term, it's pretty easy to tell whether a company makes the cut. These are the old-fashioned, largely faith-based screens.

Kazanjian: *Again for tobacco, you're not excluding the store that sells it?*

Domini: No. In each of these cases, it's the manufacturer or in the case of nuclear power and gambling it's the service that we're concerned with.

Kazanjian: *How about the store that sells guns?*

Domini: Not the store that sells guns, but the manufacturer of the gun. That really is pretty much where the social investment industry in general is on this, aside from the occasional exception. Other items we look at include community, environment, diversity, employment, product, and this beautiful category called "other." In each area we have several yes or no questions.

Kazanjian: *Take me through some of those.*

Domini: Under community, one of the questions is, "Have you given 1.5 percent of pre-tax profits to charities in each of the past three years?" If the answer is "yes," it means you're in about the best 12 percent of our universe. When we launched this whole process, we asked for 3 percent of pre-tax but found that a 3 percent threshold captured less than 1 percent of the companies in our universe qualified. Even these questions have changed over time. The questions are systematically ascertainable, with or without the company's help.

Kazanjian: *What if the answer is "no"? Are they automatically excluded?*

Domini: None of these things automatically puts you in or out. It's just a matter of data collection.

Kazanjian: *What's another question?*

Domini: "How many women are on the board of directors or among the top five in line management in terms of pay? It's unusual to get zero as an answer today. Only about 7 percent of the companies we follow have no women on the board or no women in the top five in terms of line management. A zero response is indication you either have a really hostile environment in which women cannot come through the ranks, or a management and board that does not make any effort to bring women in. We're not trying to say that white men can't run a company, but rather that 75 percent of the work force and 75 percent of the consumer base is not a white male.

Kazanjian: *What else are you looking for in the diversity category? How about the disabled?*

Domini: There is no systematically ascertainable data on the disabled. For instance, one of the directors of General Mills is blind. It doesn't say he's blind anywhere, so it's not systematically ascertainable. But we do rate positively those companies that have been awarded recognition by advocacy groups for their hiring and promotion of the disabled.

Kazanjian: *What about sexual orientation?*

Domini: Sexual orientation is one of the more controversial things that we research. We view it as a positive when a company has language in their EEO statement that makes it explicit there will not be discrimination based on sexual orientation. Many companies do not have that language in their EEO statement. We also view it as a positive when they extend benefits to same-sex partners.

Kazanjian: *The environment is another hot topic. Where do you weigh in on that?*

Domini: If you've paid a state fine of $100,000 or more, or a federal fine of $1 million or more in any of the last three years, or if you've been part of a class action suit, that's a negative, among many. We have about eight indications of concern and about six positive signals. If a company has over 30 super fund sites, we view that as a concern.

Kazanjian: *Please define "super fund" for readers who might not be familiar with that term.*

Domini: It's a federal clean-up campaign resulting from laws stating you have cradle-to-death liability for any waste you ever touched.

Kazanjian: *Any area we missed?*

Domini: We have written an extensive document, over 70 pages long, that shares the questions and reasons why they are asked, but this gives you a sense of the approach. Before KLD came along, this kind of research was done on a "I happen to know that" basis. You may happen to know that Disney buys products made in sweatshops, but you may not know that Sears Roebuck does, as does every single small-appliance manufacturer. In fact, virtually all American consumer goods are made in sweatshops. The "what I happen to know" approach doesn't really amount to much of anything. You have to be much more systematic. Our approach is.

Kazanjian: *What about the quality of the product itself?*

Domini: It's hard, but we look for things such as qualifying for ISO 9000, getting awards for quality, and spending 5 percent or more of revenues on research and development. We think that indicates a corporate culture that's committed to staying ahead of the curb on product development. We also see if there are any recalls of a serious nature, product liability suits, or boycotts.

Kazanjian: *How do you use all of these questions and the responses you get? Obviously no company is perfect, so it must come down to a subjective decision.*

Domini: The final analysis is very subjective, but the systematic research process helps. In the end we stand back, review the data, and make the call.

Kazanjian: *What's the biggest "sin" companies commit?*

Domini: The old faith, or sin, screens are alcohol, tobacco, or gambling, although alcohol is fading as a concern. That one doesn't get very high concern ratings in our shareholder surveys.

Kazanjian: *Has the tobacco concern intensified over the years with the barrage of lawsuits and new research on whether it is an addictive substance?*

Domini: Tobacco has become almost a South Africa. It is something that drives people to ask their 401(k) provider for a socially responsible fund. It is a search for tobacco-free choices that causes many investors to seek us out.

Kazanjian: *You said you follow 850 companies. Do you find more companies meet your social screens now than you saw when you first started the firm?*

Domini: Certainly the number increased when South Africa ceased to be a screen.

Kazanjian: *What challenges does your industry now face?*

Domini: Today the barrier to socially responsible investing that needs to be addressed is the perception you're not making the world a better place, which I think you are. Because of socially responsible investing, there is now ongoing systematic corporate accountability research. This just didn't exist until socially responsible investors began demanding it. These demands are leading to a system that is like a dense fabric. For instance, KLD relies on a nonprofit Northern California concern called Cannicor for information on mortgage loans. Cannicor looks at the Home Mortgage Disclosure Act data to establish whether or not banks are making mortgage loans to minorities. That's their mission in life; they're a watchdog for that. We buy their research, which helps us evaluate the banks in our universe. In this way, socially responsible investors create a dense structure between research, activism, grass roots groups, and top management. That's the research impact. As a shareholder, the fund also files shareholder resolutions. These allow us to assist activists to leapfrog management and go to the board of directors, especially because the fund owns significant positions in some of these companies. We filed with Johnson & Johnson and R.R. Donnelley in 1998 on the Mexican factories they operate. Now we've turned our attention to the sweatshop area. This is different, though, since our companies do not own these factories, but only buy from them.

Kazanjian: *You are an activist shareholder.*

Domini: We either empower the activists or are activists ourselves.

Kazanjian: *And you vote your proxy accordingly?*

Domini: We do. If you go to my Website (www.domini.com) you'll see an online report on how we vote. We went online because someone I know told me, in casual conversation, that they called the 800 line at Fidelity and asked them to support a resolution with a particular company. They were told Fidelity doesn't reveal how they vote their proxy. That seems a little high-handed, since it is the public's money after all. These are issues shareholders care about.

Kazanjian: *Do you think companies like having you as a shareholder?*

Domini: I think it's a two-edged sword. Companies are generally pretty used to hearing from activists. I file eight or ten resolutions a year. Some companies like being held by the fund. Home Depot put in their annual report one year that they were a member of the Domini 400 Social Index. I think some companies like us, some don't care, and others don't like it at all.

Kazanjian: *Do you change the companies in the index very often?*

Domini: No. We try to model it on the S&P, in terms of portfolio turnover and industry weightings. Companies come off either because they fall off the social screen or because of a capital change, merger, acquisition, or spin-off.

Kazanjian: *Do you believe in indexing as a way to invest, or have you just chosen that as a matter of convenience?*

Domini: Both. I am an active manager at my investment firm, where I deal with very high-net-worth individuals. Indexing is a technique that demands a portfolio of at least $25 million.

Kazanjian: *When you're putting an index together, whatever index, you don't really look a lot at the specific fundamentals of every company in terms of valuation. I assume that's true with the Domini 400 Social Index too, in that you're evaluating companies strictly by the social screen. But what about for your individual accounts? Once you've gone through the social screens, what else do you look at before deciding whether a stock is worth owning?*

Domini: A good preface to that statement is there are 1,000 ways to figure out whether a stock is worth owning. A thousand of those ways are successful and 1,000 are dismal failures. It all depends whether you are applying them correctly or incorrectly. I will not sit here and tell you that it is stupid to evaluate book value relative to inventory turnover. My bet is there is somebody in the world for whom the formula has worked. Having said that, I don't particularly think any method has an edge. Now, I will quickly move to contradict myself by saying I do feel the biggest secret to making money is avoiding losing money. This is hard to do. When I'm actively managing a portfolio, I try to remove risk. I define risk in a pretty old-fashioned way—if I think something will happen and I am wrong, that's risk. I do believe social criteria eliminate a great many risks. For instance, it forces you to move away from industries with cyclical risks. The nonqualifiers tend to be old-fashioned, heavy industrials with environmental, employment, and other kinds of problems from a social investing perspective. You move away from companies that are possibly yesterday's industries and emphasize the companies in tomorrow's industries. Those tend to have the strongest employment programs and most innovative products. It also biases you toward companies of higher financial quality. I work with high-net-worth individuals who need low portfolio turnover. I'm buying companies I hope to own forever.

Kazanjian: *How many stocks would an average private account have?*

Domini: Twenty-five. My biggest bet is on management. Not on the price of sugar or oil, the state of the economy, or whether or not Congress decides to pass a bill that empowers something to happen. I want top-flight management. Taking it to its extreme, Coca-Cola says it has a unique product and a magic formula nobody knows about.

Really, the company sells sugar water. You and I could sit down for a half hour and figure out a sweet liquid we could sell to compete with it. Why is Coke such a successful company? Because management put the factory in the right place, distributes the product in the right place, and makes good decisions about advertising. That's the key way I reduce risk. I try to own something where the management in place has a history of making the right decisions.

Kazanjian: *Is the entry price point a concern to you?*

Domini: Yes. You could probably come up with the 70 or so companies on my shopping list pretty easily. They tend to be big and seasoned. I want proven success and quality. The pricing decision is pretty simple. I figure that sometimes I can buy Coke and sometimes I can't. I can't buy it when it's priced high relative to other stocks, and I can buy it when it's priced low. But when it's priced low, I have to make a decision about whether or not it's because everybody knows something I don't know. I'm buying Colgate Palmolive now, which is successful for all the same reasons as Coke. Why is Colgate down? Because there's been a worldwide collapse in Brazil, which was an important distribution area for them. That's not the kind of thing that's a long-term problem.

Kazanjian: *Are you valuation agnostic, as far as the fund is concerned?*

Domini: Yes. Money is added to stocks because they're in the index. The financial criteria they have to meet are pretty minimal. They must be at least $5 a share, liquid enough to be in an index fund, and have positive earnings in the last two years. This last criterion has kept us out of the Internet arena. When you buy an index, you're betting on the economic engine of the United States. It is a reflection of the U.S. economy.

Kazanjian: *You talked about wanting to buy and hold a stock forever. What makes you decide to sell?*

Domini: In terms of the index funds, it's because of mergers, acquisitions, and falling off social screens. In my actively managed separate accounts, it's also because I was wrong about the basic thesis. I might have purchased a company because I felt it had top-quality management and subsequently lost confidence in them. A number of years ago I owned Heinz. I got nervous when the CEO kept hitting lists for how well he was paid. And then there was the fact that he kept making acquisitions and getting into new products that didn't really pan out as well as he thought they would.

Kazanjian: *How often does a company fall off the index?*

Domini: We average 5 percent portfolio turnover, but it has been closer to 20 percent the past two years due to the mania for turning three companies into one, or vice versa. This is also true for the S&P 500.

Kazanjian: *Even though your fund has outperformed the S&P 500 by a hair since inception, we often hear you should never combine your personal beliefs with investing.*

Domini: Why shouldn't you? People say you shouldn't because you have to give up some performance.

Kazanjian: *And that's traditionally what we've seen.*

Domini: That may be, but the Domini Social Equity Fund is ahead of the S&P by an average of eight basis points a year.

Kazanjian: *Most of your competitors have underperformed the index.*

Domini: There have been a number of very poorly written articles on this. Many of the socially responsible funds are balanced funds, meaning they own both stocks and bonds. They shouldn't be compared to the S&P. Morningstar recently did an analysis and found socially responsible funds were twice as likely to get a top rating than were conventional funds. Perhaps the industry got a slow start, but the underperformance claim is just not true anymore.

Kazanjian: *Do you believe everybody should invest in socially responsible funds like yours, or just those who share your beliefs?*

Domini: I don't think I would have anybody if I didn't have performance. That's sort of a baseline. I think about half the population agrees with me because in 401(k) plans, where I go head-to-head with funds such as the Vanguard S&P 500 Fund, I get about half of the assets. There's still a chance to create an accountability system through ownership of publicly traded companies. We're headed toward an abyss unless we create a structure within which corporations have goals besides just making money. That's the Domini Social Equity Fund's long-term goal, and I can't conceive of any reason anybody wouldn't share that goal.

Kazanjian: *How have your separate accounts performed compared to the S&P?*

Domini: They've outperformed the S&P.

Kazanjian: *You've been doing this for quite some time. It seems as if this whole issue has only recently come into the spotlight. Are you* *seeing a lot more interest in socially responsible investing and is more money being invested this way?*

Domini: I really think there are several things going on. One, Americans are planning for the future and thinking about how to invest. Two, there's also been a real shift in public sentiment on corporations. They are viewed with suspicion, as incredibly greedy, and as the problem. And three, I'm a little Pollyanna-ish, but I think most people would like to do what they can. This is something they can do. There is a starfish story where one child throws the starfish back in the water and says it made a difference to this one. That's what we're trying to do. You can't solve everything, though you must solve what you can.

Kazanjian: *Obviously, this is an issue companies are becoming more concerned about, too, don't you think?*

Domini: I feel the European leadership is way ahead of American companies here. I don't know if it's because they have real social safety nets in Europe and are able to come to America and say, "Sure you guys can buy five televisions and we can't. But you can't walk down the sidewalks. You come to any one of the cities here in the Netherlands and you can walk down the sidewalk all weekend and you won't see a piece of litter, and you'll be able to sit at a bar without seeing a drunk."

Kazanjian: *Do you buy foreign stocks?*

Domini: No, but I have a real interest in learning more about what's been going on in Europe.

Kazanjian: *Even with all the attention on political correctness and social responsibility in the United States, are you concerned we're not moving as rapidly as we could?*

Domini: One thing America has done marvelously compared to the rest of world is seriously addressing diversity. I don't think diversity is on anybody else's radar screen, whether it's race, gender, sexual orientation, physical capacity, or mental capacity. We're way ahead of the rest of the world on those issues. In terms of environmental impact or the safety of products, we're just making changes willy-nilly, figuring if it goes wrong, we'll change it. I don't know what we're thinking. We're saying, prove this global warming, and prove there's a problem with genetically modified organisms. Europeans are saying prove there's no problem with petrochemicals. Prove they're safe to our atmosphere. They've gone the other way.

Kazanjian: *You have a lot of technology and financial services stocks in the fund. Are these companies more socially responsible, or is that just a coincidence?*

Domini: Technology, communications, and financial services don't have as many environmental or diversity issues. Newer industries, such as technology, don't care what you look like or where you grew up. If you've got the brains, they've got the job.

Kazanjian: *You said originally you went around and wanted others to start a fund like yours. Are you seeing more funds like this becoming available?*

Domini: Definitely. You're also seeing splinter funds emerge that specialize in women, gays, the environment, or animal rights. But these are tiny. The funds that have the largest shareholder base are those that apply broad social criteria and a clearly defined investment strategy. It's really catching on. In fact, Domini Social Investments was the ninth fastest growing mutual fund in America as of 1999.

I often wonder whether all of the recent attention being placed on socially responsible funds is a short-term fad or a long-term trend. Judging by the recent flood of money into these investments, I'd guess this genre of investing is here to stay. According to the Social Investment Forum, a non-profit membership group, assets in socially aware investments now total $2.7 trillion. That's up 82 percent since 1997. But, as Amy readily admits, even the most die-hard believers won't invest in funds that don't have strong performance to go along with their causes.

I also found it interesting to note that even though Amy runs an index fund of some 400 companies, her private accounts remain concentrated in around 25 stocks. That's a similar trait shared by most of the other Wizards in this book. I got the sense that when it came right down to it, especially as a private manager, Amy was more concerned about whether a stock was a good investment overall, not just politically correct in every way. In other words, my guess is Amy would rather own a profitable company with a few sins, than a sin-free company with bleak prospects for the future. This kind of investing makes much more sense to me than approaches that rate companies solely on their business practices, without much regard for the other important fundamentals. ∎

WARREN LAMMERT

JANUS FUNDS

Few fund families have been as hot in recent years as Janus, and Warren Lammert is one of the Denver-based company's most successful managers. Lammert originally joined Janus in 1987, following a stint as an analyst at Fred Alger Management, the firm run by fellow Wizard David Alger. He was drawn to Janus by another Alger alumnus, Tom Marsico. But one year later, Warren left to get a master's degree in economic history from the London School of Economics. He came back to Janus as an analyst in 1990 and took over management of the Janus Mercury Fund in 1993. He's been beating the market ever since.

At 38, Warren is a shining star among the growing crop of promising young investment managers. He has free reign to buy any stock he wants, regardless of size or location, although as his fund gets larger he's focusing more on mid- and large-cap names. Warren works closely with the other Janus managers to come up with investment ideas, since part of his incentive bonus is based on how well his colleagues perform. It's a structure, he says, that encourages teamwork. It's also one reason many Janus funds seem to list the same stocks among their top ten holdings.

Warren still uses a lot of the same intensive research skills he learned at Alger. He develops detailed financial models for every company under consideration and gets information from a range of independent sources, such as suppliers and competitors, before buying. He also meets regularly with company management. Although Warren believes in diversification, he tends to concentrate in his favorite industries and individual issues. He has been more willing to take a chance on pure-play Internet stocks than some of his Janus colleagues, and is a longtime fan of the cable industry, which he has followed for the past three years.

Away from the office, Warren works out his tensions by playing ice hockey, which he views as a necessary escape from the hectic pace of Wall Street.

Kazanjian: *I guess you have your father to thank or blame for getting you into the investment business.*

Lammert: Exactly. I was an exchange student in Holland my senior year of high school and chose to defer matriculation at Yale by a semester. This was in 1980, when gold rose above $800 an ounce, the Russians invaded Afghanistan, and U.S. inflation went to double digits for the first time in many decades. The economic picture looked pretty bleak. I decided to take a semester off, do more reading in economics, understand what was going on myself. My father said that was fine, but made me get a job. I was hired by A. G. Edwards in my hometown of St. Louis. I worked there through that summer and the fall semester for a terrific guy Mark Keller, who later became head of the research department.

Kazanjian: *What sparked your interest in going to Holland?*

Lammert: I thought it would be a great experience to live in a different country and see how things work somewhere else. That's what drove me to be an exchange student.

Kazanjian: *You must have a deep-rooted interest in economics. You studied it as both an undergraduate and graduate student.*

Lammert: I've always had an interest in business. I ran a lot of businesses as a kid, like lemonade stands. I even sold mint toothpicks and seeds door-to-door.

Kazanjian: *That sounds a lot like me! I was a young entrepreneur as well. After A. G. Edwards, you went on to Yale?*

Lammert: Yes. In high school, I was also interested in politics and thought for a while I wanted to be a politician. That partially sparked my interest in economics. I was head of the Missouri Teenage Republicans group before becoming a Libertarian. I'm still very much a Libertarian. I went to Yale, came back to A. G. Edwards the next summer, and spent still another summer working at a small St. Louis brokerage firm called Newhard Cooke. I've gone back and forth over time between wanting to pursue a career in business and the stock market and having an interest in academics and teaching. In my senior year of college I got involved running a student pizza-delivery business. It was a great experience but very time-consuming. I think I graduated with a 3.4 GPA from Yale. That kind of killed my academic ambitions. I wasn't able to get into grad school at that point. I decided to look for a job on Wall Street and was fortunate to gain an interview with Fred Alger Management, which I thought was in management consulting but turned out to be in the investment business. I hit it off very well with the fellow I interviewed with. We talked about economics and had a great chat. I wound up with a job there as an analyst.

Kazanjian: *David Alger, the current president of that firm, is also featured in this book. You must have worked with him.*

Lammert: Yes. He's a terrific guy and very bright.

Kazanjian: *What was it like there?*

Lammert: It was exciting. David and his brother Fred were very driven people who really wanted to perform. They were emotionally invested in that performance, so it could be a stormy place at times. If you had a stock in the portfolio that wasn't working, they were all over you. At the same time, it was fun. David is 15 or 20 years older than I, but he would organize games of throwing paper balls into trash cans, hopping on one foot, twisting around, making the shot across the room. The games probably relieved some of the tension. There was a lot of pressure to perform, but it was a fun place socially.

Kazanjian: *Isn't there always pressure to perform in this business?*

Lammert: Tremendous pressure. At Janus, Tom Bailey, our founder, is a very driven person. However, having been a portfolio manager himself, he knows how to deal well with pressure. When you're doing well, he reminds you you'll be schlock again. When you're doing poorly, he'll tell you five stories about how his worst times were much worse than this.

Kazanjian: *What's the history of Janus?*

Lammert: Tom Bailey started the firm with a couple of partners back in 1969. In 1984, he sold a large interest to Kansas City Southern because one of his partners had cancer and needed liquidity. It's been a wonderful investment for them. Tom struck a deal that allowed him to retain control of the Janus board as long as he owned more than 5 percent of the stock.

Kazanjian: *Is Tom still involved in the firm?*

Lammert: Very much. He lives in Aspen, but is in the Denver office three days a week. I'm going to visit a company with him in a few days. He doesn't take primary responsibility or build models, but in addition to running the business, he gets involved with the investment process.

Kazanjian: *How did you originally hook up with Janus?*

Lammert: My first boss at Alger was Tom Marsico. I worked for him about one and a half years. He then left to come to Janus. We continued to be good friends, and he invited me out for an interview. At the time, Janus had $900 million in assets. There were three portfolio managers—Tom, Jim Craig, and Ben Niedermeyer. I was the first analyst to support those guys. Helen Hayes, another colleague from Alger who now manages our international funds, joined me a month later. The Algers thought I was crazy to leave their firm, which at that point had $3 billion in assets compared to $900 million for Janus.

Kazanjian: *You stayed at Janus a couple years and then went back to school again, right?*

Lammert: I joined Janus in January 1987. Partly because I didn't get settled well socially in Denver, and partly because a good friend of mine died in a strange accident, I began to think about what I wanted to do with my life. I had a long-term interest in academics and decided to give that track a shot. I left Janus in May 1998 to go to the London School of Economics and get a master's in economic history. I didn't get entirely away from the business because I wrote my thesis on the rise and fall of the stock market in 18th-century England and on the effects of the Bubble Act, which I argued delayed development of the stock market in Britain for about 60 years. I had a good time there and entered the Harvard history Ph.D. program following my year in London. At Harvard, I started doing some work on the side as an analyst for Leigh Severance, who shares office space with us at

Janus and has his own firm. I had a lot of fun working with him and stayed in touch with my friends at Janus. They were doing well and felt they needed another analyst. They asked if I would consider coming back. Along about midterm I got tired of studying and spending hours in the library writing solitary research papers. I enjoyed the give and take and feedback you get in the market much more. After one semester at Harvard, I returned to Janus.

Kazanjian: *That was January 1990. What were the assets then?*

Lammert: Around $2 billion. Today we are $222 billion and growing. When I first joined the firm in 1987, I think I was employee number 32. Now we have some 2,000 people.

Kazanjian: *Tell me about the structure at Janus.*

Lammert: We have a team of analysts who support all of the portfolio managers. We have a group of analysts who focus primarily on overseas companies under Helen's direction and a couple who focus on small- and mid-caps. We also have a larger team covering the bigger companies. Every analyst can reach across these disciplines, which we think is healthy.

Kazanjian: *Janus is known for having a very team-oriented environment.*

Lammert: Individual portfolio managers have total responsibility and the final say for their portfolios, but it's very much a team effort, in terms of doing research on companies. There's great give and take on ideas and a financial incentive for us to work together. This group gets along extremely well. We socialize together, and there's a wonderful absence of internal politics that I have not seen in any other place. I think we're really blessed in terms of the smooth internal functioning of the firm.

Kazanjian: *How has the firm changed from when it was smaller to now?*

Lammert: It's a much different dynamic. I don't interact with everybody everyday the way I used to, at least not face-to-face. But we're still on one floor in our Denver building. We pretty much have open offices and people do circulate quite a bit during the day. We have a couple of formal meetings every week, which is new, to make sure we actually get in front of each other. The truth is, our informal interactions are probably the most important.

Kazanjian: *If you take a look at the various Janus funds, you find they all seem to hold the same stocks, especially in the top ten holdings.*

Lammert: We do tend to share our best ideas. As I mentioned, we're compensated to work together. By and large we share a similar philosophy, in terms of looking for outstanding companies that can grow their earnings over time.

Kazanjian: *Why does the firm want you to work together. Isn't competition healthy?*

Lammert: We're not concerned that our performance looks the same, but we're all trying to do the best job we can for our shareholders. We have lively disagreements about companies and their prospects, but at the end of the day we all want to do the best we can. We want every Janus manager to perform well. My primary driver is how the Mercury Fund and the other assets I'm responsible for perform. But there's also a component that depends on how the other portfolio managers do. We think this achieves better results for our shareholders. I think it's a positive situation. We're able to communicate well, so the best ideas wind up being shared. That's one reason all of our funds are in the top quartile on a trailing 12-month and 3-year basis. I think that shows this is a team effort. At the same time, there are individual differences. If you look at the results of the Janus Funds on a year-by-year basis, you'll see very substantial differences in performance, even if there are some common holdings.

Kazanjian: *Janus, as a firm, has been growing like a rocket. Your strong performance is attracting billions of dollars. Is that something shareholders should be concerned about?*

Lammert: There are definitely pluses and minuses. Certainly we suffer in our ability to move in and out of stocks easily. If we like a company, we tend to own a meaningful percentage of the stock. As a result, if we're wrong, the costs are higher. We are probably constricted to a certain extent on the size of companies we can invest in. The positive side is that we have critical mass and are able to develop a serious research effort. We now have 32 analysts and 21 portfolio managers who are out visiting with companies and sharing and debating ideas. It's a huge benefit to be able to really do the research work and build detailed models in-house.

Kazanjian: *How did you come to manage the Janus Mercury Fund?*

Lammert: I'd been an analyst for seven years and had managed private accounts since 1991. I built a good record, and they gave me the Mercury Fund in 1993. I managed the Janus Balanced Fund for about a year before that.

Kazanjian: *How much do you manage altogether now?*

Lammert: About $21 billion. Close to $12 billion of that is in the Mercury Fund.

Kazanjian: *What's the difference between Mercury and other Janus funds?*

Lammert: I'm able to find the best opportunities I can wherever they are from both a geographic and market cap perspective. As the fund has grown, I've lost some flexibility on the small-cap side, but can certainly buy mid- and large-caps. By charter I can own anything. I think that's helpful. Our technical prospectuses give all of our funds tremendous flexibility. I have the most flexible charter of any Janus Fund.

Kazanjian: *So far, Janus has closed four of its funds—Janus Venture, Janus Global Technology, Janus Twenty, and Janus Overseas. Is there a point when you would close Mercury because it got too bloated in assets?*

Lammert: I think so, but we have a way to go. Janus Twenty closed at around $24 billion. I think I'd have to get to about that same point before size were an issue.

Kazanjian: *You have the flexibility to buy foreign companies. In the past, you've kept as much as 30 percent of the portfolio in international stocks. What's the attraction?*

Lammert: The entire process is bottom-up. I look at individual company opportunities one at a time. Sometimes I'll find companies that happen to be headquartered overseas whose growth prospects and/or valuations are more attractive than those I find in the United States.

Kazanjian: *Tell me about your overall investment approach.*

Lammert: It's a completely bottom-up process. I look for great opportunities one at a time. I tend to concentrate on what I regard as the more dynamic areas of the economy. I spend a lot of time analyzing technology companies. At Janus, I have also covered pharmaceutical and biotech stocks. Those are all areas I tend to spend quite a bit of time looking at, since I understand them well. I also try to leverage the work of my colleagues who have expertise in other areas. I'm flexible and attempt to learn about other industries over time. I'm willing to go anywhere, but I have a fondness for attractive growth companies that have emerged out of the technology and medical industries.

Kazanjian: *Those are your two primary areas of focus?*

Lammert: On a long-term basis, yes. But I'm willing to own anything from an auto stock to a chemical stock.

Kazanjian: *You've also been investing a lot lately in the cable industry.*

Lammert: Cable is a business that three years ago seemed like a strange thing for a growth manager to be interested in. It had become a fairly mature and heavily regulated business providing television signals to consumers. Then the business began to change in a fundamental way. Cable companies started to upgrade their networks from one-way analog networks to two-way digital networks. They also expanded the capacity of the cable pipes. As they moved to these two-way digital platforms, they improved the basic cable TV product. As you go from analog to digital, you get about a ten-to-one expansion of capacity on the cable pipe. In a traditional analog setting, you could put one TV program on about a 6 MHz piece of spectrum. At 600 MHz, you can put 100 channels on an analog system. When you go to digital compression, and get a ten-to-one compression, that same 600 MHz pipe can provide up to 1,000 channels of content. That's a tremendous transformation. It means the cable companies can offer a much richer selection of content and services, such as video on demand. They also have the chance to get into two entirely new businesses. First is the telephone business, which is three times the size of the cable business in the United States. The cable operators are able to offer multiline service at discounted prices. Also, these two-way digital networks are able to offer, high-speed Internet access that's 100 times faster than a standard telephone line. So the cable companies now have three revenue streams that they're able to leverage off the same platform. That transforms what three years ago was a mature, slow-growing, single-digit growth industry into a very dynamic growth business again.

Kazanjian: *What was the Eureka moment when you made this connection?*

Lammert: This is a case where I was able to leverage the work of my colleagues. Jim Craig, who runs the Janus Fund and is our chief investment officer, was first to develop an interest in cable. We were all excited by Bill Gates's investment in Comcast. That signaled he believed the cable pipe could have this new role as a primary driver of bringing communications and the Internet into the home.

Kazanjian: *What percentage of your portfolio do you have in cable?*

Lammert: About 12 percent on a pure-play basis, although I also have large positions in various media companies.

Kazanjian: *Is cable your largest overall sector?*

Lammert: It's very large, but traditional technology is still a bigger focus at 25 percent of the portfolio. I'm including telecommunications-equipment companies in that number.

Kazanjian: *Where does the Internet fit in?*

Lammert: I would still break out the Internet separately. My pure-play Internet exposure is about 15 percent.

Kazanjian: *You own some of the upstart e-commerce companies, such as Amazon.com and Yahoo!.*

Lammert: I'm a very strong believer in the future of the Internet. I try to take advantage of volatility and emotional extremes to acquire these companies.

Kazanjian: *How many stocks do you own in the portfolio altogether?*

Lammert: About 60.

Kazanjian: *In looking through your annual reports, that's a much smaller number than you had just a few years ago.*

Lammert: Going back to 1994, I tended to own around 100 names.

Kazanjian: *Why did you cut back?*

Lammert: I decided it was better to focus on a smaller list of companies. I had the number-one capital appreciation fund in the nation in 1994. The longer list worked at the time, but I wasn't happy with my performance in 1996–97. I decided to focus more on my best names. That has certainly paid off.

Kazanjian: *Do you concentrate primarily in your top ten holdings?*

Lammert: I do try to focus on my best ideas. The top ten currently make up about 43 percent of the portfolio.

Kazanjian: *Do you always remain fully invested?*

Lammert: I don't, per se. Tom Bailey likes to quote Adam Smith from his book, *The Money Game*: "To win you must first not lose." He believes in taking your responsibility as the steward of somebody else's money seriously. I try to invest on a company-by-company basis as I find opportunities that are truly compelling. To the extent I have opportunities I'm excited about, I'm fully invested. There are times when companies become fully valued. In that case, I'll sell my positions. If the flow of ideas isn't there, I'll raise cash. I try to let the ideas compel me to invest the money, instead of just wanting to be fully invested. Lately, I've had more ideas than cash to put to work, which is a good thing.

Kazanjian: *Denver, where Janus is based, has become sort of a financial Mecca. What's the environment like?*

Lammert: When I first moved here, I thought our location was a disadvantage, even though there was already a significant presence by other investment managers, including Founders, Berger, and Invesco. I think Denver is now the number-three or -four center for money management in the country. This means every company that goes out to meet with investors comes through Denver. Any disadvantage we might have had from not being in New York or Boston has gone away. Fortunately, we've always had a philosophy of going out to see companies in their offices. That's more helpful than passively sitting here waiting for someone to come through and sell you on their stock.

Kazanjian: *What do you look for in a company?*

Lammert: I look for companies that can sustain superior earnings growth. There are two kinds: steady unit growth companies, like a Wal-Mart, which has a proven concept that can grow geographically into new areas. A technology company with a great product it can sell more units of, thus expanding the market for its products, also falls into this category. I also love life-cycle change companies, which is a term we used at Fred Alger as well. The cable companies are good examples of that. It's an industry that is perceived to be mature, but has a catalyst for change that can reignite growth. Those are often the most exciting stories because you can get paid twice, both for earnings growth and through a reevaluation of the opportunities by Wall Street.

Kazanjian: *How do you define a growth stock?*

Lammert: It's a company that's able to grow the economic value of its franchise. Most often it's a matter of growing reported earnings. Other times it's cash flow or franchise value.

Kazanjian: *When you find a company that interests you, what specific things do you look at before buying?*

Lammert: I'll generally develop a very detailed model. An analyst will also be assigned to the company to help me understand the business better. We look at the key drivers of revenue and what's happening to costs and margins. That generates more questions. We'll then talk to company management, refine the model, and sometimes meet with management to better understand the fabric of their organization. Next, we talk with competitors. Management will always tell you what's right. That's what they're paid for. If you want to hear the real story, it's helpful to talk with competitors to learn about the skeletons in the closet. We also speak with customers.

Kazanjian: *Do you get an honest assessment?*

Lammert: Everybody's biased. Management is biased in a positive way, competitors are biased in a negative way. Customers also have their own bones to pick. Not everybody can be entirely candid. You get a mix of views and have to filter out a lot.

Kazanjian: *Who gives you the best information between the company, competitors, and customers?*

Lammert: Ultimately the most important source is management. They tend to be relatively straight because their reputations are on the line.

Kazanjian: *Are there particular management characteristics that tell you this company is led by capable management?*

Lammert: It's hard to line them up in a box. You want people who are smart, have a history of delivering, and can communicate well. We try to meet people at a variety of levels of management to see if they've really built what appears to be an effective organization.

Kazanjian: *When you make a mistake about management, what's usually the biggest problem?*

Lammert: In many instances, top management tries to build meaningful business empires, but loses touch with the realities of the business.
I think trying to achieve growth and build a business at a fast pace
sometimes drives people to create a fantasy that can't happen. You really have to watch out for that in the growth universe.

Kazanjian: *Does that mean you are cautious of companies growing too
rapidly?*

Lammert: I'm looking for companies that can achieve rapid growth,
but I'm wary of the potential for people to stretch beyond the
realistic.

Kazanjian: *Aren't Amazon and Yahoo!, two of your holdings, examples of companies that are shooting for the moon?*

Lammert: I'm very aware of the risks. That's why I have a portfolio of
60 stocks and don't place all my bets on Amazon. I've spent a lot of
time with the people at Amazon. I think they're assembling a tremendous, high-class, motivated, exciting organization.

Kazanjian: *How do you determine whether a stock is selling at a fair
price, or do you care?*

Lammert: I ultimately look at the value of the enterprise that's being
created. I'm trying to find companies that are attractively priced relative to their ability to grow earnings. That's a shorthand for a dividend discount model.

Kazanjian: *In layman's terms, tell us how you would figure that out
for a company.*

Lammert: Broadly speaking, I like to see forward earnings looking out
a year or two. Then I determine the price-earnings multiple I'm being
asked to pay, relative to what I think is a sustainable growth rate for
the business.

Kazanjian: *How long do you own an average holding?*

Lammert: Turnover is on the order of 100 percent, which means my
average holding period is one year. But that hides a lot of things. The
reality is if I own 60 names, probably half will be in here for three
years. The other 30 will turn over either because they disappoint me
or the valuation does not reflect the company's realistic earnings
potential.

Kazanjian: *The people reading this book don't have access to your an-alysts or earnings models. What are some of the most important things they should look for when buying individual stocks?*

Lammert: They must understand the business and have a real view as to why it can grow and prosper over time. They need to believe in management, and in the game plan, and should spend time looking at the numbers. I don't think building an earnings model is hard. It just takes time and practice to learn. Individual investors should focus on a small number of companies and really get inside to understand the business.

Kazanjian: *What goes into an earnings model?*

Lammert: You start with the results a company reports on a quarterly basis, look at revenues, cost of goods sold, the tax rate of the earn-ings, the cash flow being generated, what's happening to the cash, etc. If you can find a couple of main revenue drivers that can be mapped out to get more granularity [concrete details or substance] it's worth doing that. If it's a pharmaceutical or biotech company that has a major new product in the pipeline, you must do the arithmetic. How many patients are there who could potentially benefit from this new treatment? You then need to know what price the product can be sold for, whether it will be marketed with another company, and how big the drug can be relative to existing revenues. It's that kind of exercise.

Kazanjian: *Any other characteristics you look for?*

Lammert: I'm really just trying to understand the individual busi-nesses. We benefit from a corps of many analysts who really do hard work and debate the merits of people's assumptions on the business plans. There are several analysts here who don't believe in Amazon. That's good for me because I'm hearing different points of view. I de-velop milestones to look for as the story develops that help me decide whether to stay with it or not.

Kazanjian: *Janus is a pretty young organization.*

Lammert: Yes. Tom Bailey is the senior guy. Jim Craig, our director of research, is in his early forties. I'm 38. Most of the other portfolio managers are my age or younger.

Kazanjian: *That means most of you have never managed money pro-fessionally during a severe bear market. Is that a problem?*

Lammert: Probably. Tom Bailey grew up in this business during the 1970s. Between 1974 and 1980, the real value of stocks after inflation went down 50 percent. I think employment in the securities business went down about 70 percent during that period. Tom knows from experience that stock prices can head south as well as north. You can go through long periods of time where it's hard to earn a return for your shareholders. I've been very fortunate being in the business during an unusually long bull market sparked by a wonderful economy, low inflation, and terrific real economic growth.

Kazanjian: *Do you think we'll have another major bear market like the 1970s?*

Lammert: I don't doubt that we will. I don't necessarily see the confluence of negative economic factors as you had back then, which included the Vietnam War, the Arab oil embargo, and some pretty awful economic policies that helped precipitate the fall. Of course, our ability to look into the future is limited. I'm an optimist on the long term. We really do have a dynamic economy built on technical innovation, greater capital investment, and more effective financial market structures that help redeploy capital in our economy more effectively. I think we're in a period of wonderful innovation, especially in the technology, pharmaceutical, and biotech fields. This will pay great dividends for investors over the next decade.

Kazanjian: *Does it worry you that there are so many young portfolio managers, many much younger than you, running billions of dollars? The old-timers say you young folks won't know what to do when the markets goes down.*

Lammert: I was a senior analyst and senior member of the team at Janus through the 1987 crisis when stock prices went down 30 percent in a day. You had the phenomenon of younger portfolio managers then, too. Most economists were convinced the reduction in people's assets would cause a collapse of consumption. They said we'd have a significant recession or depression. The reality is people muddled through. The market didn't do much after the collapse in October through the end of 1987 and gradually began to improve in 1988. We wound up having a good year in 1989. The overall economy never rolled over. People didn't panic after the initial collapse and take that much money out of the market. In contrast to the concerns and worries of the doomsayers, people often surprise us with their resilience.

Kazanjian: *If you weren't managing a fund, just out there looking for someone to manage your money, would you give it to a younger manager?*

Lammert: I think I would look at his or her record, try to understand his or her philosophy, and how he or she looks at stocks. I'm not sure I would let age be the dominating factor for me. It's important to maintain an ability to look at the areas of change in the economy. People who say they would never invest in the Internet are making a mistake. People who get too exuberantly carried away with the Internet may also be making a mistake. Just as you do with companies, you must look at the individual track records.

Kazanjian: *Does your background in economics help you pick companies and manage money?*

Lammert: It helps me deal with the emotions of the market. By studying economic history, I've seen periods when investors got too carried away and how it has paid to have faith in the market to generate value over time. That's helpful. But company research really requires hands-on, practical experience. Economic theory may give you some useful background and help you think about some questions to ask, but good analysis really requires digging in and understanding individual enterprises, why they exist, how they serve the customer, and what their strengths and weaknesses are.

Kazanjian: *What's the most important investment lesson you've learned?*

Lammert: Do the work yourself and think for yourself. You've got to remain appropriately cynical and wary, but at the same time seize your opportunities.

Kazanjian: *What do you do away from the office?*

Lammert: I have a family, a two-year-old and four-year-old. That keeps me busy. I've always played ice hockey. Before I had two kids, I played three times per week. I love sports. I ran a marathon last year. I find sports and exercise are necessary antidotes to the stress and pace of this business.

Kazanjian: *How many hours a day do you work?*

Lammert: Probably ten. I'd like to work more, but with a family that's not possible.

Kazanjian: *Whom would you say your fund is most appropriate for?*

Lammert: A long-term growth investor who has confidence in new technologies and is willing to suffer some volatility.

With all of the attention being given to the Janus Funds these days, Warren's biggest challenge may be keeping up his great performance in light of all the new cash flowing in to his fund right now.

One interesting development at Janus is that the fund family, known for its heavy emphasis on growth, recently launched a value fund. The company claims the move is designed to broaden its line of offerings. But could this growth shop be changing its stripes by distancing itself from the high-priced stocks that have lead to skyrocketing performance in recent years? While some observers think so, I have my doubts. After all, it would be hard for Warren and his colleagues to find companies with the strong growth they demand by looking through the value heap. ■

KEVIN LANDIS

FIRSTHAND FUNDS

Which manager runs the top-performing fund in America over the five-year period ending in 1999? It's Kevin Landis, by a landslide. His Technology Value Fund has bested the S&P 500 by almost 28 percent annually since its inception in 1994. No other fund comes close. Even more interesting, it is the first investment portfolio Kevin has ever managed professionally, fund or otherwise.

Kevin came into the fund industry in a most unconventional way. The 38-year-old spent several years in the technology field before taking up investing as a hobby. He quickly realized he was making more from trading than from his day job. He got together with a friend from his investment club, Ken Kam, and the two decided to start their own mutual fund in 1993. Ken had his own medical-device company at the time and as little experience in the investment field as Kevin. Their journey on the way to starting this fund, which is detailed in the interview, was quite brave, to say the least. This was definitely what you'd call a bootstrap operation. In fact, for the first couple of years, the entire operation was run out of Kevin's home.

From the start, these partners planned on building a family of funds focused exclusively on investing in technology and related stocks. Their company, Firsthand Funds, is located in San Jose, California, in the heart of the Silicon Valley, so they are close to many of their investments. The firm now has six different funds, with more planned for the future. While Kevin and Ken initially ran the funds together, Ken left to start his own firm in 1999, although he still serves as an outside consultant.

Kevin is clearly an optimist on the entire technology industry. While he has no clue what will happen with these stocks over the next month, week, or even year, he's convinced more money will be made in technology than in any other sector over the long haul. And, for those willing to stomach the risk, he's perfectly comfortable recommending that investors keep 100 percent of the stock portion of their portfolios in technology.

Kazanjian: *You certainly have the most unconventional background of anyone in this book, but I guess it's fitting for someone running a technology fund. After all, you were born and raised in the Silicon Valley and your dad worked in the electronics industry. Did you want to get into the technology field as a kid?*

Landis: Like most boys, I went through phases of wanting to be a fireman, astronaut, and pro football player. I eventually decided I was pretty good at math and wanted to do something technical. When I was at U.C. Berkeley, pursuing my electrical engineering degree, I discovered I had a real affinity for economics and business. After graduation, I worked for my dad in the family business for about four years. He was an engineer working with other engineers trying to solve their problems by selling them the proper test equipment for the right kinds of components. I was one of his manufacturer's reps. While I worked in that business, I studied for my MBA in the evenings at Santa Clara University.

Kazanjian: *Why did you decide to pursue an MBA?*

Landis: I really missed school. Late in my college career, I found my economics and finance courses to be a lot of fun. If you're an engineering student and you've managed to get through multivariable calculus, compound interest is a snap. I had a real affinity for these classes.

Kazanjian: *You're obviously attracted to numbers. You must be a left-brain person.*

Landis: No question about it.

Kazanjian: *What did you do after getting your MBA?*

Landis: I was an analyst for Dataquest, which involved writing about emerging technology markets. Dataquest is a high-technology market research firm. I worked in the semiconductor group. My job was to forecast the demand for equipment such as printers, disk drives, and computers. I then had to translate that into semiconductor demand. For example, in the late 1980s, when laser printers were just starting to become adopted rapidly, I took several printers apart and did a complete inventory of all the chips inside. I figured out how they worked and what their bill of materials looked like from a semiconductor standpoint. I then talked with the printer group for their forecast of how many printers were shipped from 1988 to 1992 and how the mix was changing away from simple dot matrix computers. I also talked to the designers of these devices to learn how they would be different in the next five years. I ended up with a report showing how the printer market was going to evolve, how many there would be, and therefore how many DRAMs the printer industry would buy in the future.

Kazanjian: *That sounds like information a stock investor would need to know to figure out which company stood to profit the most.*

Landis: Absolutely. It was a very intellectually satisfying process.

Kazanjian: *How do you make predictions like that with any degree of accuracy?*

Landis: I learned a few basic market research techniques in business school. If you wanted to forecast the market for toothpaste, you had to know how many people would be brushing their teeth several years out, how often they would brush, how much paste they would squeeze on the brush, and how much they'd leave in the tube when they threw it out. These kinds of simple linear approximations were utterly useless to me at Dataquest. We had these new devices that didn't exist two years before. I got used to dealing with a lot of unknowns and had to make many rational assumptions.

Kazanjian: *How on target were your forecasts?*

Landis: Of course, the ones I remember were brilliantly insightful and highly accurate. I got a couple of forecasts wrong. I noted that the PC industry was becoming a snap together industry where just about anybody could get in the business. All you had to do was buy chip sets, microprocessors, DRAM, monitors, and keyboards to build it up. I looked at the laser printer business and saw how laser printers were the next big thing that was coming. I said anybody who can snap together a PC can snap together a laser printer. You can buy your print engine at Canon, all the chips from various suppliers, and away you go. It didn't happen that way. Hewlett-Packard was aggressive on price, Adobe wasn't aggressive on pricing PostScript, and that combination led to HP's really dominating the printer business in a way I did not expect. On the other hand, there were things I thought were just so obvious I'm upset I didn't act on them. I thought once Microsoft got Windows right, not only would everybody adopt it, because it let you run more than one thing at a time, but also Microsoft would do well in all of its other software businesses. Looking back, I can't believe I didn't buy Microsoft when I was so passionate about how the world was going to go.

Kazanjian: *Wouldn't you agree that technology is the most difficult thing in the world to forecast because it is constantly changing?*

Landis: I would, but there's a conundrum. Tech companies are all about making new things possible. It just looks like magic because it couldn't have been done before. In reality, it was possible, only no one had figured it out. By definition, technology companies are always creating new markets.

Kazanjian: *What happened after Dataquest?*

Landis: I went to S-MOS systems as a new product marketing manager. I talked about bringing new products to market and helped to shape them.

Kazanjian: *So far I haven't heard you mention anything about investing.*

Landis: I dabbled in the market a bit at Dataquest. Remember, back then I was just out of business school, having learned that markets were efficient, most stocks were fairly priced, and you were foolish to try to beat the market. The professors concluded you should always buy index funds. It makes good logical sense.

Kazanjian: *But does it hold water?*

Landis: That depends. I've come to realize a few markets are very efficient. The foreign currency market is very efficient. The used-car market isn't. People pay different amounts of money for similar cars. It has to do with the flow of information and how hard or easy it is to make these calculations.

Kazanjian: *Is the stock market more like the currency markets or a used-car lot?*

Landis: The market for technology stocks is inefficient, like the used-car lot, so a good money manager can add a lot of value.

Kazanjian: *When did you first decide to explore the markets for yourself?*

Landis: As an analyst at Dataquest, I had to take questions from clients, many of whom were from the financial industry. I realized they didn't have a lot of sophistication, by and large. Also, I was kicking around investment ideas with my investment club and other folks who were in high tech.

Kazanjian: *Speaking of the investment club, that's where you met your former partner, Ken Kam. When did you start your club?*

Landis: We founded the Winners Circle Investment Club in the spring of 1987. Ken and I were two of the five original founders.

Kazanjian: *Did you focus solely on tech stocks?*

Landis: Not totally. One of the lessons we learned is that you ought to be totally devoted to something you know well. We leaned into the crash of 1987 like a Mike Tyson uppercut. We were wrung through the school of hard knocks. Along the way, I read about the philosophies of Peter Lynch and Warren Buffett. I tried to apply their ideas to high tech. By the time I got to S-MOS, I was pretty good at investing in tech stocks. I got to the point where I was making as much, if not more, money as an investor than as a product manager. After a little more than two years at S-MOS, I realized my true calling was as an investor. That's what I wanted to do.

Kazanjian: *Did you start sending your resumé out to Wall Street?*

Landis: No. I saw other analysts follow that track at Dataquest. They started off as junior analysts and got into the game of musical chairs, waiting to move up the ladder. If they didn't lose all their hair or have a heart attack, they eventually could help someone run a portfolio, and maybe go out on their own. That seemed like a lot of hoops to go through to get where I really wanted to be, which was managing a mutual fund. I realized that taking the direct path, though it was a hard one, was the better way to go.

Kazanjian: *So you and Ken decided to start the firm together?*

Landis: We had been talking and exchanging investment ideas. He felt the same way I did. Unlike me, he had just sold his own medical business and was independently wealthy.

Kazanjian: *When did you decide to start the firm?*

Landis: I quit my job in July 1993. That was the last time someone else gave me a paycheck. We commenced operations in 1994.

Kazanjian: *Most money management firms begin running separate accounts and eventually move into funds. Why did you decide to start with funds from the get-go?*

Landis: One of the things I noticed about my dad's business is that it didn't scale well. If he was successful, the companies he sold for became successful enough that they didn't need him as their rep anymore. He could literally work himself out of a job. I resolved that my business would scale very well. There are two great aspects to the mutual fund business. Number one, when you initially open your doors, you can accept money from just about anyone. Number two, if you are successful, you can easily continue to add shareholders. We have tens of thousands of shareholders today. There is absolutely no way we could do that managing individual accounts. We also wanted to build a base by having many professionals from the technology industry as shareholders. We planned to use them as our network of contacts, which would help us to succeed even more.

Kazanjian: *Your idea, then, was for the firm to focus solely on technology investments?*

Landis: Yes. I would focus on electronic technology companies, while Ken would focus on the medical side, since that was his area of expertise.

Kazanjian: *What was the process like for getting your mutual fund started and approved?*

Landis: It was daunting. When you start a fund, you have to fill out Form N1A. The estimated time for completion, the last time I looked, was 1,000 hours. If you have to hand that job to a lawyer at $250 an hour, you're looking at $250,000 just to get out of the gate. Instead, we spent about $50,000 in legal fees and acted as our own legal secretaries and paralegals to get our filing out.

Kazanjian: *How did you navigate your way through the complicated form?*

Landis: We called the SEC and asked a bunch of stupid questions. Then we ran around like a bunch of bumpkins and asked everyone some frighteningly naïve questions.

Kazanjian: *How long did it take to get your registration together?*

Landis: We filed our papers in January 1994 and didn't get approved until late December of that year.

Kazanjian: *What were you doing during that time?*

Landis: We elected to do a private placement. We took ten key investors and invested $134,000 and ran it as a mutual fund. Not a mutual fund open to the public, but a mutual fund nonetheless. That got us operationally into the routine of pricing our share every day and investing the money on an ongoing basis.

Kazanjian: *How much would it cost someone to start a mutual fund today, just for legal fees and registration?*

Landis: On a shoestring budget, $100,000 to $150,000 to get it open, and then you need at least another $100,000 to capitalize it.

Kazanjian: *Did you start off slowly?*

Landis: Yes, we worked out of my rented house in Milpitas for the first couple of years. We spent that first full calendar year, 1995, going back to our Rolodexes and telling everybody who'd gotten stock picks from us for years, "Now's your chance to invest with us." That year, we had a little less than 200 investors and about $2 million in assets.

Kazanjian: *How was your performance that first year?*

Landis: For that stub period of 1994, we were up 25.3 percent. In 1995 we were up more than 61 percent. We were the number-one mutual fund in the third quarter of 1995 with a return of more than 30 percent. Nobody knew it because we weren't activated in the Lipper database. We realized that we might never be the number-one fund for a quarter ever again. We made a concerted effort to figure out how to tell the world about it. A reporter for the *San Jose Mercury News* interviewed us and wrote our story. That article came out

Wednesday, December 20, 1995. The phone absolutely rang until it had smoke coming out of it. That article launched us on a whole new projectory. We realized the power of the press. We also had a powerful story, applying the value discipline of Buffett and the invest-in-what-you-know philosophy of Peter Lynch to the Silicon Valley and high tech.

Kazanjian: *Today you have some $2.3 billion in assets and six funds, not to mention a high-rise office in San Jose. Are you finally making money?*

Landis: The management company is profitable, but we're looking for more office space and I just hired another analyst. That brings the staff here to 14. I think we have a winning approach and formula. I'm not yet in the mode to maximize profits.

Kazanjian: *For someone reading this, who wants to get into the investment business, would you recommend starting a fund from scratch, based on your experiences?*

Landis: If you climb a mountain, and know in advance all you must go through to get to the top, it makes it emotionally difficult to even start. When people ask me that, I'm honest about everything I had to overcome. My original business plan didn't call for me to return 60 percent to shareholders two years in a row, or to get that feature article. I tell people interested in starting their own fund what it cost, how long it took, and all the other things I shared with you. In the end, most people considering the idea decide not to do it.

Kazanjian: *Let's talk more about your investment process. Your marketing line has long been that you're better able to choose good technology investments because you're right in the Silicon Valley. Is it really important for investors to live in the middle of it to make profitable decisions?*

Landis: No, but it sure helps. I think of it as a home-field advantage. If you are in a research triangle in North Carolina, Plano, Texas, or Maynard, Massachusetts, you have your own home-field advantage there as well.

Kazanjian: *Are most of the investments in your portfolio headquartered in the Silicon Valley?*

Landis: Fewer than half, as a matter of fact. I simply buy good stocks, regardless of where they are.

Kazanjian: *Your original fund is the Technology Value Fund. Most people have a hard time associating value with technology.*

Landis: Technology has many uncertainties. Even good companies can sometimes report disappointing news. If you're a value investor and know the companies well, the market offers you a lot of attractive entry points on great stocks. One winning approach is to identify quality companies, in good markets, and buy them when they hit a bump in the road.

Kazanjian: *How do you know whether it's just a bump or a major crack that's about to emerge?*

Landis: That comes down to how well you understand the business. At that point, you can't rely on analyst reports, because you'll be reading nothing but downgrades.

Kazanjian: *How many stocks do you own in the portfolio?*

Landis: I tend to be more concentrated than others, with between 40 and 50 names most of the time.

Kazanjian: *You place heavy bets on certain stocks. Are those your best ideas?*

Landis: Yes. It's not unusual for my largest position to be in the high single digits and even into the double digits. If I'm right about my largest position, it can easily run up into the double digits.

Kazanjian: *What is your overall investment strategy?*

Landis: I like to own the best companies involved in the strongest technology trends.

Kazanjian: *Do you begin the process of putting your portfolio together by first deciding which trends you think are going to be most advantageous?*

Landis: I ask myself, "When somebody writes the history of what happened five years from now, what trends will emerge?" I then try to understand which companies will be heavily involved in making that happen. Next, I figure out what I'm willing to pay for those stocks.

Kazanjian: *Looking ahead, what trends do you see as being most profitable?*

Landis: One is DVD. I think DVD players will come into the consumer electronic space and take over the well-worn VCR. Another trend is digital photography. This technology is getting relentlessly better and will trump current chemical photography. People will move to it very quickly. Another is the flat-panel monitor, which will displace the CRT. You're probably sitting in front of a CRT now. Five years down the line, you'll be using a flat panel. It takes less power, gives a sharper picture, and is easier on your eyes. A bigger trend is the whole area of wireless, which is really picking up speed again. Most people on this planet have never made a phone call. I think that will change over the course of our lifetime. Wireless is not just cell phones. It's satellite communications and many other things as well.

Kazanjian: *How do you determine who the winners and losers will be in each of these areas?*

Landis: You have to look at the trend and determine what you know about it. For example, digital photography and DVD are mostly consumer technologies, which means although the units will be large, there will be significant pricing pressure. You must figure out how a company can profitably participate in that environment, which means they're either a low-cost producer or don't manufacture cost-sensitive parts. You might pick a chip company that has its decoder chip in almost every single DVD player. That's how I'm doing it, through a company called Zoran.

Kazanjian: *What about wireless? What kind of angles do you see there?*

Landis: We have a fairly big investment in Qualcomm. Qualcomm is involved in developing the CDMA standard, which is the better mousetrap of wireless. It doesn't matter who sells you your next cell phone. If it's a CDMA phone, Qualcomm gets paid. That's not the only way to play it. You could pick a cell phone provider and place your bet there. You could invest in component suppliers, too. There's a company in North Carolina, RF Microdevices, that supplies power amplifiers to these phones. It's a highly focused pure play on cellular phone components. That's a tough business because of pricing pressures, but these guys have figured out how to make a profit at fairly low price points.

Kazanjian: *What kind of analysis do you perform on these companies?*

Landis: I meet with management, but that doesn't really give me the whole story. It's rare that management sits down and immediately 'fesses up to being incompetent or substandard. You always get a good story. It takes more detective work. You get their story and then go check it out. If all detectives did was get somebody's story and never check it out, they wouldn't be great detectives, would they? You talk to customers, competitors, suppliers, and figure out if they are as locked in as they think.

Kazanjian: *Do you believe individual investors must understand the technology a company is involved in before buying the stock?*

Landis: I absolutely believe that. I also feel individual investors are best served by buying a combination of individual stocks they feel strongly about and mutual funds to round it out and lend diversification.

Kazanjian: *You haven't talked about the Internet.*

Landis: That's the mother of all trends right now. I was getting there. While there are some early leaders and franchise winners, it's still anybody's game. I think it's safer to bet on the infrastructure companies. That way, you're just betting that traffic will continue to grow. It takes some of the risk out of picking the pure-play winner and you can get better valuations that way.

Kazanjian: *You haven't purchased any of these IPO or dot.com companies?*

Landis: Not really, certainly not for the Technology Value Fund.

Kazanjian: *Is there any other advice you can offer on how to analyze these companies?*

Landis: I look at a company's products, how competitive those products are, the market its selling into, and how bullish I am on that market. It ultimately comes down to examining the company and asking what it's capable of doing a year or two down the line. From there, you figure out what you're willing to pay for the stock.

Kazanjian: *What about balance sheets? A lot of these companies aren't making money and have a lot of debt.*

Landis: Unless the balance sheet is really weak, it honestly doesn't go into the calculation. People don't buy tech stocks based on balance sheets. They buy based on what the income statement will look like down the road. That's what growth stock investing is all about. Still, I need to know a company is financially solvent. If it's losing money, I need to be sure it isn't burning through cash. I'm mostly concerned with how fast the earnings engine will grow and where it will be down the road.

Kazanjian: *Do you buy both large and small companies?*

Landis: Yes. When you look at a trend you believe in, you then try to figure out which companies are likely to win. You don't know who will show up on your radar screen. Clearly, you hope to find a small pure-play company with incredible intellectual property barriers, but that doesn't always happen.

Kazanjian: *Once you've found a company you're interested in, how do you determine whether it sells for a price you want to pay?*

Landis: I'll typically build a simple spreadsheet that shows me what the recent income statements look like. Then I build pro forma income statements stretching out into the future based on my forecast for how the company can grow. This is where management can really help, based on their targets as to where they'd like to get gross margins, operating income, spending, and overhead. If a company shows strong earnings visibility, I might conclude investors will pay 1.5 times the current market multiplier. Today, that would come out to 40 times earnings. So I'll take the expected earnings in my spreadsheet and apply it to that multiple.

Kazanjian: *How do you estimate what PE people are willing to pay?*

Landis: I take a look at the peer group's market multiple and what I think the growth rate going forward is likely to be.

Kazanjian: *Are you pretty strict on that?*

Landis: The market has a way of giving you discounts on good and bad companies. The trick is to deal just with the good companies and take advantage of those discounts. If I think the market will pay $50 for a stock five years from now, and it currently trades for $40, I'll probably pass, since the upside is limited.

Kazanjian: *Why are technology stocks so volatile?*

Landis: Because they are all about creating new things. As technology companies create new things, they open new markets. It's hard for people to figure out what to expect from those markets. Expectations get whipsawed back and forth.

Kazanjian: *When do you decide to sell?*

Landis: There are three cases, although they usually sound like two: Case number one is easy. A good company just becomes outrageously overpriced because of all the hype. Iomega comes to mind. Don't fall in love with your stock. If it gets too expensive, get out. The other two cases tend to get lumped into one, which people describe as "deteriorating fundamentals." In variant one, you made a good decision and bought a quality company. Before the world could see you were right, bad things happened and it fell apart. Another version of deteriorating fundamentals that a lot of people sweep under that first rug is that you just made a bad decision. The company's not going anywhere and was a lousy company to begin with. In either case, you have to admit you made a mistake and chalk it up to experience.

Kazanjian: *How often are you selling stocks?*

Landis: You'd be surprised. This is high tech. Companies get leap-frogged all the time. Markets that you really thought were going to be the next big thing fail to show up. A lot can happen.

Kazanjian: *What's your average holding period?*

Landis: I've owned the successful ones for three or four years. My turnover is around 100 percent a year.

Kazanjian: *Do you put all of your money in technology stocks?*

Landis: Yes.

Kazanjian: *Should the average investor follow your lead?*

Landis: That requires an emotional examination. Technology is volatile. Volatility is the price you pay for the higher expected returns. Opportunity and the unknown go hand-in-hand. You must figure out how much of your money you can stand to see bouncing around like this. If you're the kind of person who calculates your net worth each day, you probably don't want too much in tech. You'll give yourself a lot of worry lines. Your time horizon also matters. People think volatility means risk. It does if you sell in short order. The value of your house can be very volatile, but you don't care if you're going to live there for at least five years. Who cares what it does from one day to the next? It's the same thing with technology stocks. You have to remember everybody is manic about high tech, and you should always brace yourself for the possibility that a few months down the road, there will be a major sale in tech stocks.

Kazanjian: *When do those sales normally come around?*

Landis: If you can find somebody who's got the answer to that, tell them to give me a call! One thing I'll add is that technology equals growth. You must be invested in technology to realize growth. A large portion of the economy's growth comes from tech.

Kazanjian: *Do you expect a positive overall market for technology stocks over the next several years?*

Landis: Over several years, absolutely. If you said over the next three or four months, I'd shrug and admit I don't have a clue.

Kazanjian: *What do you do away from the office?*

Landis: I drive around and check to see how many cars are parked in the parking lots of the companies I'm investing in. I'm not a 24-hour-a-day undercover cop, but I keep my eyes open.

I've known Kevin for several years and am continually amazed at his success, both as an investment manager and businessman. Granted, he's had a lot of forces working in his favor. Perhaps most important, technology has been the number-one performing sector for years, and he has ridden that wave. But I've long felt that Kevin's success was due to more than just being in the right place at the right time. He seems to really have a knack for picking winning stocks and trends before the rest of the crowd.

It's also impressive to hear how knowledgeable Kevin is about technology in general, which serves him well when analyzing stocks. That's not surprising since, although he's relatively new to investment management, he grew up around the technology industry. He is able to evaluate his holdings as a professional in the field, instead of basing his decisions solely on outside research.

What can we surmise from Kevin's investment process? First, it's important to invest in technology that will be popular several years from now, instead of buying what's hot today. Then you must make sure you're paying the right price for these stocks.

Of course, seeing the future is hard for even the most experienced professional to do. And while even Kevin isn't exactly sure which technologies will rise to the forefront in the coming months (although he gave us a few guesses), he remains convinced that the sector in general will continue to be an outstanding performer for years to come. ■

RICHARD LAWSON

WEITZ FUNDS

When Rick Lawson decided to become an investment manager in 1990, he hooked up with Wally Weitz, the man he considered to be Omaha's best investment manager next to the city's other famous "Wizard," Warren Buffet. Wally gave Rick a list of books to read on value investing. After quickly absorbing all of this information, Rick was back offering to work for Wally as an unpaid intern, just so he could get his foot in the door. Rick was so good at finding winning stocks, he was soon on the payroll and got his own fund, Weitz Hickory, in 1993.

Weitz Hickory started like a rocket, soaring 34 percent in its first year of operation. But it fell almost as quickly the following year and ended 1994 down more than 17 percent. From that point on, however, it has been a straight shot up. Hickory has trounced the S&P and most other funds across the board. Even more impressive is that Rick predominately owns small-company stocks, which have been out of favor pretty much since the fund's inception.

The financial press finally picked up on Rick's record and started doing stories on Weitz Hickory in 1998. New money began pouring in at such a rapid pace that he was forced to shut the fund's doors to new investors by the middle of that year.

Rick, 42, says he's always been a value investor at heart, even before he hooked up with Wally Weitz. His dad is also in the investment business, so he grew up around the industry. Unlike most other small-cap fund managers, Rick concentrates on just 30 to 40 names and isn't afraid to put more than 5 percent of the portfolio in a single issue. Still, because he buys low-priced stocks, the fund has been far less volatile than most of its peers. But Rick is quick to point out that he doesn't purposely buy small-cap stocks. He has the freedom to own whatever he wants. He's looking for good companies that he can buy cheaply and hold on to for a long time. It just so happens that almost all of the ideas he's run across are small.

Kazanjian: *Since your father is an investment manager, I guess you grew up around this business.*

Lawson: Yes. But for one reason or another, I originally wanted to be an engineer. At Rice University, I double majored in chemical engineering and economics. It didn't take long to figure out I was a better engineering student than an engineer. I ended up going to work for Procter & Gamble doing product development, which was somewhere between engineering and business. I was trying to understand what products customers wanted and helped to create those products. After about two and a half years, I concluded I really wanted to get more into the business side of things.

Kazanjian: *So you went to Harvard for your MBA?*

Lawson: I did. After that, I worked for a management consulting firm in Boston that focused on issues of market analysis and marketing strategy.

Kazanjian: *You obviously had a keen interest in marketing.*

Lawson: I definitely wanted to know how markets and businesses work; what's a good market, what's a bad one. I learned a lot at both of my early jobs. But over time I concluded I didn't really want to be a consultant for the rest of my life. There was too much emphasis on selling and building client relationships. I was more interested in thinking about the businesses.

Kazanjian: *Why not start your own business?*

Lawson: You've got to have a good idea to do that. My wife and I ultimately decided we wanted to move back to the midwest and were both out looking for jobs in Minneapolis, Kansas City, and Omaha.

As it turned out, she got a job with First Data in Omaha, and I followed. I assumed I would get a marketing job, but after a few months of beating my head against the wall, I concluded that wasn't what I wanted to do. I thought about getting into the investment management business, which I had considered off and on over the years. That was in 1990.

Kazanjian: *How did you hook up with Wally Weitz?*

Lawson: I looked around town trying to decide where I wanted to work and quickly concluded it was with Wally. I liked the way he structured his business and how he thought about investing. It seemed like the best of the opportunities in town.

Kazanjian: *How did you first meet him?*

Lawson: Because my father's in the business in town, I was able to talk with several investment managers in the community. Wally had a great reputation.

Kazanjian: *Why not just join your dad?*

Lawson: His firm runs separate accounts and is a partnership. I have a great deal of respect for my father and would have loved to work with him. However, it quickly became clear that working for him probably wasn't going to work out. As a two-person partnership, bringing in the son of one of the partners was not an ideal situation.

Kazanjian: *So you invited Wally to lunch?*

Lawson: Exactly. It was an informational meeting. I told him I was interested in the business and asked if there were any books he could recommend for me to read. He gave me a list of the classics on value investing. A couple of weeks later, I called him back and said, "I've read the books. I'd like to get together and talk with you again." We went back and forth like this for a while. I finally asked if he'd be willing to let me use some space in his office to see if I could add some value. He agreed.

Kazanjian: *You worked for free, then, like an unpaid internship?*

Lawson: Yes.

Kazanjian: *Were you a value guy at heart before all this, or was it a function of working with Wally?*

Lawson: I was definitely a value guy. My father is a value investor, and that basic philosophy has always made more sense to me than anything else. I read Benjamin Graham's *The Intelligent Investor* and several other related books early on. They all clicked with the way I thought about things.

Kazanjian: *Obviously you were trying to work your way into a job with Wally.*

Lawson: I wanted to prove myself, get a job, and help Wally pick stocks. It took about three months before he finally decided to put me on the payroll.

Kazanjian: *Was he running all of the money at the firm by himself at that time?*

Lawson: There was one other analyst, who had been hired relatively recently, so Wally wasn't really looking to bring on someone else.

Kazanjian: *How did you talk him into hiring you?*

Lawson: It's hard to say exactly. Part of what I tried to do was learn a lot from Wally and talk to him about how he was thinking. I also forced him to think about some of the decisions he was making by asking him questions. I see the buy-side analyst's role as a very difficult one because you not only have to come up with good ideas, you have to come up with ideas that are relevant to the person you're working for. Then you must present them in a way that they can be listened to and used. Those are really three separate skills. In the end, I guess you'd have to ask Wally why he hired me.

Kazanjian: *Clearly, you impressed him. Did you start out managing money right away?*

Lawson: No. Most everything we do here is in the form of pools of one sort or another. Wally began managing private partnerships and then added mutual funds. Today, mutual funds represent the largest part of our business. Early on, I was basically an analyst helping Wally come up with investment ideas.

Kazanjian: *Did he have the Weitz Value Fund at that point?*

Lawson: Yes. That mutual fund was up and there were three equity partnerships. One of those partnerships has since evolved to become the Weitz Partners Value Fund.

Kazanjian: *You started the Weitz Hickory Fund in 1993. How did that happen?*

Lawson: After a couple of years of doing this, I started begging Wally to allow me to have a fund of my own. I wanted to have the experience of managing other people's money and to develop a track record. Because of the way we were structured, it really wasn't a big expense to start up a new fund. In response to my prodding, he let me launch Hickory.

Kazanjian: *Why is it called Hickory?*

Lawson: I grew up living on Hickory Street and my parents still live there. It seemed like an appropriate name.

Kazanjian: *Was it designed to be a small-cap value fund?*

Lawson: No. It was designed to be my fund. By that I mean I wanted something that would be consistent with the way I manage money, which is really very similar to Wally's approach except I'm more aggressive. I tend to be more concentrated in my stock picks. I'm also more fully invested and have a small-cap bias.

Kazanjian: *You have the latitude to buy anything, though?*

Lawson: That's right.

Kazanjian: *Nevertheless, most people, including Morningstar, consider Hickory to be a pure small-cap fund.*

Lawson: That's right, and if you look at the history of the stocks I have owned, it would certainly qualify as being a small-cap fund.

Kazanjian: *You're saying that's purely coincidental?*

Lawson: It's coincidental to the extent that there is nothing in the prospectus that forces this to be a small-cap fund. However, philosophically, I believe it is easier to find value among smaller companies.

Kazanjian: *Your first year out was great. Your return was 34 percent, or double the S&P 500. But 1994 was a different story. Hickory fell 17 percent, while the S&P was flat. What happened?*

Lawson: There were two main factors that made it tough. A couple of industries that were important to me had bad years. One was the cable industry, which faced rate reregulation. This was implemented in a way that was more onerous than people originally expected. That made for a very difficult year among cable companies. It was also a time when interest rates were being raised by the Federal Reserve.

That made for bad performance among financial companies, and I owned a lot of financial companies.

Kazanjian: *After that bad spell, it's pretty much been a straight ride up for you. The assets in your fund grew like a rocket in no time, thanks to a string of great press. How did you get to be so popular?*

Lawson: We have never done much to generate new assets. We run no-load funds, so there's nobody out distributing them, and we've never advertised. All of our growth has come from word of mouth, to the extent that organizations such as Morningstar say positive things, or there's positive press. For one reason or another the stars aligned in 1998 and a lot of people noticed us.

Kazanjian: *How much money was in your fund in 1997?*

Lawson: At the end of the year it was just over $20 million.

Kazanjian: *And it just shot up from there?*

Lawson: By the end of March 1998, assets hit around $44 million, which seemed like a lot. By the end of June the fund was just over $200 million. Over the next six weeks assets went from $200 million to $500 million.

Kazanjian: *Why was everyone running in all of a sudden?*

Lawson: There were two or three sparks. There was an article in the Sunday *New York Times* in April 1998. Then there was a Morningstar write-up and some articles in June and July that created more attention. *The Wall Street Journal* talked about the fund as being the number-one performer for one and five years as of the end of June 1998. That certainly had an effect.

Kazanjian: *What was the atmosphere like around the office back then?*

Lawson: Absolutely insane. We went from taking 1,000 prospectus calls for the firm overall during all of 1997 to about 1,000 calls in January 1998. We thought that was pretty crazy. The week *The New York Times* article hit, we took 1,000 calls. Then there was a day in July when we took 1,000 calls. It was very crazy.

Kazanjian: *Were you working the phones yourself?*

Lawson: I was answering the phones myself. Everybody was answering the phones.

Kazanjian: *This money that was coming in so quickly. People were obviously following performance. Is that a good way for people to choose mutual funds?*

Lawson: Yes and no. I don't think it's totally crazy to look at funds that have done well as a starting point. But I think it's much more important to understand *why* they've done well. You need to understand the investment philosophies and strategies that have been used and decide whether those strategies make sense for you as an investor. You also must determine if those strategies have staying power and are likely to have a reasonable chance of working well in the future.

Kazanjian: *You closed your fund once it got up to around $500 million. Why did you choose that number?*

Lawson: There was no magic to the arithmetic. The investment philosophy I've always used depends on concentration. I don't believe in owning lots and lots of stocks. I think it makes sense to concentrate on those opportunities that seem most attractive. I've also always found it easier to locate value among smaller companies. I want the opportunity to buy small companies. If you say that you're going to concentrate and buy small companies there's clearly some size that's too big. It's not clear what that size is, but it just felt as if $500 million were a reasonable point at which to close.

Kazanjian: *Do you worry this money's hot and as soon as you have a down quarter they'll all leave?*

Lawson: To a certain extent. One of the things I like about having a closed fund is I feel that the longer I can demonstrate my style and approach to a group of investors, the better the odds of their deciding to stick with me even when I hit a cold streak.

Kazanjian: *Are you able to manage the portfolio the same way today as when you had $20 million?*

Lawson: Not identically. I think there are certain companies that are now too small for me. That never used to be the case. It just doesn't make sense for me to think about a $100 million market cap company anymore, because the odds are I won't be able to buy enough for it to matter.

Kazanjian: *Do you feel as if closing the fund has helped? There is research to show that many funds tend to go on to be underperformers once they close.*

Lawson: I don't think that in the long run it should work that way. I think perhaps what you see is the effect of all the money coming in over the short run. That's sort of a leftover effect from before the fund closed. I think in the long run there's just no question that if you don't close you'll get too big. That will definitely hurt long-term performance.

Kazanjian: *Would you open your fund again at any point?*

Lawson: I would never say never, but the basic reasons for closing haven't changed.

Kazanjian: *If you had a mass exodus of people pulling out, would you open it then?*

Lawson: Sure. There are two drivers that could lead to reopening. One would be assets shrinking and no longer having the need to keep it closed. The other would be having enough experience with a larger size that would tell me that the larger size still works and therefore it's not as much of an issue. I see that as a decision that cannot be made anytime very soon.

Kazanjian: *Is there any way to get into your fund now?*

Lawson: If you are a current shareholder you can add more money to the fund. If someone were to give you a share of Hickory, you would be a shareholder. There's really no other way.

Kazanjian: *Are there any plans for you to start another fund?*

Lawson: The basic logic of why you close it would suggest that starting another fund would be pretty counterproductive. What we're saying is there is some right amount of money for my investment style. If I were to open another fund then I'd be managing more money. That doesn't really accomplish anything.

Kazanjian: *That's what a lot of fund families do, though. They'll start a clone of the same fund after closing it. A version two, if you will.*

Lawson: I know they do but that just doesn't make a lot of sense, does it?

Kazanjian: *Why do you like small-caps so much?*

Lawson: It gets to how I think about value. I believe it's easier to find value among smaller companies. They are more likely to be misunderstood or for investors to have given up on them for the wrong reasons. They are also more likely to be mispriced for one reason or another. Therefore, the odds of finding something that's seriously undervalued are much greater among smaller companies.

Kazanjian: *How do you define a smaller company, in terms of market capitalization?*

Lawson: I don't worry about it a whole lot. I don't even calculate the median market cap of the fund. I guess most people think of it as $1 billion or less, but I will look for value anywhere.

Kazanjian: *You are one of a small handful of managers who have been able to beat the S&P 500 over both the past three and five years. Most small-cap managers have significantly underperformed because the sector has been out of favor. What have you been doing that the others haven't?*

Lawson: Maybe it's because I think of myself as a value manager first and a small-cap manager second. It's hard to say. I don't know that I have a good answer to why others haven't done better. I just do what I think makes sense and it's worked.

Kazanjian: *A lot of small-cap managers lament that they own good companies, but Wall Street is ignoring them, which is why they are underperforming. Is that just an excuse, or has it really been hard to find good small stocks that are going up in this market?*

Lawson: Maybe the answer is that I'm looking for deep discount to value and I'm looking for value that's growing. If I actually find that combination, I have two ways to win. Sometimes the value grows and the discount to value stays the same. In that case, the stock goes up as value goes up. Alternatively, the gap between the current stock price and the underlying value of the company could shrink, which would also cause the stock price to go up. By looking hard for both those things I'm more likely to get one or the other to work well. I definitely haven't had a lot of trouble finding interesting stocks to buy.

Kazanjian: *How do you define value?*

Lawson: I think of myself as an absolute value investor. By that I mean I am trying to define value on an absolute scale. I ask whether I would like to own a company at its current market price, assuming that I never had a chance to sell it to anybody else. When you think about value from that perspective, all that really matters is the long-term discounted free cash flow.

Kazanjian: *What's discounted free cash flow?*

Lawson: It's just a function of how much cash you should expect the company to be able to pay out to its shareholders over its life, discounted back to the present.

Kazanjian: *How do you figure that out?*

Lawson: I feel the best way to identify good opportunities is to answer three questions. Number one, how good a business is this? That's a qualitative question. I'm looking for businesses that have a sustainable competitive advantage, some kind of edge that will allow them to do well over a long period. The next question I try to answer is what the company is worth. I try to calculate value from lots of different dimensions and estimate it in many ways. I usually don't have to make heroic leaps to come up with a value that seems pretty reasonable. I might use book value as a gauge of value. In the case of a cable company there are private market value transactions that take place that give you a sense of what other people think value is, and you can make comparisons to that. There are many different ways to do this.

Kazanjian: *What's the final question?*

Lawson: Why is this stock cheap? If I can identify some reason why all the smart people on Wall Street don't want to buy the stock today, that gives me a lot more comfort that the analysis I've done in questions one and two is reasonable. If I can't find the reason the stock is cheap, I wonder whether maybe I've misestimated how good the business is or misestimated value.

Kazanjian: *I've always wondered that same thing. I talk to a great many value managers and they are all looking for cheap stocks. It makes you wonder why stocks get cheap in the first place. Aren't cheap stocks lousy stocks?*

Lawson: I would say there are two dimensions that give you the opportunity to find cheap stocks. One is misinformation. Perhaps you have an edge. You've figured something out that others haven't. I think that's possible, but that's hard to do. It's certainly difficult as you get bigger and have more money under management. The other way to think about it is to understand why stocks get traded and treated the way they do. I would argue that for a number of institutional, cultural, and just human reasons there are certain stocks that people don't want to buy right now. Often it has to do with timing. For example, a company may have a problem right now. Anybody looking at the company would admit it. However, some would say it is a temporary problem because it's a good business. They're confident that sooner or later the situation is going to change. A lot of managers can't buy a stock like that because it might not go up in the next quarter and they'll look bad. Many investors are very worried about quarterly performance. I take the attitude that if it's a good business and it's cheap, I'm happy owning it for the next three to five years. I don't care when the problem gets solved, as long as I'm comfortable it will be solved. But I do want to buy when it's cheap.

Kazanjian: *Does that mean there's no such thing as an efficient market?*

Lawson: How do you define efficient market? I think information is moved around the market very efficiently. I think everybody knows stuff pretty fast. But I think the market has blind spots and is manic depressive. Therefore, I believe there are great opportunities to buy businesses on the stock market for less than they're worth.

Kazanjian: *In general, what are the qualitative aspects that lead you to believe a business is a good business?*

Lawson: Mostly I'm looking for a sustainable competitive advantage. I want to see something about the business that will allow the company to earn high returns over a long period of time. There's no one answer to what creates that. It may have to do with the industry structure that makes it a natural. I'm also looking for businesses where there's pricing power, a cost advantage, and some edge that I believe will be around for awhile. It's an advantage to be selling to lots of customers who view the product or service as such a necessity that they're willing to pay money to get it. I could give you lots of examples, but there's no simple one-line answer to what makes a good business.

Kazanjian: *Is management important?*

Lawson: Management absolutely is important, but I will draw a distinction between the quality of the business and the quality of management. I in no way want to minimize the importance of management. If you don't trust management, don't think they'll do a good job, then it's a lot harder to feel really good about the company. But you can have good management and not have a particularly good business. Alternatively, you could have a great business and management is only so-so. I'd like to have both.

Kazanjian: *If you could have one or the other, which would you rather have?*

Lawson: A great business.

Kazanjian: *How about balance sheets and financial statements?*

Lawson: I find that, in many cases, really good businesses that are also interesting stocks don't have particularly good balance sheets. It may be because the good business has been around long enough that somebody has figured out how much cash flow it generates and has messed up the balance sheet by doing a reversed buyout. Maybe management is just running the business with a lot of debt. I don't find the standard balance sheet ratios of debt to equity to be very useful.

Kazanjian: *Debt doesn't bother you, then?*

Lawson: Debt needs to be thought about relative to the overall value of the company and the cash flow generating capability of the business. I think every business has a right amount of debt. But that's more a function of cash flow than it is of book equity.

Kazanjian: *On the valuation side, I didn't hear you talk about PE ratios, book value, and those other value-oriented yardsticks I'm sure you read in Ben Graham's books. Do you look at that kind of stuff?*

Lawson: PE ratios and book value are two of the valuation techniques I use in trying to think about the value of a business. Given my focus on long-term discounted free cash flow, I care a lot more about the cash flow generating capabilities of a business than it's reported earnings. For instance, I'm comfortable owning cable and cellular businesses that have never had much of any reported earnings. These companies could make money if management would allow them to, but cable executives are pretty averse to paying taxes. They always find a way to make sure they don't report earnings.

Kazanjian: *I guess that means you don't follow Graham's teachings religiously.*

Lawson: In my view, if you think about what Benjamin Graham was saying, he really had three main points. You should think about buying a stock as buying a piece of a business. So understand the business. Think about the market as this "Mr. Market" that sometimes wants to buy your stock and sometimes wants to sell your stock and take advantage of those changes in mood. Finally, look for a margin of safety. Pay less than what you think a business is worth. Those are the three main points I've taken away from Graham. How you calculate value is a question that different people have answered in different ways over the years. To me, the only way it really makes sense is to figure out what you would be willing to pay if you had a chance to buy the entire business.

Kazanjian: *Take us through an example of a company you recently purchased and the decision-making process you went through.*

Lawson: Let's use Valassis Communications. This is the company that prints freestanding coupon inserts that show up in the middle of your Sunday newspaper, usually near the comics section. Today, there are only two companies in the country that print freestanding inserts—Valassis and a unit of News Corp called News America. If you go back to 1993, there was a third company that tried to get into the business. It started offering the service and was out selling a similar product. The entrance of the third company created a price war where all three competitors were lowering their prices trying to get business, and Valassis's stock got hit. What I learned is that because of the way these booklets get distributed, if you distribute a thin booklet that has maybe 16 pages, the newspapers charge you a certain amount for distribution. If you then make it a fat booklet, say 40 pages, the newspapers charge you a bit more, but not in proportion to all the extra pages you have. Therefore, if you're somebody with a lot of customers and print fat booklets, you'll make more money than if you're printing thin booklets. That dynamic made it very hard for the third competitor to get anywhere. It was losing money hand over fist. It was obvious to me the third competitor would eventually have to get out of the business. It was losing so much money and couldn't even get to the break-even point. I saw that as a great opportunity to buy Valassis, because once its competitor was gone, it would be able to make very high returns on invested capital. I viewed this as being a good business facing a temporary problem. Lo and behold, that's basically how things worked out. The third competitor did get out of the business, and pricing has slowly recovered. Valassis's profitability is temporarily affected at times by the price of paper, but that's about it. Valassis had another aspect that I thought made it attractive. Because of a previous LBO, Valassis was recording a lot of goodwill amortization on its income statement. If you looked at how the business really worked, it was able to generate, and still generates, more free cash flow than reported earnings. That's not a very common relationship. By and large companies generate a lot less free cash flow than they generate in reported earnings. I thought that because of all this free cash flow investors were misvaluing the company and I think that has continued to be the case.

Kazanjian: *When you have a losing stock, what's usually the biggest mistake you make?*

Lawson: There are two issues. I guess I need to know what you mean by "losing." I almost never succeed in buying a stock at the very lowest price it sees. It's not at all uncommon for me to buy a stock, have it go down, buy some more, have it go down more, buy some more, and over a period of months or longer see that I've lost money on the company. To me, that is not a mistake. It's just a question of not getting the timing exactly right. As long as the fundamentals are sound, that's often an opportunity to buy even more of something that turns out to be a wonderful long-term investment. Not everything I buy works out that well. There are times when I have misread the situation and do regret buying a stock. Often I've misestimated the value of the company. I would say the main mistake I make is in thinking that a business is better than it is for one reason or another. I occasionally don't see that there are some forces on the horizon that could affect the business.

Kazanjian: *Do you try to hold your companies for a long time?*

Lawson: I like holding for as long as I can. I continually reevaluate my businesses. I have in my head a value when I buy a business, and I continue to look at facts as they come in to decide whether I want to adjust that number up or down.

Kazanjian: *This value is based on the free cash flow?*

Lawson: Yes, and all the other techniques I use to try to estimate value.

Kazanjian: *When would you sell a stock?*

Lawson: Basically, I want to own as many stocks selling at really big discounts to value as I can. If I can find a 40-cent dollar, that's wonderful. I want large positions in stocks like that. Over time, if things work out, the discount to value will shrink and the stock price will go up. Because the stock price is going up, the company becomes a bigger proportion of the portfolio. In my ideal world, as a company starts selling for 80 cents on the dollar, still a discount to value but not nearly as big a discount, I no longer want to own it. So I'm constantly looking at every holding to see whether I want to add more or trim back because it's no longer as attractive as it used to be.

Kazanjian: *Is there a point where a bad stock goes down so much that you say, "I better get out of here and cut my losses?"*

Lawson: I don't think that way. Because I'm constantly revaluing businesses, it is certainly conceivable that I will say, "Oh, gee, I misvalued this business. I made a mistake in thinking about it. It really isn't as cheap as I thought, and therefore I want out."

Kazanjian: *What's your average holding period?*

Lawson: The turnover has tended to fall in the high 20 percent range. That means I hold a company for an average of three to five years.

Kazanjian: *You hold a concentrated portfolio of some 25 names. How much will you keep in a single holding?*

Lawson: I have had positions that are more than 10 percent of the portfolio. If I feel strongly that it's a great business and totally misvalued, I'm not uncomfortable doing that. There are constraints that arise from the tax rules on how much a mutual fund can have in various stocks. [For instance, the IRS says nondiversified funds such as Weitz Hickory can keep no more than half of their assets in positions that each make up more than 5 percent of the total pie.]

Kazanjian: *Where do you find most of your ideas?*

Lawson: There's no simple way to answer that. I read a lot, I see a lot of Wall Street research. That's never the endpoint, but sometimes that's a good beginning. Over time you get to know industries, you talk to a lot of people in the business. I see myself as a big sieve. I'm catching lots of information, and I know the kinds of things I'm looking for. If I find something that looks as if it might be interesting I'll do a lot more work on it of one sort or another.

Kazanjian: *You seem to concentrate in certain sectors. Is that just a coincidence?*

Lawson: In some industries you'll find a company that looks interesting, and because of the structure of the industry there will be opportunities for other similar companies. The cable industry is a good example. The cable company that services Omaha is not that different from the company that serves Des Moines, but they are different companies. In some cases you can find a combination of companies that Wall Street views as being similar, but they really have different dynamics. When the whole sector is out of favor, that can create opportunities. I don't start by saying I want to go buy some medical stocks and go find a bunch of them. I might at one point say it feels as if there should be some opportunity in this industry because it's out of favor for what seems like bad reasons. Then I'll go look and see what might be attractive.

Kazanjian: *What are the sectors you like right now?*

Lawson: At this point I don't really have as much of a sector focus as I've had in the past. I still own a lot of financial services companies, but they represent a number of different business models. Other than that, I still own some cable and cellular companies, although they have become less significant to me than in the past because there just aren't as many cheap companies as there used to be.

Kazanjian: *You definitely used to load up on them. Have you cut back because you feel cable and cellular stocks are overpriced?*

Lawson: I'm not sure I'd call them overpriced, but they're no longer significantly underpriced. We've gone from a period when these industries were completely out of favor to where they're much less unloved.

Kazanjian: *Do you pay attention to the market itself and interest rates?*

Lawson: Not really. You don't ignore anything, but I'm really trying to focus on businesses and the valuations of those businesses.

Kazanjian: *Would you raise cash at any point if you were negative on the market?*

Lawson: As long as I can find companies that I want to own at prices I want to own them at, no, I would not raise cash by selling stocks I like.

Kazanjian: *Have you run into a situation like that before? Or do you think there are always stocks that are good values out there?*

Lawson: My sense is that there's almost always something you can find. There have been times when I was more excited about the number of opportunities than others, but by and large there's almost always some industry or set of companies that the market has wrongly given up on.

Kazanjian: *Do you personally visit companies?*

Lawson: I do. I think it's important to understand the management, where they're coming from, and to get a feel for the business. I think you can get that information lots of different ways. Clearly one of the ways is to go visit companies.

Kazanjian: *Is there a point when you would move into larger companies?*

Lawson: Yes. If you look at my holdings, I've never been exclusively into small-caps. I am driven by where I see opportunity.

Kazanjian: *You also buy some private placements. That's pretty rare for a mutual fund. Isn't liquidity a problem?*

Lawson: I would never allow private placements to become a large percentage of the fund's assets. At this point I don't think they've ever been more than about 5 percent of total assets. I wouldn't allow it to get much more than that. Liquidity does not concern me that much. I can't imagine getting to a point where I have to sell the other 95 percent of my holdings. I don't view stock picking as an active trading activity. I'm looking to buy companies that I can own for a long time. So, yes, I think about the liquidity and whether private placements are a good or bad thing. But it's not my first and foremost consideration.

Kazanjian: *Small stocks in general have underperformed in the past several years, although they have recently started to perk up. What's your outlook for small-cap stocks going into the new millennium?*

Lawson: It looks to me as if the sentiment toward small-caps relative to larger-cap stocks is quite negative and that the valuation of small-caps relative to larger-caps are very attractive. These factors should create a good environment for small-caps. Small-caps are very out of favor. I don't know what the catalyst will be for them to turn around, but I'm willing to bet that small-caps should be an easier area to find good value than large-caps over the next few years.

Kazanjian: *What percentage of a portfolio do you think investors should keep in small-caps?*

Lawson: I'm not sure I'm the best person to ask that question since I do all my own investing in the fund I manage, and it's thought of as a small-cap fund. I really don't think about it that way. The way I think about investing is that you should find an investment style and approach that you feel comfortable with and use it. If that means all your money is in small-caps, fine. If you find a large-cap manager you think is really good, and you feel comfortable with that approach, that's fine too. I don't get into this asset allocation stuff. I don't think it is that helpful.

Kazanjian: *It's interesting to me that most managers don't put all of their money into their funds, as you do. Do you think they should?*

Lawson: I believe fund managers should put a significant portion of their money in their fund, unless they are managing a bond fund.

Even then I would certainly think all of your bond investing should be done through your fund.

Kazanjian: *Do you buy any individual stocks?*

Lawson: No.

Kazanjian: *Your fund has a pretty high minimum of $25,000. Why is it so high?*

Lawson: Weitz has always had high minimums for two reasons. One, we've always done all of our own administration and had high minimums in self-defense. We didn't want a situation where we got really hot and were inundated with lots of new accounts. Last year demonstrated why that was a good thing to worry about. The other advantage to high minimums is that it's less likely an investor will just write us a check on a lark. They're going to think about it more. We like that. We want people who've thought about us and why they're investing with us. We think that creates a better relationship and makes for better shareholders.

Kazanjian: *Is Weitz Hickory the only portfolio you work on right now?*

Lawson: I have always helped to come up with stocks for all our funds. Wally and I talk and share ideas all the time. I consider my analytical work as being available and helpful to all the stock funds we have here.

Kazanjian: *Do you and Wally think alike?*

Lawson: We're very similar in our approach. As I said earlier, Hickory is a more aggressive version of the investment style Wally uses with the Value Fund. We're not identical, but we're more than compatible.

Kazanjian: *Do you think individual investors are better off in funds, or should they just put together a concentrated portfolio of stocks as you have?*

Lawson: It really depends to a certain extent on the capabilities of the individual. How much time does he or she have to think about investing? Is he or she the type of person who can do investing for him or herself? I think there are a lot of people who are perfectly capable of looking around them, finding good businesses, and being patient about their investments. If you're that kind of person, I see nothing wrong with investing for yourself. On the other hand, it's very difficult for many people to be good investors. They react too much to short-term news, they don't have the patience to allow a good business to be recognized by the market, and they get too concerned when the stock market goes down. I think for people like that, letting someone else manage their money makes sense.

Kazanjian: *If you're going to manage your own money as an individual, how many stocks do you think you need to own?*

Lawson: I keep 25 to 35 names in the fund. If I were managing a portfolio just for myself, I'd be comfortable with between 10 and 15 stocks.

Kazanjian: *The conventional wisdom with small-cap stock funds is that you should be more diversified because of the inherent risks of small-company stocks. You obviously don't buy that.*

Lawson: No, I don't. Risk is a funny term. I don't think there is a good quantitative way to measure risk. To my way of thinking, the best way to minimize overall stock market risk is to buy good businesses at a big discount to value. If you do that, your true risk of losing money over the long run is not that great.

Kazanjian: *Why do you think so many active fund managers in general underperform the index?*

Lawson: There are some real institutional issues that make it difficult for money managers to focus on long-term investment results. Too many of my peers are actively measured on their quarterly performance. They are legitimately worried about losing their job if they're different. To outperform you must be different. If you are willing to be different, occasionally that means you'll be different for the worse. Many people just can't do that. They cannot bear that risk because if they underperform for a period of time they're going to lose the money they manage. One of the advantages I have is I really am able to focus on long-term results. I know there will be periods when I underperform. That's okay.

Kazanjian: *I guess what you're saying is that managers who actively try to beat the market every single quarter are almost doomed to fail.*

Lawson: I really believe that. When you become focused on beating the market every quarter you start asking the wrong questions and looking for the wrong things. You're no longer investing—you're trying to figure out what stock will go up next quarter. You're not trying to find a good business that's undervalued.

Kazanjian: *Back to value, you own shares of Berkshire Hathaway. That's certainly not a small-cap stock. It's a company run by one of your Omaha neighbors, Warren Buffett. Have you ever met him?*

Lawson: No, not yet.

Kazanjian: *He's a value investor, too. In fact, you two seem to have a lot in common.*

Lawson: The kinds of characteristics that I talk about are at one level pretty similar to what Buffett looks for. He, on the other hand, is looking for what I consider to be really stable businesses where there's not a lot of change. Coke has been Coke for a long time. I am more comfortable with businesses that are experiencing change, as long as I feel I can understand what that change is and I'm on the right side of it. A cellular company business that didn't exist 20 years ago is perfectly reasonable for me because I understand how the change is working in favor of the business. I end up looking at a different universe from what he does. We're similar in terms of thinking about stocks as a business, looking at long-term discounted free cash flow, and seeking a sustainable competitive advantage.

Kazanjian: *You get compared to Buffett a lot. Are you tired of that comparison?*

Lawson: Yes, I am. I don't think anybody should be compared to Warren Buffett except Warren Buffett. Let's wait 30 years before you compare me to him. I just don't think the comparison is valid at this point. I haven't been doing this long enough.

Kazanjian: *When it comes to evaluating smaller companies do you find you can trust the information you get from management as much as you can with a large company?*

Lawson: It's important to check, double-check, and look at all information you get from lots of different directions on all companies. The kinds of issues you run into may be different with smaller companies, compared to larger companies. There are issues in both cases. Many times investors really don't know what is going on in larger companies, because they are made up of so many different divisions. I doubt there is anybody on Wall Street who truly understands all of GE's businesses. To a large extent, investors have to trust what management tells them, regardless of the size of the company.

Kazanjian: *If I had been a shareholder in your fund when it had only $20 million in assets, how do I now know that at $800 million you're* *still performing as well as if you still had $20 million? Do you think your bigger size is penalizing those who were with you from the start?*

Lawson: That's a hard question. Only time will tell. You at least have the evidence that I'm willing to worry about it because I've closed the fund. I would worry more in a situation where it goes from $20 million to $800 million to $8 billion with no sign of slowing down. I also think about how this performance is generated and whether it's reasonable to expect the techniques used in the past will still work with a somewhat larger asset size. For example, there are fund managers who have been very successful flipping IPOs. They'll buy a lot of IPOs and sell them almost immediately. That's a strategy that does not work when you are managing billions of dollars.

Kazanjian: *Do you buy IPOs?*

Lawson: Almost never. It's not right to say never, because I have, but it's not a significant part of my strategy.

Kazanjian: *When you do buy IPOs, is that because you think the offering price is below the value of the business?*

Lawson: Yes. I'm not into flipping.

Kazanjian: *What about Internet stocks?*

Lawson: I believe Internet stocks represent one of the largest financial bubbles this world has ever seen.

Kazanjian: *Do you believe in the Internet?*

Lawson: I absolutely believe in the Internet, but I think the values of the companies have totally lost any contact with the underlying value of the businesses. The value the stock market is placing on these companies has very little to do with the value of the businesses. One of the reasons I'm convinced that this is a bubble is the things that people say about buying Internet stocks. The smart people who should know better are all saying, "I'm not buying this because I think it's cheap stock, I'm buying this because I have to. If I don't, I might underperform."

Kazanjian: *Didn't people say the same thing about cable stocks when they first came out?*

Lawson: I'm sure there are times when people say that, but not like this. The whole problem with bubbles is you never know how long they'll last. It's very frustrating for those people on the sidelines because you keep looking at all the stuff and thinking, "Why can't I play too?" I suspect that the effects of this bubble have found their way into the economy in surprising places. We will discover that we were more dependent on this bubble than we realized.

Kazanjian: *What will some of the ramifications be when that wealth goes away?*

Lawson: Real estate in Seattle and the Silicon Valley will suddenly be worth a lot less. It could also hurt the overall market.

Kazanjian: *How would you sum up your investment approach?*

Lawson: I buy growing, good companies at a big discount to what I think they're worth. My advice to your readers is to always take advantage of the opportunities Wall Street gives you.

According to a recent article in *The Wall Street Journal,* investors are so eager to get into Rick's closed Weitz Hickory Fund that some are willing to pay hundreds of dollars to current shareholders for a single share that can then be transferred into their name. That's because if you own at least one share, you can then make additional investments. Rick cringes when he hears this, but admits there's nothing he can do to stop this practice, especially since he currently has no plans to reopen the fund.

Rick has been successfully battling two strong tailwinds in recent years that few other managers have been able to overcome: investing in both small-company and value stocks. Choosing either approach was a losing proposition throughout much of the late 1990s. Going with both would seem to be a recipe for disaster. For Rick, it has proven to be the opposite. I guess you can chalk that up to great stock picking, not to mention big bets in companies in which he has correctly had the most conviction.

By investing only in good businesses selling at reasonable prices, Rick has quickly made a name for himself in the competitive fund industry. Not bad for a guy who just a few years ago was so desperate to break into the business that he offered to work for free. ■

NEAL MILLER

FIDELITY INVESTMENTS

Neal Miller is one of the few managers to land a job at fund behemoth Fidelity Investments as a portfolio manager without having to go through the normal ritual of working his way up through the ranks as an analyst. Of course, it didn't hurt that he was a good friend of Peter Lynch, who helped him get the job and who subsequently took him under his wing once he was on board. Neal manages Fidelity's best-performing diversified fund—New Millennium. While that name conjures up thoughts of the Internet, fast-growing technology stocks, and other 21st century industries, the portfolio also contains a sprinkling of old-world industries, including concrete manufacturers, oil companies, and even a railroad stock.

It seems Neal has a hard time finding stocks he doesn't like. His fund owns roughly 250 different names. The 57-year-old is always looking for new companies to add and scans dozens of magazines each week in search of ideas. His goal is to capitalize on big trends that might not yet be recognized by the rest of the world. Neal describes his approach as investing in the companies that will be found "in tomorrow's newspaper today." While he generally concentrates on smaller-company stocks, he also owns many larger names and doesn't feel restricted to any one area.

189

Neal was one of the first managers to venture into pure-play Internet stocks back in 1994, when a relative tipped him off to the medium's potential. What's ironic is he claims that beyond checking stock prices and research notes, he hardly ever uses the computer as part of his day-to-day routine. He joined Fidelity in 1988 running private accounts and was given the New Millennium Fund in 1992. Because the fund's strong performance attracted so much money, Miller was forced to close the New Millennium Fund to new investors in 1996. While he won't say "never," Miller tells me he currently has no plans to reopen the doors. After all, he still manages money for some of Fidelity's large private clients and doesn't want to spread himself too thin.

Kazanjian: *Your grandfathers were both successful private investors. Did that familial interest in the stock market immediately rub off on you?*

Miller: No. It was kind of a pleasant evolution. The knowledge, expertise, and sense of accomplishment I saw in my grandparents certainly had an influence, though. Growing up during the Eisenhower era, in the 1950s, I was looking at defense spending and saw great growth in utility stocks. When I became of college age, I was looking for ways to steer clear of Vietnam and the military. I wanted to stay in school at the University of Michigan for as long as I could, and fortunately I was not drafted. I had four different resumés when I graduated from Michigan, with different qualifications listed depending on the company I was interviewing with. One day, my four roommates said they saw a bunch of dividend checks come through a mail slot in our apartment. They told me there was a profession called money management. I thought they were kidding. That sounded too easy. It seemed like a hobby, not a profession. That's the way my dad treated it. The idea that this could be a job was exciting.

Kazanjian: *I think everyone would like to make a living working at his or her hobby. Where did you find your first job?*

Miller: Chase Manhattan Bank in 1967. My first meeting was with Singer Sewing Machine, which was a pension client. Stocks were just going up. There was no sense of measurement or attribution to a benchmark. That was the start of my professional career.

Kazanjian: *I take it you began as an assistant portfolio manager.*

Miller: Yes, and from there I got more involved with direct responsibility. That was a great era. Unlike many of today's practitioners, I've had a chance to experience what I call a casino stock market, pie-in-the-sky ideas, volatility, and great excitement such as we had in 1968. I saw how psychology really drives stocks.

Kazanjian: *It sounds a lot like the late 1990s. Do you see the similarities?*

Miller: I'm often asked that, and I'd have to say no. There was so much hype. I recall the president of National Student Marketing hiring a helicopter at lunchtime. He'd hover over Wall Street with a microphone and extole the great merits of the stock from the air. There was just wild speculation. People say the Internet group looks like that. On the other hand, when you talk to the likes of Jack Welch, Michael Dell, or Lou Gerstner of IBM, you get a sense of what a profound development the Internet is and how it is a hallmark of the information age. These companies are better organized to serve the consumer's needs and are in a position to increase market share and capital return. There are some fundamentals underpinning this excitement. Today's Internet stocks pale to some of the stuff you saw then. There was a company called International Travel Group that marketed Hawaiian trips to affinity groups and ended up with about a 70 percent share of all the airplanes landing in Hawaii. The stock went from 35 cents to $140 in a year. That was real exciting. There's nothing comparable right now. The barriers of entry are higher today.

Kazanjian: *Where did you go after Chase?*

Miller: The Harris Trust and Savings Bank in Chicago. I spent about 11 years there and gained a lot of confidence. The 1970s were pretty lean because under the tax structure any stock gains were taxed at about 70 percent. About the only way to get ahead was to shelter taxes rather than pay them. Equities hit a pretty bleak period. The hallmark of the Nixon era was that some policies backfired and resulted in creeping inflation. That culminated in 1980–81 with a prime rate of around 22 percent and AAA utility bonds yielding around 15 percent. I gained more confidence as a stock manager by perfecting a process and style that seemed to be working. I went from Harris Trust to Bankers Trust in 1981. From there I moved to Axe Houghton Management until was sold. After there I joined Chase Manhattan Management, which was eventually sold to UBS. While at Bankers

Trust, I met Peter Lynch, who was managing Fidelity Magellan. We chatted and exchanged a lot of stock ideas. He even referenced me in his book, *One Up on Wall Street*, as one of his good outside resources. We had a nice friendship. Peter was interested in seeing me as a candidate at Fidelity. I took advantage of that opportunity in 1988 and joined the company.

Kazanjian: *That's pretty uncommon, since my understanding is that Fidelity likes to start people out as analysts and move them up to portfolio managers. It's sort of a home-grown team.*

Miller: I was one of maybe three experienced portfolio managers Fidelity has hired. In order to see whether I could be assimilated into the organization, I was made a pension fund manager. I spent about four years doing that. Since Peter more or less took me under his wing, he carved out a portion of his asset base for me to manage, and I tied it in with my pension clients. I was like a duck in water. I really felt comfortable here from the start. I had some enormous successes and generated great numbers. I also developed a bit of a fan club here. I have a unique investment process and people wanted me to manage some of their money. Things coincided in such a way that I did get to launch my own fund at Fidelity. When we tried to figure out what to call it, one of the guys here commented that my approach sounded like the new millennium. I thought that was brilliant. So, in 1992, the New Millennium Fund was launched.

Kazanjian: *What is the normal career track at Fidelity?*

Miller: The company has an intensive recruiting effort. They start you on rotation as an analyst. If you demonstrate you've got a good head on your shoulders, understand how to ferret out opportunity, and add to the value of the funds under management, your assignments are rotated. You become involved in more meaningful and challenging groups. If that all works well, meaning, you're as good in utilities as in technology, eventually you're given an opportunity to run a fund.

Kazanjian: *Tell me how you and the other Fidelity managers work. Do you have the same team of analysts?*

Miller: We all work under a backdrop of shared resources. Most portfolio managers have their own way of constructing a portfolio and for defining what constitutes a potentially successful stock. Based on that set of eyes, ears, and filters, we then probe and interact with the resource base to flesh out opportunity using the experiences we've had. Like the others here, I don't have dedicated assistants. I work by myself. On the other hand, I contribute to the mix by generating ideas. I'm always trying to separate the wheat from the chaff and to quantify the future. To be able to sound out these ideas against the resource base here has had great results.

Kazanjian: *I know you run the fund yourself, but if you're looking at a stock you might be interested in, do you ask a Fidelity analyst to research the company for you?*

Miller: If you ever came at the world that way you'd get thrown right out the window. Basically, I bring them the idea, tell them the scenario, and ask if it makes sense. I'll hope the answer is, yes. They then may ask whether I've considered some other angles that might involve other companies or groups or stocks that tie in with this. The process then fans out. One good idea can result in investing in an entire sector, investing in a group of companies, in the business that supplies the raw material, the business that does something to the material, and then the enterprise that markets it.

Kazanjian: *One idea feeds many others. That's what your friend Peter Lynch has always pointed out. Do you find you're in competition with other Fidelity managers, or do you all work together to achieve superior performance?*

Miller: I think what kills any institution with a lot of assets under management is what you might call gravitation toward a central tendency, and it's a huge pitfall. This often happens when you have a team management approach. In that case consensus compromises the brilliance of the individual members. We don't have that here in any respect. To become a portfolio manager, you must have a certain process, a unique way of sorting out opportunity and finding investment ideas. At Fidelity, we're all experts in different things. We do get together to meet with companies. I'll ask questions along a track I'm familiar with, and so will the others. The outcome is much richer because what might not make sense to me may fit right into another manager's puzzle.

Kazanjian: *Let's get back to the New Millennium Fund. What's the main idea behind that fund?*

Miller: I'm looking for companies that will be in tomorrow's newspaper today. At the time we started it in 1992, the word millennium sounded as if it was long into the future. That's the idea.

Kazanjian: *What is your investment approach?*

Miller: Basically, I view investing as a three-step process. You get a good idea, you price it right, and you test the assumptions you made, in terms of whether the original set of parameters will be fulfilled. To expand on that, you start with the raw material. If the company does something with that material, it adds value. You then get the product out into the marketplace. What I'm trying to do is look for events— bottlenecks or exceptional backdrops where the raw material prices might decline—that can change market opportunities. These events can cause market opportunities to increase or decrease, depending on the circumstance, so you're always going back and forth, reevaluating your original parameters. It's simplistic stuff, but I think about it every day. They say an inefficiently priced growth stock will give you the greatest opportunity for return. That's true if you can find a company that's suffering and has been neglected by Wall Street. For it to work, though, there must be a wind blowing to fill the sail and turn it into a sailboat, meaning a favorable marketing backdrop. The company needs management that wants to harness this energy. Given that, they can excel and surprise Wall Street. The consensus will be moving up when the company's results come in. Data from the 1950s onward suggests that if you were to move ahead in time and look back, there's a one-to-one relationship among return, stock prices, and that surprise factor. So I'm always interested in companies that can be overachievers. I'm a growth stock manager and I like to find companies that are focused on this opportunity.

Kazanjian: *How do you go about finding good ideas?*

Miller: For me it's an intellectual challenge. I really enjoy conferences, company meetings, opening my eyes and ears, and perusing magazines. I subscribe to more than 300 magazines. I'm always looking for anomalies, things that don't fit into an existing pattern, with the idea that this can suggest a contertrend, or a new wedge of future opportunity. When you get an idea, you have to develop a business plan for the company and put a proper valuation on it. I've also learned that using time efficiently is a key variable in success.

Kazanjian: *It sounds as if you're a contrarian.*

Miller: Yes and no. I'm a contrarian to the extent that I like cement stocks, which haven't had a good run for 30 years. I'm a contrarian to the extent that I'm looking for something that's fallow today, but all of a sudden has a new opportunity backdrop because of a new product, legislative initiative, or demographic profile. Or there might be a social proclivity. In other words, red is in so red cars will be selling better. I'll then look for the guy who makes the paint with the right glow.

Kazanjian: *What are some of the magazines you subscribe to?*

Miller: I'm all over the place, from *GQ* to *Demolition* magazine. I don't read them, I peruse them. Last night I flipped through *Terror* magazine. What you're trying to do in investing is figure out where things might be off or on center. What's happening in Malaysia and other places? What ties in with different political leanings? That's another component to this. When you're trying to see the future, or deliver tomorrow's newspaper today, you have to assume risk. As I say to my clients, "If I know I'm going to be jumping from a burning building every day, I'd rather jump from a half floor up than from the fourteenth floor." You want a magazine like *Terror* to know how to reduce the floors you're jumping from.

Kazanjian: *Your approach sounds very eclectic.*

Miller: I can take it either from the bottom-up or top-down. The two are equally weighted. In technology, where the key is the development of new products, it's pretty much a bottom-up process. In the Internet space, for example, I must understand the need for scaleable storage, how that scaleable storage could take place, what glue holds it together, what kind of infrastructure, bandwidth, and gadgets are needed, etc. You could say that's top-down, but I don't think so. I'm not good at what you might call sector rotation. I'm solidly in the camp of issue selection. I don't think I have ever once in a presentation talked about my portfolio's industry concentration.

Kazanjian: *How do you spot tomorrow's headlines?*

Miller: By looking for anomalies and having a compulsive case of curiosity. I turn over rocks and if I spot an anomaly, such as good management, I'm engaged and in overdrive. Then I try to find out whether there's an opportunity and align myself with the analyst resources here.

Kazanjian: *You were an early investor in the Internet.*

Miller: I started to get in around 1994.

Kazanjian: *What brought you there?*

Miller: I noticed that the Internet was shrinking the physical world and making it more convenient. I was first introduced to this by my nephew at the University of Washington who was coauthor of an old growth forest overview. He said the paper wouldn't have been possible without the ability to exchange information on the dates involved, the dimensions of size, and so forth without the Internet. Number one, he couldn't afford it. Number two, he couldn't have been on the same page with others simultaneously discussing it. He told me to keep my eyes and ears open for anything and everything having to do with the Internet. That was the starting point. Along the way I had the good fortune of meeting David Wetherell of CMG, College Marketing Group, which is now known as CMGI. He said the Internet would enable direct marketers to sharpen their focus, have a one-to- one marketing experience, and to reach their final audience with a group of products much more efficiently than you could on the phone. I was hot to trot with this idea of keeping my ears open on the Internet. It turns out Wetherell was the right person to compare notes with. He's quickly tapped into the power of Internet through CMGI, which is a composite of companies in the direct marketing area. The Internet is the hallmark of the information age. It's going to enable people to get higher returns on capital and gain market share in their respective enterprises. A lot of my focus has been on the utility part of the Internet, like Real Networks, which is in streaming media. I have also been interested in companies that allow you to be less reliant on your keyboard for interacting with the Internet. By focusing on the utility companies, you know that no matter who wins they'll need these services.

Kazanjian: *You also have had heavy weightings in media and leisure, which isn't surprising. However, I was surprised to see companies such as Union Pacific and Global Marine. You also mentioned your interest in concrete manufacturers. Those are certainly not thought of as new-millennium companies.*

Miller: I'm always looking for a becalmed sailboat race and a weather pattern that will stir things up. I'm trying to find an experienced team at the helm to cope with that weather pattern and win the race. To find that sailboat race, I peruse magazines for anomalies that might lead to some scenario showing me both that there is a storm coming up and these are the boats that might win. In the case of Global Marine (a provider of offshore drilling services), dwindling oil and gas reserves and the need to replace those depleted reserves are my weather pattern. What has given Global Marine's racing yacht an edge is its product innovation—technology has sharply reduced oil and natural production costs, thus opening otherwise uneconomical territory to development. Union Pacific is a bit of a departure. I've always been intrigued by special situations. Union Pacific is a quasi-monopoly that has doubled its strength through its acquisition of Santa Fe. The acquisition didn't go well. There was massive congestion, which caused service problems, lost business, and ultimately an earnings short fall. You want to invest in a monopoly when there's adversity, because they always have pricing leverage and people try hard to get them back on track, no pun intended, knowing there's no alternative. Union Pacific is one of the few examples in that position. That's how I got into it.

Kazanjian: *When you find a company you're interested in, what type of analysis do you do to decide if you want to own it?*

Miller: One thing you have to come to grips with is the business plan. What are the critical variables of success? Then you have to examine the reputation of management. If they do a good job, the company's products will be embraced by others. You look at what kinds of systems are in place. Are they off center? Is everything finely tuned? Next, very important, and this is the eclectic side of me, you check where the company and the industry have been before. In the case of cement, it was hot stuff 30 years ago. You then ask if there is any chance of resurrecting that psychology. You're most objective before you make a decision. In the end, you hope the business plan leads you to believe the consensus is too cautious, the stock is inefficiently priced, and the company is prone toward an earnings surprise. You then go back to your starting point, when you're most objective, and outline your price targets over an interval of time.

Kazanjian: *Do you look at balance sheets?*

Miller: I'm aware of them. I'm sensitive to the balance sheet and look to see if gross margins are rising or falling behind, whether they have the capacity to internalize this opportunity, etc. But, I don't start with this.

Kazanjian: *It sounds as if you mostly want to be comfortable with the business in general, as opposed to the specifics of the operation.*

Miller: Yes, but I'm comfortable because I've kissed a lot of frogs and made a lot of mistakes.

Kazanjian: *From a valuation perspective, how do you determine whether you're paying a fair price for the stock?*

Miller: The system I use assumes it's all relative. I look at where the group's selling and where the company's selling in relation to past history. I go back 40 to 50 years.

Kazanjian: *What happens from there?*

Miller: I'm looking for companies that will come out with an earning surprise. Then I ask what I have to pay for that surprise. For me, it's a relative valuation. Is the stock at the high end of its range or the low end? Again, I go back as far as I can.

Kazanjian: *You must have a flexible approach. You own some stocks that would be considered more value-oriented, selling at low PEs, and others priced quite high.*

Miller: Everything is time sensitive. It's certainly a quarterly process for Union Pacific to demonstrate it's out of the woods. In the case of oil-service stocks, they are selling near scrap value and could take a while to come back. The Internet stocks are also a long-term proposition.

Kazanjian: *What makes you sell a stock?*

Miller: There are several reasons. One, the expectations are fulfilled. At the start of the journey I have a certain price target in mind. Once it gets there, I might sell. Another is the wind that you're trying to track that fills the sail goes away. Once it disappears, you're dependent on the company or a Wall Street analyst to describe what's happening, and I don't like that. It could be the business plan as outlined doesn't materialize, or a stock goes up faster than it should given the time interval that's needed to get things straightened out. If I'd bought Union Pacific and it doubled the next day, it would be gone.

Kazanjian: *Isn't the Internet an area where the consensus is almost too optimistic?*

Miller: I don't know. I was just talking with a couple of companies today and couldn't believe what I was hearing. It's like a mongoose going through a snake. The thing's just been swallowed, and it's a big bulge. People don't realize that bulge is ahead of them. The question for the Internet, more than whether earnings can materialize, is to what extent new vistas are realistic.

Kazanjian: *Do you think pure-play Internet leaders of today will also be leaders of tomorrow?*

Miller: I don't have a clear answer for that. Everyone's talking about the first mover advantage and the various segments of the Internet. I think you have to go with people who are visionaries and keep yourself honest. Then you try to figure out the barriers to entry.

Kazanjian: *There are a lot of areas you like. Is there any sector you completely avoid?*

Miller: Not at this point. I'm not good with sector rotation. I'm especially bad at anticipating commodity price swings, so I tend to shy away from banks, insurance companies, and precious metals. However, if somebody tells me that they're going to reduce the price of gold by $200 an ounce through the leeching process, I'm real interested in that.

Kazanjian: *You're obviously trying to keep a constant pulse on the best places to be. You must like a lot of things, since you have roughly 250 stocks in your portfolio.*

Miller: Yeah, I'm like the guy who started with eggs and ended up with a flock of ducks. I love to be surrounded by a huge group of companies. It's always been my style. It's Peter Lynch's style as well.

Kazanjian: *But the conventional wisdom is that you don't want your portfolio to be too diversified because then your best ideas get diluted.*

Miller: I'm trying to see the future and at the same time reduce risk. I'm a big subscriber of diversity. I don't know which idea is going to work real well. I just know that usually I'm on to stuff that's pretty powerful. If one out of three works, I'm in great shape. If I bet on one and there's a weed in the garden, that's not good.

Kazanjian: *Fidelity funds in general tend to be more diversified than most.*

Miller: I don't think there's any particular generalization that you can make here. Some managers run small portfolios. There's no generalization that prevails.

Kazanjian: *But funds that are very diversified tend to perform like the indexes. Yours obviously hasn't. You've far outperformed the S&P 500. Is that because all of your stocks have been good, or do you concentrate on your best ideas?*

Miller: It really varies. I buy a lot of small obscure companies, such as Ag-Chem. This company has a patent technology that uses a satellite signal to tell the agricultural equipment how much pesticide to release on the field. From being in touch with these guys, I learn about agricultural products, rain, and so forth. Each company has a purpose and might contribute more or less, so I'm always pointed in a number of different directions.

Kazanjian: *It seems like a lot of work to keep up all of those names.*

Miller: You have to love this job and eat, sleep, and breathe it. It helps to have a lot of experience. I work awfully hard. That's not a self-serving comment. I just do.

Kazanjian: *How closely do you monitor your holdings?*

Miller: The tools for following companies are just extraordinary here. I take pride in knowing the management of each company, their strategy, where the people have come from, and where they want to go. The best situation you can find is one where management sees the opportunity at hand and feels so strongly about it they're buying back stock. But getting too close to management can compromise your objectivity. Over time I've tried to separate the relationship and closeness I have with some of these people with the stock price. Knowing the person is one thing; the stock price is something completely separate.

Kazanjian: *What is a typical day at the office like for you?*

Miller: I typically start by watching CNBC. I want to know what the foreign markets are doing. Then I come to work and peruse three to four newspapers. I look at the calendar that is presented to me electronically at Fidelity. I see the management from at least two to three companies every day. We then have a lunch or a social occasion where I can talk to other analysts and managers. Today, we had a lively discussion on the motivation for selling gold and debated what the future for South Africa looks like. During the rest of the day I interact with my pension clients, review my portfolio reconciliation, see how I did versus the market, and prepare for tomorrow. At night, I go through my magazines.

Kazanjian: *You closed your fund to new investors in September of 1996. What were the assets at that point?*

Miller: Something like $1.3 billion. Now we're up to $2.4 billion.

Kazanjian: *Why did you close the fund?*

Miller: There are capacity limitations. If I get a good idea, I want to have it focused. At a certain point, you can have so much money that you lose focus or have to scale up to bigger companies. While that was a concern, it was not really the cause for the closing of the New

Millennium Fund. Rather, I was suffering from extreme cash flows. Trying to monitor the cash flows and get the money deployed without shortchanging existing shareholders was becoming a problem. I was moving my own stocks, since I buy many smaller companies. I was spending all of my time deploying money. It was getting the best of me. I asked for help, and the institution responded by closing the fund.

Kazanjian: *Was it hard to get Fidelity to agree to the closure?*

Miller: This was not a decision made in isolation. We previously acknowledged this could be a possibility, and the machinery was already in place to close the fund whenever it seemed appropriate.

Kazanjian: *Do you still tend to concentrate on small-company stocks?*

Miller: Yes. More important, I want companies that are focused on a major opportunity. Microsoft is as focused on software as Lin Broadcasting is on cellular radio. Focus doesn't necessarily mean big versus small, but it's generally difficult for bigger companies to be focused.

Kazanjian: *Are there any plans to reopen the New Millennium Fund?*

Miller: Not currently.

Kazanjian: *Over the years what would you say has been your biggest investment lesson?*

Miller: Believe it or not, and I know this sounds selfish, but it's listening to myself.

Kazanjian: *Intuition?*

Miller: Yes. Somebody told me that the best people at the CIA are people who get a hunch, ask about five questions to flesh the hunch out, and worry from that point forward. They're always challenging their hunches. When you don't start challenging your hunches, you run the risk of being sweet-talked into a different position.

Kazanjian: *Based on your current assessment and observations, do you believe the stock market will continue to do well in the new millennium?*

Miller: Yes. I think it's the golden age for asset accumulation. People are worried there won't be enough to provide for their future and are saving to provide for themselves. The majority of people are in their peak earning years and will be for the next ten years. I think it's a golden age for equity investments.

Kazanjian: *Do you still work with Peter Lynch?*

Miller: Off and on. We got together the other night and were debating a lot of things, like whether small stocks will eventually outperform large stocks and whether people will move away from funds and into individual securities. I'm not sure we came up with any good answers, but it's pretty exciting.

Kazanjian: *Has your investment process evolved over the years or have you always done it this way?*

Miller: It's always been the same. I've never strayed, and I doubt I ever will.

Neal clearly has an eclectic investment process, to say the least. He owns by far more stocks than any other Wizard in this book. I would also guess that he subscribes to more periodicals than anyone else. I found him to be a somewhat difficult interview at first, since I had a hard time grasping exactly what his investment approach was. I later realized that was merely a function of the fact that he likes so many stocks for so many different reasons. As a result, it was impossible to pin him down to a specific approach that one could articulate in a simple formula.

He kept describing his approach as looking for "tomorrow's head-lines" today. I guess that's what all managers hope to do. But Neal goes above and beyond traditional Wall Street research, reading in-dustry trade publications, for example, to spot future trends long be-fore his peers hear about them through the more traditional media. I think that's a technique we can all learn from. How many of your in-vestment decisions are based on what you read in your own profes-sional trade journals?

I also think Neal should be applauded for convincing Fidelity to close his fund at such a relatively small asset base. Fidelity is often criticized for letting its funds grow too large. Neal's New Millennium was among the first to shut its doors. While that's great for existing shareholders, it unfortunately means that his expert skills are cur-rently out of reach to the rest of us. There's always a chance his fund will reopen, or that he'll start another one. While he admits that's a possibility, he says there are currently no plans for either of these events to take place. ∎

WILLIAM MILLER

LEGG MASON

Who has the best record of any mutual fund manager in America? Most folks would guess it's Peter Lynch. But the true title holder is Bill Miller. Bill has whipped the performance of the S&P 500 each and every year since 1991. Peter Lynch was able to do it for only seven years in a row.

Bill manages the Legg Mason Value Trust, a fund that has blossomed to more than $13 billion in assets. That's really no surprise. After all, when you're the greatest living fund manager, a lot of people want you to run their money. Value Trust outperformed the S&P 500 by almost 15 percentage points annually over the three-year period ending in 1998, and by almost 10 percent during the previous five years.

Bill's approach has been criticized by some, who claim his fund's name is misleading. Although he insists he's a die-hard value manager, the 49-year-old owns such high-flying growth stocks as America Online, Dell Computer, and MCI WorldCom. How do those qualify as value stocks, you might ask? According to Bill, it's because they were cheap when he bought them and, unlike some of his peers, he's willing to hold on until he deems them to be too expensive.

A former philosophy student and longtime market observer, Bill joined Legg Mason as director of research in 1981. He comanaged the

Value Trust from its inception in 1982, and has run it solo since 1990. He also runs the small-cap Legg Mason Special Investment Trust. Bill still studies the great philosophers and finds that many of their teachings apply to his work as an investor.

In talking with Bill, you can sense right away that he's well schooled and ardent about sticking to his approach of unearthing companies selling below intrinsic value. It's no wonder fund rating service Morningstar named him its domestic equity fund manager of the year in 1998. I think you'll find his approach to value investing is both logical, refreshing, and exceedingly effective.

Kazanjian: *You started off as a philosophy student, but one of your former professors says he used to find you in the library reading* The Wall Street Journal *instead of the world's greatest philosophers.*

Miller: I was always interested in things financial. When I was nine or ten years old, I was watching my father read the financial pages of the newspaper, which had a different visual aspect from the sports pages. I asked him what *that* was. He said those were stocks and stocks' prices. I then asked what that meant. He pointed to one name and said, "If you look here you'll see it says plus one quarter. If you owned one share of that company, you would have 25 cents more today than you had yesterday." I said, "What do you have to do to get that 25 cents?" He said, "Nothing, it does it by itself." It was that conversation that got me interested in the markets. I thought, "Wow! you can make money without doing any work. That's the business I want to be in. I probably had come in from mowing the grass for 25 cents for two hours, so this stock thing sounded like a pretty good deal. It was much later that I realized only the market rate of return took no work. Getting an extra rate of return was a different matter. Then, as an undergraduate in college, I majored in economics and European intellectual history.

Kazanjian: *How did you wind up studying for a PhD in philosophy?*

Miller: The decision to go to graduate school was driven more by the lack of finding anything else that was terribly interesting. Economics, both 30 years ago and today, is highly stylized and basically a mathematical exercise. When I looked at other alternatives, law school seemed to be a huge waste of time, since you spent three years trying to figure out where to put commas in documents. Business school would have been more interesting, but I had an army obligation. While I was in the army, a friend was at the Harvard Business School and I was stationed for a short time near Boston. I visited him and saw he was spending two years studying cases that seemed to be very commonsensical. At the end of the day it was a case of determining what I found most interesting. I thought philosophy was intellectually interesting, so I studied that.

Kazanjian: *Despite your early interest in stocks, I understand your father actually discouraged you from getting into the investment field.*

Miller: It was the worst advice I ever received. When I got out of the army in 1975, the market had just finished its worst period since the Great Depression. It wasn't the kind of thing you would have recommended as a profession that was full of opportunity.

Kazanjian: *You left the PhD program before getting your degree. What happened after that?*

Miller: I went to work for a company in Pennsylvania called J.E. Baker in 1977 as assistant to the CEO. I was a jack of all trades, doing whatever he asked. Initially, it was a lot of number crunching on acquisition stuff. He was looking for somebody who had a conceptual grounding in economics.

Kazanjian: *When did you join Legg Mason?*

Miller: In 1981, as the director of research.

Kazanjian: *How did you make that transition?*

Miller: It was fairly seamless in that my wife was a broker at Legg Mason. She joined the firm in 1975 to help put me through graduate school and I knew the principals. It was and still is a fairly small firm based in Baltimore. They talked to me about joining the research effort, which didn't interest me much. Then they talked about diversifying into money management. I found that to be much more appealing. By that time I was treasurer at J. E. Baker and enjoyed overseeing the company's investment portfolios. Chip Mason, Legg Mason's CEO, planned to start a fund that would reflect the firm's research ideas. I joined in October of 1981, and we started Value Trust in March or April of 1982. My predecessor as director of research, Ernie Kiehne, and I comanaged the fund. He was the senior manager. Our initial portfolio consisted mostly of stocks Kiehne had followed for a long time.

Kazanjian: *When you first started, had you even invested in the stock market yourself at that point?*

Miller: Yes. When I was in the army some friends sent me money saying, "You always talk about the stock market, and you think you can invest in it. Here's some of our money, see what you can do with it." We formed a little investment partnership and I invested for them in the early and mid–1970s, before joining Legg Mason.

Kazanjian: *When you joined the firm in 1981, what was your investment philosophy?*

Miller: The same as it is now: value. However, it's much more sophisticated now than it was then.

Kazanjian: *Where did that value orientation come from?*

Miller: From my reading. I've read all the stuff I could about investing for as far back as I can remember. I've always thought the right way to do something is to determine who's best at it and see what he or she does. It seemed fairly clear to me that Ben Graham was the intellectual leader of the security analysis field. Then, reading about Warren Buffett and seeing how he had survived and prospered during the difficult period from the late 1960s to the early 1970s was a real eye-opener. It also always made intuitive sense to me to try and buy things at the best possible price in relation to underlying value. I remember talking to Bob Torray [who is featured elsewhere in this book] ten years ago. He believed that if you explained value investing to people, they either got it or they didn't. You couldn't convince somebody it was a good way to invest if they didn't instantaneously see that. Most people, for whatever reason, seem more psychologically attuned to buying companies that are growing, have great prospects, or for whatever reason have something people can get excited about. Valuation tends to be a much less important factor for most people than it is for me.

Kazanjian: *I want to dig deeper into your investment approach in a moment, but given the kinds of companies you own, one might wonder whether you still follow the rules of Graham and Buffett.*

Miller: We are absolutely valuation purists. But we are not valuation simpletons. A lot of people have taken what Graham said in interviews or wrote in *The Intelligent Investor* and extracted the simplest possible rules from that. If you actually get into *Security Analysis* or some of the interviews Graham gave late in life, you see there's much more to it. I was going through some of Graham's later interviews and saw one where he was asked before a Congressional committee whether stock prices were too high and what stock prices depended on. His comment was they depended on earnings, but most important, on future prospects and to a minor extent on current asset values. Most people believe that if you talked to Graham he would be most focused on current asset values and least on future prospects. But that's not what he said. As to Buffett, if you read his stuff, our methodology is virtually identical. Buffett says he tries to buy things at the cheapest price relative to future cash flows. He doesn't precisely calculate the cash flows. As he says, he would rather be vaguely right than precisely right. We do a more extensive and detailed analysis, but it's the same thing.

Kazanjian: *Are you saying people have misinterpreted Graham's teaching?*

Miller: I don't think they have misinterpreted it. They just take too narrow a view of it. Graham believed in low PE ratios and low price to book value. All of that is correct. It's just not the full story. It would be like asking Michael Jordan how much money he makes. If he said he made $200,000 a year, that would be true. But he also makes a whole lot more than that. That's the same thing with Graham. It's true that he was a low PE guy, but he was a lot more than that.

Kazanjian: *How was the performance of the Value Trust starting out?*

Miller: The performance was great. Our general methodology in the early 1980s was much simpler than it is today. It was more in line with looking at such factors as low PE, low price-to-book, and low price-to-cash flow ratios. What we now call accounting-based factors were the critical valuation drivers. Because we started in 1982 at the bottom of a recession and were very disciplined in our approach, our performance was outstanding. We didn't realize it at the time, but low PE, low price-to-book, and low price-to-cash flow stocks perform best from the bottom of a recession to the peak of an economic cycle. Then, from the peak of a cycle to the bottom of recession, at least on historical basis, they're dreadful. We happened to catch it at exactly the right time. From 1982 into the spring of 1986, we were the single best performing fund of all funds in America, better than Fidelity Magellan. Then from 1986–1990, from the peak of the cycle to the bottom of the next recession, we performed very poorly, as did most other accounting-based value funds. We lagged badly in 1990. My partner retired at the end of 1990. I took over as the sole portfolio manager in 1991. We've beaten the market every year since then.

Kazanjian: *How do you define value investing today?*

Miller: I take it right out of the textbooks. If you go to any finance or investment textbook and look up value or valuation, it will say the value of any investment is the present value of the future free cash flows of that investment. I can't find any textbook that defines value differently. They all get it from John Burr Williams, whose initial PhD dissertation in the 1930s later became the book, *The Theory of Investment Value.* He called it the "rule of present worth." The only way you can compare two distinct investments, such as aluminum and computer companies, is to look at them on a comparable basis. The only reasonable comparison is between the returns you expect to earn from them. That's what I'm trying to do. Investing, as Buffett said, is putting money out today with the expectation of getting more back tomorrow. The question is how do you do that? We believe the best way to determine the most reasonable expectation of what we're going to get back from an investment is to forecast and discount back the free cash flows.

Kazanjian: *Where do you find your ideas initially?*

Miller: They come from all different sources. Many come from the new low list. We look at anything that looks cheap statistically and do a lot of computer screening. That's a starting point for many value investors, but some of my peers put a lot more weight on the statistics coming out of computer screens than we do. We just use them to get a universe of names to investigate more deeply. We get ideas from spectacular blowups in the market (Waste Management or HBOC/ McKesson in 1999 are good examples) or from companies that are perceived to have lost out in some competitive battle, such as Toys 'R' Us. Plus, people who know our style are always serving up ideas. Ninety-nine percent of them aren't interesting, but occasionally we find one that's worth doing some work on.

Kazanjian: *Stocks on the new low list are obviously companies no one wants right now. They have problems. What makes you decide it's okay to buy? Are you hoping for a turnaround?*

Miller: We do a lot of turnarounds, but we tell our analysts to avoid the word "hope" in their research, and instead prefer "believe" or "expect." Normally, companies that are perceived right out of the box as terrific companies with strong competitive advantages will not make it into our portfolio because they never hit one of our valuation metrics and therefore don't come to our attention. As a result, we've missed many great companies that it turns out were undervalued, Microsoft and Charles Schwab being prime examples. They are stocks that always looked expensive, so we never took an opportunity to analyze them in-depth. If you think about it, the only way you can earn an excess return by owning a particular company is if the market hasn't valued it properly. If the market has it properly valued, you will earn the market rate of return or the rate of return of the underlying company, whichever is lower. The market has got to be systematically wrong about the prospects of a particular business in order for you to earn an excess return on it over any extended period of time. When growth investors do really well, they do so because the companies grew faster and longer than people believed they would. To most value investors, a company is undervalued because the market has overly discounted some negative event or is too pessimistic about something that's weighing on the stock price.

Kazanjian: *How do you know that it's just an overreaction and not more serious?*

Miller: You analyze the business. You have to get into actually figuring out what the company does and what its competitive advantage is. Most important, you must understand the long-term economic model of the business. How much capital does it require to operate? What returns are normal in that industry? Where is the company positioned in the industry? How can its management execute in a way to deliver the business model?

Kazanjian: *Let's talk about some of the holdings in your portfolio. You own a lot of names that you would not normally find in a value fund, such as America Online and Dell Computer, companies that have really fueled the portfolios of many growth funds as well as yours. Tell me how those stocks justifiably fit into a value portfolio and how you came to find them originally.*

Miller: The important thing to understand is when we say we are value investors, both of those words are important to us—value and investing. First, we don't believe many people who call themselves value investors do very sophisticated valuation work. Second, and more important, they sure don't invest. They trade. They buy stocks and flip

them out if they go up 50 or 100 percent or trade up to some historical valuation metric. They're sort of fundamental traders. What captures people's attention when they look at our portfolio are names
such as Dell, AOL, Gateway, and Nokia—stocks that are being
bought mostly by growth investors. We bought these things when
they were really cheap. We've made 30 to 40 times on our money in
both Dell and AOL. Most investors rarely hold companies long
enough to make 30 to 40 times their money. They're lucky if they
make 50, 100, or 200 percent. We've got not only 10-baggers, but
20-, 30-, and 40-baggers. [This is a concept popularized by former Fidelity Magellan manager, Peter Lynch. A 10-bagger, for instance, is
a stock that has appreciated tenfold.] You get those only if you actually invest in companies as opposed to trading them and trying to
guess when the stock is going to pull back. We don't spend time trying to guess stock price action. We spend our time trying to value
businesses.

When we analyzed Dell, for example, in February 1996, that was
a period when you had rumbles of Fed tightening and everybody
thought we were going to have a recession. Investors had sold tech
stocks down to levels that looked to us to offer an opportunity. Most
value people at the time were buying paper, steel, and aluminum,
which also were down in the dumps. When we did all the valuation
work on those companies, we concluded they were not terribly attractive or mispriced by the market. Their business fundamentals were
poor and were likely to remain so. On the other hand, when we
looked at Dell, trading at the time around $1–2 on a split-adjusted
basis, we saw a company that had a superior business model, excellent competitive advantages, growing at 25 to 30 percent a year, earning 30 percent on invested capital, and trading at five times earnings.
Why would we ever buy a paper company at five times what they
hope to earn if paper prices go up if we can buy a terrific company at
five times today's earnings? When we got further into the detail of the
business, it looked to us that the market had systematically misunderstood the potential of the company. Historically, PC companies
traded between 6 to 12 times earnings. Even when value investors
were buying PC companies, they would buy at 5 to 6 times earnings,
and sell when they got to 12 times earnings because that was the peak
multiple these companies historically had attained. When we analyzed
Dell, we concluded it was worth at least 25 times earnings as a business. If you were to buy the whole company, you would pay up to 25

times earnings, whereas the market had peaked valuation out historically at around 12 times. We thought it was worth about five times
what the market thought it was worth. It's highly unusual to find
things that appear to be that mispriced, so we loaded up on it. As it
turned out, we were right. We actually underestimated the ability of
management to execute what turned out to be a very superior business model. Fortunately, because what we do is dynamic valuation,
our models are updated every quarter or more often as we get more
fundamental data. We're always trying to figure out the underlying
business value and the intrinsic value of the company. Earlier in 1999,
Dell reached a level where we thought it was moderately overpriced,
so we sold a fairly significant portion of it.

Kazanjian: *Was it a similar story with AOL?*

Miller: AOL was much more controversial when we bought it in the
fall of 1996. People thought AOL was going bankrupt, and the stock
had lost three quarters of its value from May to November. Our
analysis was that the company was worth roughly double what we
were paying for it. We do scenario analyses of the companies, since
we don't have any idea of what the future's actually going to look
like. We try to map out the possible futures, assign probability
weightings to them, and figure out which one appears to be most
likely. Then we determine the value under that scenario. Under one
scenario, we figured AOL could be worth multiples of the central
value we had calculated. As it turned out, the company brought in a
new president and began to execute on a model that even today I
think people misunderstand.

Kazanjian: *That was when AOL was having significant capacity problems and people couldn't log on. Scenario one must have been that
everybody would switch from AOL to other carriers, which is what a
lot of Wall Street was thinking.*

Miller: That was certainly a scenario, but when they were being sued
by the state attorney general and there were stories in the news every
day about how people couldn't log on, we found it fascinating that
they were not losing subscribers. The value proposition was very
powerful. Ordinarily, if you bought a product or service that you paid
for up front and then couldn't use, you'd ask for your money back
and switch to somebody else. But AOL's customer base continued to
grow. That told you there was a very different value proposition
going on here. It's like when they went from old Coke to new Coke.

People wanted the old Coke back. They didn't want the new Coke. Here, people didn't want CompuServe or the Microsoft Network. They wanted AOL. When we analyzed traffic patterns, we found 80 percent of the customers on the Microsoft Network used it just as a portal to the Internet, whereas 80 percent of AOL's customers stayed on the proprietary service and did not pass through to the Internet. This again supported the view that there was tremendous value in the service. We knew people wouldn't stay with the company forever if they couldn't get on. So we analyzed how long it would take AOL to solve this problem. There were two different issues. One was technological. Could they deploy enough technology over the requisite time horizon to solve the problem? We believed the answer was yes. Second, could they finance it, since it required lot of up-front capital and they didn't have a lot of money? Would it put too much strain on their financial condition? Our answer, after analyzing the situation, was that adequate financing would be available. We made a big bet on AOL, and fortunately we turned out to be right.

Kazanjian: *Since you bought both Dell and AOL, they're up 20–40 times your original cost. Without these two stocks, your fund would clearly not be where it is today.*

Miller: There's no question that without our two largest holdings going up the most, we would have done worse. Back when I was director of research, we used to put together a Thanksgiving list, 12 stock picks for the forthcoming year. It had a really good record of beating the market. *The Wall Street Journal* began to pick up on it in the early 1980s. They published our Thanksgiving list on Thanksgiving Day. A reporter called me the third year this occurred and said, "I went back and analyzed all your lists. They did beat the market, but there are 12 stocks on each list." I said, "Yeah, I know, one for every month." He said, "If you throw out last year's two best performers, you wouldn't have beaten the market. The year before that the only reason you beat it was because you had a big takeover." I replied, "If the assumption is we don't own the things that enable us to beat the market, then it follows that we won't beat the market. But we do own them." It's like AOL and Dell. We do own them. Part of the process is selecting that stuff. The other thing people misunderstand about our process is that we've owned Dell and AOL for only three years. We've outperformed every year since 1991, long before we owned Dell and

AOL, and we've outperformed over the entire 18-year history of the fund.

Kazanjian: *Some of your critics have faulted you for holding on to companies like AOL and Dell after they become overvalued. Because of that, they claim you're not really a value investor.*

Miller: Well, those people are wrong, in my opinion. If these stocks were significantly overvalued, we would sell them.

Kazanjian: *How do you figure out what a company is worth?*

Miller: We use what we call a multifactor valuation methodology, which is a mouthful for saying we look at the value of the business every possible way we can. We use PE, price-to-book, price-to-cash flow, but we adjust those numbers. Six years ago, when companies were told they had to put their postretirement health care benefits on the balance sheet and take a charge for them, General Motors' book value went from $55 to $5. What's the sense of price-to-book when one day it's $55 and the next day it's $5? The company hasn't changed, only the accounting metrics. We adjust the accounting metrics for the underlying economic reality. We do all the cross-sectional analyses of trying to figure out what the historic parameters have been. Most important, we do a scenario analysis of the business. We project cash flows out anywhere from five to ten years under a variety of scenarios. One scenario would be where the current growth rate continues. Another, where the company does a lot worse. Another is where it does better. We then try to figure out what we call the "central tendency of business value." Each scenario analysis gives us a different number and then we see how those numbers cluster. If they all cluster around the same thing, then we have a pretty high confidence in the particular valuation range.

Kazanjian: *How often do you reevaluate these intrinsic value numbers?*

Miller: We evaluate every company as often as we can, especially when new information becomes available. The underlying business value doesn't change dramatically unless the inputs change. We compare price and value all the time and are always looking for new ideas that are cheaper than what we already own.

Kazanjian: *What most often causes you to make mistakes?*

Miller: Usually the inputs are wrong. For instance, we bought Waste Management in early 1999 when the stock was trading in the $50s. We believed it was worth $60 to $70 based on all the inputs we had from our model. As it turned out, the inputs were totally wrong. Management's guidance about the year was wrong, so the baseline off which we calculated growth rates and discounted it back to calculate free cash flows was wrong, as were their cash-flow numbers. Even their historical reported numbers were wrong. That's why the stock went from the low $50s to the low $20s. The market adjusted this down for what appears to be the new economic reality. This gives you a sense of how sensitive these numbers are to input changes when you do forward-looking valuation work, as we do.

Kazanjian: *As we speak, AOL is still about 15 percent of your portfolio. What would make you sell that stock?*

Miller: If it looks as if our valuation work is wrong, or if the stock gets to a price that's dramatically above its business value, as it did in March and April of 1999. The difference and weakness in our approach is we would never look at AOL today if we didn't already own it. It would not hit any of our measures and metrics. By most valuation tools, it does not look cheap. The only way you can get to the detail is by actually looking into the business to analyze the economics and project the future cash flows.

Kazanjian: *Several months back, you mentioned you sold a significant portion of Dell, but not all of it. Why didn't you sell the entire position if you thought it was overvalued?*

Miller: That's when you get to the point of balancing risk and taking taxes into consideration. We have billions of dollars in gains in both Dell and AOL. We want to avoid delivering massive capital gains to our shareholders if we can. We will never sacrifice returns so people don't have to pay taxes, but we're trying to maximize their after-tax rates of return.

Kazanjian: *That is a risk for new shareholders to your fund since they weren't around when the gains were realized, yet would have to pay taxes on them once you did sell out.*

Miller: Absolutely.

Kazanjian: *What are some other reasons you would sell a stock?*

Miller: We have a threefold sell discipline. The first one is if the company's fairly priced. Our turnover has been running between 10 and 15 percent a year for the last several years. That means our implied holding period is anywhere from 7 to 10 years. We really are investors, not traders. We look at whether a company is undervalued on a 5- to 10-year basis. If it is, we would earn an excess return by owning it. It might be overpriced on a three-month basis, but not on a three-year basis. Fairly priced means we cannot earn an excess return by owning this company over the forecast time horizon. Second, we will sell if we find a better bargain. We try to remain fully invested. If we find something that's more undervalued on a tax-adjusted basis than what we already own, we'll sell the least attractive thing in the portfolio.

Kazanjian: *How do you determine what the least attractive holding is?*

Miller: It has to do with intrinsic value. Every company has an intrinsic value that we calculate. If one stock trades at a 10 percent discount to intrinsic value, and we find something that's at a 40 percent discount to intrinsic value, one is replaced with another, because the stock with a 40 percent discount gives us a greater risk-adjusted return over the forecast time horizon. Even though we own names that look as if they're "growth" stocks, every single company has a calculated intrinsic business value.

Kazanjian: *What's the third reason to sell?*

Miller: If the investment case changes. Perhaps the government comes in and says it's going to change the reimbursement rates for nursing homes. Guess what? All your cash flows are going to change. Or if you own cigarette stocks, which look cheap until you factor in the litigation environment. Sometimes we learn the world evolves differently from what we thought. If we were owners of AT&T, which we're not, and they committed capital to buy TCI and Media One, if it didn't look to us as if they were going to earn above their cost to capital, that would totally change the value of the business.

Kazanjian: *Do you pay much attention to the market, interest rates, etc.?*

Miller: We pay a lot of attention to it. The justifiable valuation of a market with 7 percent inflation is radically different from the valuation of a market with 2 percent inflation. We pay attention, we just don't forecast it. We observe it and adjust our models for the current economic environment.

Kazanjian: *How patient are you with companies that don't move up for months or years?*

Miller: We will own a company as long as we're confident of the business value and in management's ability to execute those values. As long as we trust management and believe it's dealing with us in a fair way, we will hold the stock. Circus Circus [now called Mandalay Resort Group] is a good example. We owned it for three years, and it did nothing but go down. As it turns out, we were too optimistic about the environment in Las Vegas and how that would develop. Even though the stock performed poorly, we kept buying it because the stock price declined more than the business value. We will stay with companies for long periods as long as we're confident of the business values. [Mandalay shares doubled during 1999.]

Kazanjian: *Tell me more about the additional analysis you do on companies before buying?*

Miller: We do virtually anything we can to help us add value. We talk to management, suppliers, competitors, and analysts. Because we are long-term owners of these companies and don't blow out the stock because it misses a quarter or underperforms for X period of time, management tends to be more open with us than with other shareholders or analysts, in terms of talking about longer-term business strategies and issues. Most people don't care about that.

Kazanjian: *You also manage the Legg Mason Special Investment Trust, which focuses on small- and mid-cap stocks. Is there a difference in how you analyze smaller companies, compared to the larger ones?*

Miller: No, the process is exactly the same.

Kazanjian: *How much do you have in the Value Trust fund right now?*

Miller: About $13 billion, and another $4 billion in a fund that shadows the Value Trust.

Kazanjian: *How many stocks do you own in the portfolio?*

Miller: Forty to forty-five.

Kazanjian: *Why do you stay so concentrated? A lot of value guys are pretty diversified because they don't know which of their ideas will work out.*

Miller: That's because they don't do the research. I'm not disparaging them, but you can't do in-depth research on 300 companies. It's hard enough to do it on 40. You can't turn your portfolio over and own hundreds of names and do much in-depth research. You're relying on stock factors such as PE, price-to-book, and price-to-cash-flow ratios, along with historical correlations to drive your returns. I'm not criticizing that. If that works, more power to them. But it's not what we do.

Kazanjian: *Is there a point where size will be a problem? Your fund is getting very large, and you don't own many names.*

Miller: One of the things we try to do here is be rational. One way to approach your question is to look at evidence showing that when your average assets under management are roughly equivalent to the average market capitalization of what you own, size begins to impact performance. That's why if you're running a small-cap fund, and you've got $500 million in your fund, you can't own market caps much smaller than $500 million or you're going to own too much of the company, and the market impact costs will be too great. The average market cap in our fund right now is about $50 billion. Under that scenario we could take in twice the amount of assets we currently have without size impacting performance. Another way to look at it is the S&P 500 has about $10 trillion of assets. The S&P 500, as you know, outperforms most managers most of the time. That means there's $10 trillion of assets under management that outperform almost everybody. But they own 500 stocks. We own 50 stocks. Therefore, we could theoretically outperform with $1 trillion, which is ten times what Fidelity Magellan has in it right now.

Kazanjian: *You have now bested the record of Peter Lynch, by beating the S&P 500 for nine straight years. That feat has brought a lot of attention to your fund. Do you worry that many shareholders have bought in because of your performance and may therefore watch you more closely than they do the average manager, so that if you underperformed for any period of time, they'll pull out and be disappointed?*

Miller: I don't feel pressure from that. I have a concern that shareholders are buying the fund not fully understanding our strategy. Shareholders who chase performance are not the kind of shareholders who are most suitable for this fund. There are funds set up to shoot the lights out every year. That's their job. We're trying to earn the highest possible risk-adjusted returns for our clients on a long-term basis using a valuation driven methodology. We're not going to change our strategy or style if we underperform for a bit, and we undoubtedly will underperform. If people are surprised by that, they should look at another fund.

Kazanjian: *Why do you think so many managers do underperform the S&P 500?*

Miller: Because there isn't any evidence that their investment methodologies and management styles lead to outperformance. There are two different issues here. First, what's the evidence that your general investment style will outperform? Most people don't have a strong warrant for whatever they're doing. They may or may not have some academic basis for historical correlation between growth and outperformance, or valuation and outperformance. They don't line up their portfolio to comport with old academic studies. They pick and choose. More important, I think too many people underperform because they have a money management style that makes no sense. Namely, they try to forecast variables that are unforecastable. Nobody can forecast interest rates or GDP numbers. People who base their portfolio on forecasts are basing it on something that is inherently subject to large error. Then they compound the error by turning the portfolio over roughly 100 percent or more a year, which means they are trying to react to data in an area where the market has the greatest advantage. The market is most efficient in the short run. All the academic evidence and theory indicates this. That's why day traders are destined to lose money.

Trying to guess the short-term stuff or react to it makes no sense. If you look at the S&P and ask yourself why it outperforms most people, it's not because the S&P has a superior stock selection methodology. They select 500 stocks out of 10,000 public companies. They're not selecting these on the basis of trying to beat other money managers. They're trying to get companies that represent the overall U.S. economy. They want companies that are leaders in an industry, niche, or sector, that have been around for some time, have adequate trading liquidity, and have financial characteristics such that they'll be in business ten years from now. That's about it. Why does that beat 95 percent of money managers? It's not the stock selection, it's the money management strategy of the S&P. It's long-term, has low turnover, is tax-efficient, and doesn't change company or industry weightings. It just lets them evolve. You'll hear money managers say all the time, "I'm overweight this, underweight that, I've got too much technology, or whatever." The S&P doesn't come out and say, "Microsoft is the biggest company, so let's cut it back." They let their winners run. Technology and financial services together were 5.5 percent of the S&P 35 years ago. Now they're more than 40 percent. Why? That's the way it's evolved. Most money managers have fairly strict limits on what they're going to do and how much they're going to have in the portfolio. Look at people like Buffett. He doesn't say he's overweighted in Coca-Cola, so he's going to sell some. He just buys and holds it. If the time comes when he decides he's going to sell it, he will sell.

Kazanjian: *You're making a good case for people to just put all their money in the S&P.*

Miller: The S&P is a wonderful thing to put your money in. If somebody said, "I've got a fund here with a really low cost, that's tax efficient, with a 15-to-20-year record of beating almost everybody," why wouldn't you own it?

Kazanjian: *Bringing active management to more of a micro level, value managers especially have done miserably over the past few years, although you've been head and shoulders above everyone else. What are most value managers doing wrong?*

Miller: The growth-value distinction is a distinction without a difference. That's one of the big problems. People believe that somehow or other there are characteristics of companies that make them growth or value. I believe the growth-value distinction really describes the styles of money managers, not the characteristics of companies. Value managers put valuation as the critical driver in their style. Growth managers focus on growth and underweight valuation. What's happened to value managers, particularly in the last few years, is they have avoided technology because they haven't devoted the time or effort to understand it, and they have placed way too much weight on historical valuation metrics that have little applicability in today's environment. That's not because it's a different world or new era, but because the valuation metrics they are using came from an era of much higher inflation and high interest rates. We now have a low inflation, low interest rate environment, yet they haven't adjusted their models.

Kazanjian: *Are there certain areas of the market you like more than others, or is it coincidental that you have a heavy weighting in technology, for example?*

Miller: It's coincidental in the sense that right now we happen to find the best values in technology and financial services. We've had a consistent theme of financial services since 1982. Technology is a more recent emphasis. IBM was the first major technology purchase we made when it got so cheap, in 1994. The work we did on IBM helped us understand various aspects of this business. I think now we have reasonably good expertise across a wide spectrum of the technology sector. It just so happens a lot of value investors don't fiddle around in that area. As a result, when things go wrong in tech, stock prices can get much lower than they might in aerospace or aluminum, where the value people are.

Kazanjian: *How many analysts do you work with?*

Miller: Our total team is ten.

Kazanjian: *Looking ahead to the new millennium, how are you feeling about the prospects for the stock market overall?*

Miller: This is one of those times when the bears have the same view we do. We happen to call ourselves bullish. The bears say the returns in the market are way too high, and people have to get used to lower returns of only 8 to 10 percent a year. Our view is that stocks will provide the best rate of return of any major asset class. You can get 6 percent from bonds, 5 percent from cash, or 8 to 10 percent from stocks. That's lower than the past but it will be the best rate of return available.

Kazanjian: *What would you say you learned from your days as a philosophy student that most applies to the world of investing?*

Miller: Understanding the nature of theories of truth. Investing involves sifting through a lot of data and trying to figure out what has the highest probability of succeeding. How do you weight the data? What order do you put them in? How much credence do you give to what people tell you about things you're seeing? Philosophically, there are three basic theories of truth, the correspondence theory, coherence theory, and the pragmatic theory. What has harmed many money managers, not just value managers, over the years is that they unconsciously adopt a correspondence theory of truth, which unfortunately happens to be the wrong theory. They have a model of the world that doesn't work. Under the correspondence theory of truth, you believe your strategy corresponds to a way of investing that corresponds to some deep structure of the way the world is. How do you know when your model of the world, your methodology, is no longer operative? How do you know if it's no longer true that low PE stocks outperform? If you have the correspondence theory of truth, you're loathe to give that belief up. You say, "I know this works. It's the way the world is."

Whereas if you have a pragmatic theory, which I believe is the right theory, you say, "The reason I do this strategy is because it's been shown to work. If the evidence shows that it doesn't work anymore, I'm not going to do it." Why would you go along with something that didn't work? Pragmatic theorists use the test of usefulness and utility, not the test of correspondence.

People make up stories to justify whatever view they happen to have. The question is why? Why would you think the best companies in the world would underperform this garbage that trades at low prices? The great value of the philosophy tool kit is that it allows you to understand that investing is context dependent and the world does change. Go back to the 1950s when people believed unerringly that stock yields had to be higher than bond yields. Whenever stock yields got lower, people sold stocks. The academic evidence and practical experience were absolutely compelling. People said it fits the theory because stocks are riskier than bonds, so stocks should have higher yield than bonds, the yield being the dividend. The theory went that if you got a lower return from a risky asset class, obviously that asset class was overpriced. This worked perfectly well until 1957. Stock yields haven't been higher than bond yields since then. Anybody whose philosophy corresponded with the old rules was washed out of the business in about three years. Now people say it's obvious stocks have lower yields than bonds. Stocks protect against inflation and offer growth.

Kazanjian: *So you must be willing to change?*

Miller: You have to be willing to examine what you believe, why you believe it, and what the evidence for your belief is. You need a methodology that enables you to adapt. I wouldn't say change. Change is misleading. I'd say you must be adaptable, not for the short term but for the long term.

Kazanjian: *Do you still read a lot of philosophy?*

Miller: Yes. The most useful and helpful philosophers for investing, or really anything else, are William James and John Dewey.

Kazanjian: *What are the characteristics of the most successful companies you've owned over time?*

Miller: They tend to have low valuations and are trading way down from their prior highs because of some problem, perceived or real. They are leaders in their industries, have managements who actually care about shareholder value, and, most important, have a fundamental economic model where they can earn above their cost of capital.

Bill recently launched another fund, Legg Mason Opportunity Trust, which gives him the opportunity to buy any stocks he wants, regardless of size or price. That will free him from the "value" label, and the controversy that comes from being a value guy who buys what others consider to be growth companies.

This could be a very interesting fund, given Bill's impeccable reputation. After all, he has achieved the best record of any fund manager (in terms of consecutive years of beating the S&P 500) by running a very large fund. I expect he could do even more amazing things running a smaller asset base.

What's equally impressive is how Bill has been able to keep up his performance in light of both a strong tailwind against value and huge inflows of new cash into his fund. That, in my mind, is testament to his skills as a brilliant stock picker. Bill is definitely not a one-time wonder, like so many of today's managers who have one or two good years and then go on to have long stretches of underperformance.

By being more flexible than his fellow value managers, Bill has stood far above the crowd. He's a genuinely bright guy. My guess is until he eventually retires, it will be hard for any other manager to catch up with his enviable record of beating both the index and about every other diversified fund in sight.

As a footnote, while still remaining with Legg Mason, Bill recently became a partner in his own advisory firm, LMM/LLC. The firm is 50 percent owned by Bill, and 50 percent owned by Legg Mason. ■

WILLIAM A. OATES, JR.

NORTHEAST INVESTORS GROWTH

A s I began my conversation with Bill Oates, I immediately forgot who was interviewing whom. Before I could get out my first question, Bill asked, "How old are you? Why are you writing this book? How much money are they paying you to do this?" I instantly understood the kind of scrutiny Oates must put the management of the companies in his portfolio through. It was typical of his no-nonsense style, which I'm sure you'll sense as you read through the interview.

Bill admits he stumbled into the investment business through serendipity, since he never had any specific career ambitions growing up. He describes himself as rather ordinary. He's been in the same Boston office at 50 Congress Street in Boston's financial district for the past 27 years, where he has run the Northeast Investors Growth fund since 1980.

Bill pretty much works alone, which is probably good since he's an admittedly opinionated person. He doesn't rely on computers or fancy Wall Street research. Instead, he buys what he knows best—well-known companies with solid long-term track records and the potential to continue to grow over time. He's known for taking some unusual and controversial steps with his fund. For one thing, he makes it a point to pay out annual distributions, subjecting his shareholders to annual tax liability. He also split his fund's share price three-for-one in 1997, a move many in the fund industry criticize as meaningless. But that doesn't phase the 57-year-old manager. During our interview, he explains why he took these measures, and points out that the fund has never spent a dime on advertising, yet has grown to more than $325 million in assets.

In his spare time, Bill likes to climb tall mountains, which shouldn't come as a surprise since he tries to keep his body as active as his mind. He also jogs regularly to stay in shape. I think you'll especially enjoy his observations of the fund industry and his views about some of his younger competitors.

Kazanjian: *I know you started out at the Morgan Guaranty Trust in 1966, but did you have a long-standing interest in investing?*

Oates: I had no interest in investing. I don't think I took a mathematics, economics, or business administration course in college. I majored in American literature with a submajor in English literature and American history. I took every kind of religion, English, and history course I could get my hands on.

Kazanjian: *Did you have a career goal in mind?*

Oates: No. I played ice hockey all my life. The biggest thing I had on my mind was the next hockey game. I was on the varsity hockey team at Colby College at a time when it was nationally ranked.

Kazanjian: *How did you wind up at Morgan?*

Oates: In my senior year I knew nothing about business, but I figured that banks lent to businesses. Therefore, if you're going to lend money to a business, you probably ought to find out what the business does and how you're going to get paid back. I figured if I could somehow get into the swim at a major banking institution, it would be a selfishly broadening experience. I knew I could read the newspapers and get that part of the equation, but I lacked any kind of financial skills or the tools to evaluate what a company was worth or how to lend to it. By hook and by crook I got accepted into Morgan's training program in New York City. They took about 15 of us, not many women, mostly men. They moved us around to different departments: the credit department, the lending department, the money market department, the operational department, and the loan department. After you immersed yourself and finished the so-called training program, you were appointed to one of these areas. I ultimately ended up at the money market desk. We basically helped corporations invest their short-term cash.

Kazanjian: *How did you finally make it over to the equity side?*

Oates: I didn't. I had no experience in equities. I had no money. In 1968, I got married. I actually went to New York City with two objectives. One was to learn as much as I could about business. The other was to get married. I said to myself that if it ever came to a point where there was a cocktail party at 7:00 P.M. on a Thursday or a big project I got Thursday morning that was due at 8:00 A.M. Friday, I would go to the cocktail party. I wasn't going to get hammered down. I wanted to meet a lot of people and find someone I could spend the rest of my life with. That was as important to me as learning as much as I could about whatever business.

Kazanjian: *Why was marriage so important to you? A lot of young people, especially when they're starting out, are more interested in advancing their careers.*

Oates: I had no career to advance because I didn't know anything. I think I was smart enough to know that down the road I wanted children, I wanted to be able to do things and, most of all, I wanted somebody that I could wake up to in the morning, look at, and not jump out the window. I was lucky enough to find the right woman, and I'm still married to her today. Flashing forward, we've got three kids.

Kazanjian: *When did you get married?*

Oates: In 1968. In 1970, I applied to only one business school, Harvard, and miracle of miracles, got in. I left Morgan in June 1970, drove around the country, and walked into the Harvard Business School on September 1, 1970, thinking that I was too old, at 27, and that I knew nothing. It was totally intimidating. I can remember one day at Morgan when John Deere brought all of its high muck-a-mucks into the bank to review their revolving credit relationship. You had the president, treasurer, and so forth in a great big conference room going over pro forma sales and pro forma profit statements to prove they were solvent and a good bet for whatever money they'd borrow. Nobody questioned the figures. Sales could have been projected to go up 50 percent a year and the Morgan guys would just sit there and go, "These numbers look great. Of course, we'll renew your $10 million line of credit, no problem." Then the Deere guys rolled the papers back up and walked out. I wouldn't have known the first question to ask except I could see sales and profits escalating. I couldn't figure out percentages and nobody asked anything. I thought that was rather odd. Years later, I concluded that the Morgan guys didn't know anything more about the figures than the guys who had prepared them. A slight exaggeration, I'm sure. But nobody said, "Hey, guys, these look great. Can you just review the underlining assumptions that went into these things?" Nobody did that. I'd like to say I read *The Wall Street Journal* cover to cover, but I didn't. I read only the front page. Not the soft articles that are in column one, but the hard ones that go down the business column. It was just Greek. About four days a week I went to a fellow in the economics department who was very quiet. He always ate at his desk, smoked cigarettes, and had an infinite amount of patience. He'd tell me what it all meant. I learn better audibly than by reading. He would give me things to read, and I gradually built up a bit of knowledge.

Kazanjian: *What happened when you got to Harvard?*

Oates: I discovered that one-third of the class was older than I. That was a relief. One-third was exactly my age, and one-third was younger. During the first class, the professor in our first section said, "Before I begin this course I just want to ask a casual question." There were maybe 900 in a class in those days, and you were broken up into sections of 50 or 60. The professor said, "I'm curious. How many of you feel you are among the last five or six admitted to this year's MBA program?" About half the room's hands went up, including mine. I was convinced I was the last. Those two years were not necessarily spent studying investments but general management. I won't boast, but academically I did far better there than I ever did as an undergraduate. I was more motivated and hungry. I loved Boston and knew I wanted to stay in the area. One thing led to another, and I came to work in this very same office for Hollis P. Nichols and Ernest E. Monrad.

Kazanjian: *Was the firm called Northeast Investors then?*

Oates: The day I walked in they had a no-load mutual fund by the name of Northeast Investors Trust with $52 million in assets. It was founded by Nichols in 1950. Income was the objective, and they invested primarily in corporate bonds. Nichols had a few relatives whose money he managed outside the mutual fund, but they were not registered investment advisers. The name of the entity was Northeast Investors Trust. That was the only stationery in the box. Monrad was a lawyer versed in wills and estates, not a finance guy, and I didn't know a lot about investing. I might not even know much today.

Kazanjian: *I doubt that.*

Oates: Let me give you a bit of a timeline. Nichols retired and walked away about a decade later. In 1980, when I was 38, I told Nichols and Monrad that we had built the business to where we invested in common stocks in our individual portfolios, and if we didn't start a no-load common stock fund, all of Boston would think the only thing we knew about was bonds. We still didn't know diddly about stocks. I spent most of that summer doing legwork on the fund. We opened Northeast Investors Growth Fund on October 27, 1980. We had to have at least $100,000 in it. I think I put in the first $60,000. Of that, only about $8,000 was mine. The rest I borrowed from a bank.

Kazanjian: *What else were you doing for the firm all those years before the fund started?*

Oates: It was ambiguous. I joined to help Nichols and Monrad with the bond fund.

Kazanjian: *So when you started Northeast Investors Growth, you didn't really know how to invest in stocks?*

Oates: Well, if you're buying bonds, you're buying the debt of companies. You better find out a bit about the company you're lending money to. These companies are often public, so the research you do for bonds is about the same as for stocks. It's not as if I were wandering around in Sequoia trees on the West Coast and suddenly went over to pine trees on the East Coast. I just tilted my hat from the left side of my head to the right side.

Kazanjian: *When you started this, were you doing all the work on the fund by yourself?*

Oates: Yes, but Nichols, Monrad, and I all worked pretty closely together. For a long time Nichols called all the shots. When he retired Monrad became chairman and he called all the shots. But we all worked together. Monrad's office is right next to mine. We don't have committee meetings. We sit and discuss things periodically. We kind of think the same way, so when we get new investment ideas we talk about them. This isn't a solo shop by any means. I should say that in 1984 we came out of the woodwork and registered as investment adviser with the SEC, at which time we brought on another partner, Harry Guild. We agreed together we'd accept all individuals, institutions, churches, or schools who came to us and wanted us to help them manage their money.

Kazanjian: *No matter how much they had to invest?*

Oates: We vowed never to post a minimum.

Kazanjian: *You have separate accounts plus the fund?*

Oates: Our firm does three things. We manage a no-load bond fund, Northeast Investors Trust; we manage a no-load common stock fund, Northeast Investors Growth; and we manage individual, institutional, and family money under an entity called Guild, Monrad and Oates, Inc.

Kazanjian: *How much do you manage altogether?*

Oates: On August 1, 1972, the day I walked in here, we had $52 million. Today we have almost $3 billion.

Kazanjian: *Why were you so interested in starting the stock fund, other than broadening the firm's reputation?*

Oates: Not every human being thinks alike. I was just beginning to save a little bit of money and wanted to own stocks. If you have $20,000, it doesn't make much sense owning twelve shares of this, and eight shares of that. I selfishly started the fund as a way to co-mingle my money and buy the stocks that I always wanted to own.

Kazanjian: *Is the investment philosophy of the fund the same today as it was when you started?*

Oates: It's exactly the same.

Kazanjian: *And that is?*

Oates: This is going to sound silly, but to make money, and not blow it. Interestingly, as we speak, I am still the single largest individual shareholder in this fund, which has $325 million in assets.

Kazanjian: *Do you put all of your money into the fund?*

Oates: No, but a lot of it.

Kazanjian: *Do you consider yourself to be a growth investor? I've seen some people refer to you as a value investor.*

Oates: I'm not a value investor. It's a growth fund. With as much money as I have in this fund, I think twice before I buy or sell anything. Quite frankly, I'm investing my own money, along with my shareholders'. It's hard to get away from number one though, which is my money. I think that's a pretty good thing, incidentally.

Kazanjian: *Why not put all of your money into the fund?*

Oates: That would be quite a bit of money, first of all. I also own some stocks outside the fund. I admit that doesn't make sense. I should keep it all in the fund. I've told our individual clients I will never buy a common stock that we don't own either in the growth fund or that I don't own myself.

Kazanjian: *What do you think of fund managers who don't put a significant portion of their money into their funds?*

Oates: I think everyone's different. For example, Fidelity has as many mutual funds as there are days in the month. More. They market these things the way Procter & Gamble markets dog food. There are funds for aggressive individuals, passive individuals, women, etc. They are looking for professionals to manage pools of money as well as they can. We don't have 15 funds; we have two. We are small enough to be able to put our own money where our mouth is. It's also a big differentiating factor. We are up against the world. We're a tiny mutual fund that has never spent five cents on advertising, and we're competing against a plethora of Fidelity funds. How can we differentiate ourselves from that huge mass? Two ways. One, we have a good track record, thanks to both luck and skill. Second, we put our money where our mouth is.

Kazanjian: *Your fund has outperformed the S&P 500 over the past five years, but you didn't start out that strong.*

Oates: That's right. If you go back to 1980–82, those were rocky years in the market. You can't do as much with a $100,000, or even $250,000, as you can with $300 million. I also hope I know more now then I did then.

Kazanjian: *It seems as if your fund goes through spurts. You tend to outperform the S&P for several years and then underperform for several. Is that just a coincidence?*

Oates: I think it is. I've outperformed over time, and that's what counts. I happen to personally espouse an investment philosophy that goes like this: I've always felt that the minute anybody takes a dollar out of his or her pocket and invests it in stocks, that person is taking an enormous amount of risk. Enormous. Therefore, I prefer to invest with industry leaders, long-established companies that are delivering products I understand and are necessary to life. That overall blanket ushers you over into the general corner of big-cap well-known companies.

Kazanjian: *Some of today's newer investors would disagree with you. They don't seem to think stocks have much risk.*

Oates: Look at the period of 1973–74, when the market lost around 46 percent. From 1962–82, stocks didn't do anything. Here we are at the turn of the century, and it's a whole different ball game. But it can change.

Kazanjian: *Are you able to buy stocks of any size, though?*

Oates: I can buy anything I want.

Kazanjian: *But you tend to go with the large-caps because of your style?*

Oates: Yes. I've tried to sit back and see what areas of life interest me and why. Technology is on the list because it is the future. Health care and drugs are there because people are living longer and drug companies are inventing more drugs, which leads to healthier lives. Entertainment companies, like Time-Warner and Disney, are there because people have more free time. Regional banks are important because the number of banks in the United States is shrinking, not increasing. Big banks are buying small banks, and small banks are buying medium-sized banks. If you can get yourself into a good region of the country where the work standards and ethics are reasonably high and people are reasonably honest, there are good, solid investment opportunities to be had. Those are four areas that make sense to me. They're not the only ones, but I understand these areas. Having identified the areas, I go in and look for the corporate athletes out there, the giants in the field. To the best of my humble knowledge, I see if it looks as if they'll continue to do whatever it is they do well and effectively. Then I go for them. That kind of process over the past decade has led me to more big than small companies.

Kazanjian: *Do you believe people need to own any small companies in their portfolio?*

Oates: People are all over the place. In the individual side of the business, I have some clients who simply cannot go to sleep at night owning big-cap stocks. They've got to own small, emerging, and foreign companies. It gives them the willies to think that they aren't in all these areas of opportunity. I think the segmentation of the market is really a product of Morningstar, CNBC, and the modern day in which we live, along with the mutual fund industry seeking to gather money. Part of the gathering process, as I mentioned, resembles Procter & Gamble. They've noticed that dog food is dog food. If it's packaged differently and even shaped differently, they can sell more of it. Put it in squares, triangles, or add speckles, and people think it's unique and different. They want all the flavors. Look at all the names Fidelity has put on its funds: Magellan. New Millennium. Disciplined Equity. Diversified International. This is silly. My point is that putting handles on different buckets creates a segmentation of the marketplace. Then you get Morningstar and the rating agencies bifurcating all this, dividing it, and putting people into still different buckets. The poor lowly consumer then starts to get the willies.

Kazanjian: *Does that mean you don't buy the asset-allocation academic argument, that you need a little of this, and a little of that?*

Oates: I don't want to argue against it. You'd be silly to, and you'd probably lose in an academic forum. But my zone of comfort happens to be right where we are. There's no question that the fund marketing machines have been enormously successful. They appeal to all sorts of people. I'm not knocking their success. I'm trying to understand it and to address why some people start to shake if they don't have a small-cap fund. I'm trying to understand it.

Kazanjian: *Going back to technology, do you like the Internet stocks?*

Oates: My thing is to stick with the best and the brightest, such as Microsoft, Intel, IBM, Lucent, and Cisco.

Kazanjian: *How about Amazon.com and the pure-play Internet companies?*

Oates: I own a one percent position in Yahoo!. I bought and sold Amazon.com twice and lost money both times. I don't think I'm going back because they're the pioneers of the concept but not making any money. You can't kiss all the ladies.

Kazanjian: *You do believe in the Internet, though?*

Oates: Oh, yeah. I think it's the future.

Kazanjian: *When you put your portfolio together, do you begin by making a broad market forecast?*

Oates: I'm not half smart enough to do that. I don't try to time the market. I think it's physically impossible. Anybody who tells you differently is full of baloney. Having said that, you read the newspapers, go to lunches, listen to everybody you can, and always try to figure out what the future will be. You just can't forecast it. Look at the summer of 1998. In round numbers the market closed at an all-time high on the fourth of July, and by the ninth of October, it was down about 21 percent. There wasn't one segment or sector that was spared a significant hit. No one knew that was coming. If you make an assessment that structurally the United States is in trouble, and I'm now referring back to the Vietnam period, then I would predict it might not be a good period for stocks. But who can do that? I think there are really only two decisions: Are you going to be in the market or not? If you're going to be in the market, you simply must decide what companies you are going to invest in.

Kazanjian: *You were formerly just a bond guy. Do you think people need to own some bonds?*

Oates: It again depends on your profile. Bond yields today are not really compensatory for the rate of inflation. You don't get a whole lot from the yield. If you're a family or individual, earning an honorable salary and able to live on the salary, I think you ought to have your investments in good common stocks, which don't pay much in the way of dividends. You're hoping to turn a dollar into four dollars over a period of time.

Kazanjian: *Do you believe individuals should buy individual stocks or mutual funds?*

Oates: The debate roars on that. You're talking to somebody who's done both and who does both today. My children own stock in things they can touch, use, and understand. To the extent that people buy what they really enjoy, that's not a bad deal.

Kazanjian: *Are you a buy-and-hold guy, or do you frequently trade?*

Oates: It's like going to Las Vegas. There are some people who don't know how to hold. Even somebody in my age and stage. I own Gillette personally, and I have it in our mutual fund. Gillette's high not that long ago was $64, and it's trading at $44 today. Earnings recently have been disappointing because Europe and Asia are giving them problems with one or two of their major divisions. This is a company whose earnings have grown in the range of 15 to 18 percent every year. Because of these difficulties, it appears that earnings won't be growing that rapidly in the future unless they can correct these problems. I've owned Gillette for a long time. Is it going to get back to $64? Is the company going to be astute enough to correct things over time? Who knows? The debate of holding goes on every day.

Kazanjian: *How do you come out in the debate?*

Oates: If you'd bought Polaroid way back when and just held on, you would have lost a lot of money. I don't think you hold on forever. I think you keep your nose in the wind and you sniff. The important thing is to make a judgment as to whether the product that's being produced is viable.

Kazanjian: *How do you find your stock ideas?*

Oates: By doing just what I said. I haven't touched a lot of the things that we own, but we have a Hewlett-Packard printer, our whole Internet system has a lot of Cisco parts, I've got IBM machinery, I love Coca-Cola, I use a Gillette Mach III razor, I bank at Fleet, I ski in Utah and see Zions all over the place. These are the companies I own.

Kazanjian: *But just because you like a company or use its products doesn't mean it's a good investment. You must do a deeper analysis.*

Oates: I do all the standard stuff. I get the annual report, look at the company's history, and sometimes go talk with them in person.

Kazanjian: *What are you looking for?*

Oates: Sustained earnings growth, expansion of the product cycle, increased market penetration, all those kinds of things. It's standard security analysis. You can have reams and reams of figures and pull yourself up and talk with the president and CEO of different divisions, but in the end you have to step back from all that baloney and make a judgment as to whether this is something that feels and seems good or not.

Kazanjian: *What you're saying is you must use your instincts.*

Oates: I think the best money managers have a lot of instinct and feel like a really great surgeon. Have you ever asked a surgeon how he does an operation? He can't tell you because he gets the knee, hip, or heart open and just starts doing it. I do investment work for a tremendous orthopedic surgeon and he couldn't possibly tell me how he does it. I'm not saying I'm great by any means, but I've been in the business since the mid–1960s. I've made mistakes all over the place and have improved my craft along the way.

Kazanjian: *Do you have a price discipline, in terms of how much you will pay for a stock?*

Oates: No. I have the discipline of a pig. First of all, a lot of mutual funds have very high turnover rates. I took a look at one very well-known fund and was shocked to see the turnover rate was 357 percent. You know what that means? The entire portfolio turned over 3.5 times last year. With turnover rates like that, these guys ought to have a sign posted over the door, "This is not investing, this is a sophisticated way of going to horse races." It's nuts. My turnover is about 22 percent.

Kazanjian: *When will you sell a stock?*

Oates: Number one, if I firmly believe the company's fundamentals have changed. That means it's time to pack the bag and go somewhere else. Number two, I sell mistakes. When something isn't panning out way the I thought it would, I get out of it. Three, when something as a percent of the whole becomes too big. I think having 10 percent of our fund in one stock is a bit too much. It ought to be around 5 to 6 percent. I'll hope that the success of an investment will ultimately cause you to pick the low-hanging fruit.

Kazanjian: *You have 66 stocks in the fund right now. Is that about average for you?*

Oates: I've had more. I got up to 85 once. But at that point you own too many smaller positions. If, for example, a position of $600,000 doubles, it has no impact on the performance.

Kazanjian: *You're a shareholder, so do you keep taxes in mind?*

Oates: Very much, but I think it's important to pay a dividend and make a capital gains distribution to shareholders every year. I've been criticized for this. However, I feel it represents a little weeding of the garden. If you don't sell a bit every year, you get yourself backed into a corner. If the cost of an investment is $1 million and the market value is $20 million, you can't ever sell because the taxes are so great. It's important to harvest a little every year, put a little hay in the barn, and redistribute that.

Kazanjian: *So you intentionally try to pay out gains?*

Oates: Yes. The funds have paid a dividend every single year.

Kazanjian: *You use leverage, which is something most funds stay away from. How do you use it and why?*

Oates: I use it carefully. It's a dangerous tool because if it goes against you it can really hurt. Right now I have about $10 million leveraged and the size of the fund is $325 million. I use it because we've been enjoying a period of time when money has been coming into the fund in a rather big way. What this does is let me buy ahead. If I see position I want to add to I can go out and do it today. You then hope that over the next ten days money will come in by way of purchases to pay off the loan.

Kazanjian: *What if it doesn't come in?*

Oates: That's why you have to be careful. You can get hurt. If it doesn't come in and the market starts to drop, you have to sell things that you might not otherwise sell. So far it's worked to our advantage.

Kazanjian: *Over time what would you say is the biggest mistake you've made in terms of investing?*

Oates: Things evolve. Obviously you regret every loss you've taken. In retrospect you think, "Why was I so convinced in my thinking the investment was going north—and instead it went south? Why wasn't I able to see that?" I don't think I was early enough on the tech front. Microsoft became a public company in 1986. The stock didn't do much for four or five years. I don't think I bought it until 1990.

Kazanjian: *Are there any kinds of companies you categorically avoid?*

Oates: Anything I'd say today I might regret tomorrow. Part of the problem of being older in this business, and I think I am older, unfortunately, is that you start developing biases. I've been burned twice on Amazon.com, so my instinct is not to buy it. Yet there may come a day when Amazon ought to be a part of your portfolio. That's why I say it's a plus and a minus where I am right now. The plus of Fidelity is the average age of their managers is probably 28 to 32. They can take a fresher look at some ideas because they haven't been burned in the past.

Kazanjian: *What do you think of younger fund managers?*

Oates: I think they're terrific. They're filled with good ideas and look at the world differently. Someday somebody will sit in my seat and manage Northeast Investors Growth Fund, and they'll perhaps do it in a different way.

Kazanjian: *Do you have anyone in mind?*

Oates: Not yet. There are people in my office who could do it at any time.

Kazanjian: *Would you give your money to a 26-year-old manager?*

Oates: No way. In fact, I think it's like any other transition. When I come to the end of the road, the polite thing to do would be to exit with the majority of my personal investment in the fund. That way you're not always sitting on the sidelines saying, "Why did he buy Amazon and sell Microsoft?"

Kazanjian: *Should people give their money to younger managers or stick with the older folks?*

Oates: If I were giving a talk on investments, I'd ask the audience, "Would you feel comfortable turning your money over to a 28-to-32-year-old individual to manage your money? All who would feel comfortable, please raise your hand." I'll bet you wouldn't get 20 percent of the room raising their hands.

Kazanjian: *But a lot of the great older managers I've interviewed are probably just a few years away from retirement. Wouldn't it be better to give your money to someone you know will be around for a long time?*

Oates: I think you have to watch it. Again, nothing's permanent. Part of the yearly or biyearly review you do as a fund investor is seeing whether the manager is still there. If he or she isn't, you better find out about whoever's going to take his or her place.

Kazanjian: *So mutual funds aren't buy-and-hold forever investments either?*

Oates: I don't think so. Nothing is forever. It just so happens that the incoming tide on the equity front over the past few years has lifted all boats, even boats managed by teenagers, middle-agers, and old goats. Everyone looks like a genius.

Kazanjian: *Why don't you do any advertising?*

Oates: We're too cheap.

Kazanjian: *Speaking of cheap, your expense ratio is pretty cheap too.*

Oates: Not cheap enough. It ought to be lower. It's under one percent, praise the Lord. The expense ratio will go down rapidly as the fund gets bigger.

Kazanjian: *Most funds of your size charge much more. Do you think funds are too expensive?*

Oates: That debate is in the paper every day. Those Vanguard fellows are always talking about that. If the performance is terrific, you've got to pay for the performance. If the performance is lackluster, people will redeem and go away.

Kazanjian: *Performance has been pretty lackluster for most actively managed mutual funds in recent years. There's been a lot of talk about how people should go into index funds and forget about finding active managers. Do you think active management makes sense?*

Oates: Intellectually, in the classroom, you can demonstrate that 8 to 10 percent of all managers beat the S&P 500 each year. A far smaller percentage beat it consistently. This is not many people. I think we've been fantastically lucky. It is very hard to beat the S&P 500, no matter how smart you think you are. The market is efficient, and the S&P has 500 good stocks.

Kazanjian: *Does that mean you should just index?*

Oates: I don't think it's bad to put some of your money in an index fund. I don't have any money in an index fund. I have my money in Northeast Investors Growth and about ten different stocks. Why don't I have an index fund? It's probably just ego. I think my choice of Microsoft, Intel, Coke, Gillette, Time-Warner, Zion, Bank Boston, Fleet will do better than the index.

Kazanjian: *Sounds like you're not a die-hard believer one way or the other.*

Oates: No. I think the index is great. But if you pick the right stocks you can do much better.

Kazanjian: *I understand you actually take the time to talk to your fund shareholders on the phone. That's pretty unusual.*

Oates: It's a form of promotion. I've simply tried to take a very ordinary product, a lowly no-load mutual fund, and differentiate it a bit, in a way that makes sense and will attract people's attention. It's the marketing side of me. I'll talk to anybody. You couldn't speak to the manager of Fidelity Magellan no matter how hard you tried.

Kazanjian: *Speaking of marketing tactics, you split the share price of your fund a few years ago. Isn't that pretty meaningless for a fund?*

Oates: Yes, it's somewhat meaningless, but it means a lot to my farmer friends in Macomb, Illinois. As we speak, the fund's share price is about $23. If we hadn't split the shares, we'd be at around $69 a share. It was a good event for many investors to get a statement in the mail and see they suddenly went from owning 100 to owning 300 shares. They thought it was fantastic. They felt that since the shares were cheaper they could buy more.

Kazanjian: *It sounds like a perception game.*

Oates: It's marketing. There are probably only five mutual funds in the universe that have split their shares. It's a differentiating factor. If our shares get up in price again, I'll probably do another split.

Kazanjian: *You put in a pretty long day, I hear.*

Oates: Today my alarm went off at 5:24. I got up and ran three miles with my wife outside our home in Denham, Massachusetts. I got here at 7:55. During the day I'll meet with clients, follow my companies, and talk a lot on the phone. I follow my stocks like a hawk. I read *The Wall Street Journal* and *The New York Times* cover to cover every day. I don't have a computer in my office. If I did, I'd be a basket case watching the market all day.

Kazanjian: *How often do you run?*

Oates: I'm fairly active. On Saturdays and Sundays I run, ride my bike, swim, play squash, or play golf, depending on the season. I also like mountain climbing. I climbed two 14,000-foot mountains this summer—Longs Peak, which is right outside Estes Park, and Mount Massive, the second highest mountain in Colorado.

Kazanjian: *Do you keep going to progressively larger mountains?*

Oates: The hardest mountain I ever climbed was the Matterhorn. The scariest I ever climbed was Grand Teton. I've been climbing for about a decade. I'm not sure how I got into it. It's a dangerous thing to do, and it's getting harder and harder as the body gets older.

Kazanjian: *How long are you going to stay in the business?*

Oates: I have no plans to retire, but will put a flag out when I do.

Kazanjian: *You said you can't predict the market; no one can. But do you think it's going to continue to be a good market going into the new millennium?*

Oates: I believe that the United States is one fantastic country. Our arch enemy, Russia, is dead. Think of the money, brain power, and time spent trying to win the Cold War. It's gone. You shouldn't own America's big and best companies unless you feel good about the country. Some people just don't feel good about it, and they shouldn't be in the market. My father-in-law didn't feel good about the country. He thought the Communists were going to get us. He certainly despaired over the hippie movement. He didn't like the Vietnam War. He bought mint-condition U.S. gold coins. He probably spent $250,000 on these coins. He died a decade ago. His wife died two years ago. The children lugged the coins—and they're heavy—to an honorable dealer and were appalled and shocked to receive a check for everything he'd spent a life collecting of about $118,000. Had this Harvard-educated man, who was the son of a U.S. Congressman from the state of New York, simply taken this money and put a modest $20,000 in Procter & Gamble, IBM, AT&T, you name it, the family would have done a lot better. I think of him often because he represents a certain kind of person who just doesn't feel right investing in U.S. stocks. The good economy will enable good managers to find ways to earn more for their shareholders.

Kazanjian: *Do you buy any foreign stocks?*

Oates: I would and will, but I'd much prefer to get the foreign exposure through big domestic companies. A huge percent of Coke's sales come from outside the United States, and you don't have accounting, currency, or government differences.

I really enjoyed interviewing Bill for this book. As I'm sure you gathered from his answers, he's a real character who tells it like it is. That even applies to summing up his overall investment approach: "In the end you have to step back from all that baloney and make a judgment as to whether this [the stock you're considering] is something that feels and seems good or not."

This experienced manager doesn't use exotic computer models or charts to make his decisions. More than anything else, he relies on the gut instincts he has refined over close to three decades in the business. That's something you can't learn in school, but a very valuable skill indeed. ■

JAMES OELSCHLAGER

OAK ASSOCIATES, LTD.

Several years ago, *Forbes* magazine wrote that if you want diversification and low volatility, you should stay away from Jim Oelschlager's White Oak Growth Fund. But if you want splendid results and tax efficiency, you better give him a close look. That's a great way to describe the process and strategy of this low-key manager from Akron, Ohio, who runs some of the most volatile growth funds around.

Jim's investment career dates back to 1969, when he was tapped to manage the Firestone Tire & Rubber Company's $250 million pension fund. He did such a good job, the fund had a surplus of $300 million by 1984. A year later, he left to found Oak Associates, *ltd.*, a growth equity investment management firm, with Firestone as his first client. Several other companies and individuals soon signed on, and he continued his winning ways. When folks started asking Jim to manage their smaller personal accounts, he responded by launching the White Oak Growth Fund in 1992. He has since launched two other funds, including the small-cap-oriented Pin Oak and technology-focused Red Oak, which is comanaged by Doug MacKay. Today, Oak Associates, *ltd.*, runs some $19 billion of other peoples' money.

The 57-year-old manager focuses on his three favorite areas—technology, financial services, and health care—and holds a concentrated portfolio of around 20 names. This approach can certainly subject investors to short-term performance roller-coaster rides, but over the long term it has allowed him to stand head and shoulders above the S&P 500.

Jim once thought about becoming a lawyer and earned a Juris Doctor degree from Northwestern School of Law in 1967. He was diagnosed as having multiple sclerosis in 1973, and although he is now confined to a wheelchair, it surely hasn't slowed him down.

As an added bonus for White Oak shareholders, Jim rarely trades out of his stocks, thus not confusing motion with progress. This leads to excellent tax-efficiency. In fact, given how he seems to do so little buying and selling, I asked Jim what he did to keep himself busy during the day. As you'll soon find out, the answer is plenty.

Kazanjian: *I understand that you started investing at the age of 12. How did that happen?*

Oelschlager: I had a huge paper route and was making a lot of money for a kid that age. My father introduced me to a stockbroker and had me invest some of my surplus funds, if you will, into the stock market. I kind of got hooked on it. I quickly concluded that investing was better than delivering papers in the rain and snow at 5 A.M.

Kazanjian: *What did you invest in?*

Oelschlager: My first stock was General Motors.

Kazanjian: *Why did you choose that stock?*

Oelschlager: I don't know. Seemed like a good idea at the time. It did work out though. If my initial foray didn't work out, I probably would've gone into some other business [laughing].

Kazanjian: *But in college you initially decided to get a law degree, right?*

Oelschlager: Yes.

Kazanjian: *What made you decide to do that instead of getting an MBA? What was your career plan?*

Oelschlager: It wasn't that well thought out. After getting my undergraduate degree in economics, I debated whether to go to business school or to law school and decided on law school.

Kazanjian: *You obviously had an interest in finance, since you studied economics. I assume you didn't plan to get into money management at that point?*

Oelschlager: Right.

Kazanjian: *Did you ever practice law after getting your degree?*

Oelschlager: When I was in law school I took a part-time job at the G. D. Searle drug company and stayed there after I graduated from law school. I didn't enjoy that job much and started studying for an MBA at night. There was an opportunity to move from the legal department at Searle over to the treasurer's office, and I soon was doing some investment work for them.

Kazanjian: *That was your start as a professional investor?*

Oelschlager: It was. But the hard-core stuff came in 1969 when the CFO at Firestone was interested in starting an internal investment department to manage the company's pension fund assets. The outside managers had been showing unsatisfactory performance, and the CFO thought he could start an in-house operation and do a better job. He opted to hire somebody young as opposed to going out and getting someone with a lot of experience. A mutual friend put us together. I interviewed and was offered the job.

Kazanjian: *How old were you?*

Oelschlager: Twenty-seven.

Kazanjian: *At 27 you were running Firestone's pension fund?*

Oelschlager: Another guy and I. The two of us ran it.

Kazanjian: *How much did it have in the beginning?*

Oelschlager: $250 million.

Kazanjian: *Did you know what you were doing at first?*

Oelschlager: I don't know. The CFO obviously had confidence in us, and in me. He was sort of the guiding mentor, if you will. I remember at the time having feelings of "inadequacy," and I said to myself, "The only alternative to me is another person. There's no magic book or no magic formula. And if I work reasonably hard and reasonably smart, the fund ought to do reasonably well."

Kazanjian: *Was your comanager your age, or more experienced?*

Oelschlager: He was six months older, I think.

Kazanjian: *So you were both kind of learning on the job?*

Oelschlager: Right.

Kazanjian: *Was it a stock fund?*

Oelschlager: Yes.

Kazanjian: *How did you develop your investment strategy starting out?*

Oelschlager: I suppose a lot of the developed strategy was a reflection of the investment thinking of the CFO at Firestone.

Kazanjian: *In that he dictated what you did?*

Oelschlager: No, he was very good at not dictating. In retrospect, it's amazing the amount of confidence he had in us and the latitude he gave us. It was really a unique situation, and I don't know that it's ever been replicated anyplace else. It's probably unlikely to be replicated anyplace again.

Kazanjian: *I want to talk about your current investment strategy in a moment, but how were you investing back then, and how has your approach evolved over the years?*

Oelschlager: We tried to be a little bit contrarian. We didn't follow the herd. We did what we thought made common sense. We tried to avoid conventional wisdom. Being located in Akron, Ohio, is a bit of an advantage for that. It's easy to get caught up in a lemming-type mentality, I think, if you're in a place like Wall Street where everybody's thinking alike.

Kazanjian: *What kinds of stock were you looking for and how were you choosing them back then?*

Oelschlager: It's sort of interesting because I began investing in the early 1970s, which was the era of the "Nifty Fifties." Conventional wisdom said there were only 50 stocks to own, and they were one-decision stocks because you bought them and just put them in a drawer and didn't worry about them. Almost everything else was considered inappropriate. We didn't think that made a whole lot of sense, so we avoided all those Nifty Fifty stocks and bought some of the real companies, which had real assets, real earnings, and were selling at reasonable multiples. The Nifty Fifty stocks, of course, eventually did blow up, but we didn't look so good in 1972, when they were doing very well. However, in 1973 and 1974, we looked like geniuses, even though we weren't doing anything differently. We didn't own most of the Nifty Fifty, such as Polaroid or Avon Products. We owned things such as Ford, Westinghouse, Union Carbide, and DuPont. They certainly weren't the fashionable stocks of the day, but our performance was quite good overall.

Kazanjian: *Were you beating the S&P 500 back then, or were you even concerned about that?*

Oelschlager: Yes, we were concerned about that, and, yes, we were beating the S&P. We were beating the S&P by about four points a year.

Kazanjian: *You have a concentrated style now. Did you also have a concentrated style then?*

Oelschlager: Ironically, when we took over the pension fund, we had to bring all these assets back from a variety of managers. We spent years trying to whittle down the number of stocks. At one time we had as many as 260 names, and there were always some new stocks we wanted to buy. It was really a long, laborious process to whittle that down to a manageable number. Frankly, I would have argued that it would have been impossible for us to outperform the S&P with that many names in the portfolio, but we were able to do it somehow. When we got to a point where Firestone terminated the plan and we started over from ground zero, I vowed to never have that many names in the portfolio again.

Kazanjian: *Why did you decide to keep the number of holdings much smaller?*

Oelschlager: Our objective is still to beat the S&P, and we think the best way to beat the S&P is to run a concentrated portfolio, in two ways. First, concentrated only in the industries that you think are attractive as opposed to feeling you have to have a representation in all industries just because they exist. Second, concentrated in a relatively small number of names. You know, conventional wisdom in this business says if you don't like oil stocks, which are 14 percent of the S&P, you underweight oils to 10 percent. At the same time, if you like the banks, which are 2 percent, you overweight the banks and have 4 percent. I used to tell the people at Firestone, "How would you like to explain to the first ten tire builders that walk out of this plant why you have 10 percent of your money in something you don't like and

4 percent of your money in something you like? They're going to think you're crazy, and they're going to be right. This leads to the conclusion, I think, that most managers in this business are closet indexers at heart. The reason I think they're closet indexers is because most managers know that they can't beat the market and don't beat the market. The first objective of the manager is to keep his or her job and if you don't underperform by too much, you tend not to lose your job.

Kazanjian: *Tell me about leaving Firestone. Did you say they closed the plan down?*

Oelschlager: The plan was overfunded by $300 million, which was more than the company made building tires. They needed the cash, so the chairman terminated the plan and bought annuities as required by law. He said to me, "Why don't you start over from zero?" I said, "Why don't I quit? I'll take the three women that are here with me and we'll move across town. We'll run your money on a contract basis and look for other clients." He agreed. We separated in 1985 and started our own business.

Kazanjian: *How much did you start with from them?*

Oelschlager: Basically nothing because Firestone had terminated the plan. I suppose we had about $50 million. It wasn't much.

Kazanjian: *How did you build your business from there?*

Oelschlager: Fortunately, there were a few people who were willing to talk to us, and we convinced some of them to employ us. We basically built it the old-fashioned way, one brick at a time.

Kazanjian: *And you now have some pretty high-powered clients, I understand, including the giant California Public Employees' Retirement System, or CalPERS.*

Oelschlager: We do.

Kazanjian: *How much do you manage altogether now?*

Oelschlager: Around $19 billion.

Kazanjian: *And of that, how much is in the White Oak Growth Fund?*

Oelschlager: About $2 billion. Mutual funds are a relatively small portion of our business. The other funds are Pin Oak Aggressive Growth, with $120 million, and Red Oak Technology, with $150 million.

Kazanjian: *Let's focus on White Oak. White Oak began in 1992. Why did you start that fund?*

Oelschlager: We were basically managing institutional and relatively large individual accounts and didn't have a vehicle for small portfolios. I would go to a hospital board meeting where we were managing foundation-type money, and afterwards a couple of the board members would say, "I've got $50,000 or $100,000. Would you manage it?" I tried for awhile, but it just got too unwieldy. So I decided to start mutual funds to accommodate these smaller accounts.

Kazanjian: *Where did the name Oak come from?*

Oelschlager: I've been asked that a lot. I tried to come up with a clever name, and I sure didn't want Oelschlager. I decided to pick something that was very short and easy to spell. Oak seemed like a good name.

Kazanjian: *Do your private account portfolios hold the same stocks as your fund?*

Oelschlager: Yes.

Kazanjian: *Let's dig deeper into your overall investment strategy. How do you put your portfolio together?*

Oelschlager: I start by trying to determine the industries I think are most attractive. Then I find the stocks in those industries that look best.

Kazanjian: *What areas do you think are most attractive?*

Oelschlager: The three areas I presently like are technology, which is pretty broad-based, pharmaceuticals, and financial services.

Kazanjian: *Why do you like technology so much?*

Oelschlager: I think what's occurring in technology today is equivalent to the first industrial revolution that we had in the late 1800s. I feel this is going to be just as dramatic, in terms of improving the quality of life, the standard of living, and creating some wonderful investment opportunities. Technology is leading to huge productivity gains, which in turn is keeping inflation down. This should continue to put downward pressure on interest rates and should result in a better stock market than most people expect. The really exciting news about this area is that most technology is developed in this country. We're the first to use it in our businesses, resulting in our being the low-cost producer in most places. The rest of the world needs this technology, and they're going to buy it from us. At the same time, new products are going to be coming down the pipeline. I think it's a trend that's going to last a lot longer than most people think.

Kazanjian: *Before we leave technology, why don't you give me an example of a couple of companies or types of technology companies that you would be interested in.*

Oelschlager: The Internet is going to be pretty exciting going forward, from e-commerce to a whole bunch of other functions. The companies that are building the backbone or the infrastructure, such as Cisco Systems, along with companies like Intel and Microsoft, should do very well going forward.

Kazanjian: *These are very large-cap companies.*

Oelschlager: Some of the smaller ones are going to do well, too. But the whole dot-com group is a little too dicey for me.

Kazanjian: *Why do you like the pharmaceuticals?*

Oelschlager: The pharmaceuticals, to some extent, have a similar story as the technology sector. Most of the drugs are developed in this country, and the rest of the world is going to buy them. In addition, we're all living longer. As people mature, they find they can improve their quality of life by taking some drugs on a regular basis.

Kazanjian: *What types of stocks do you like in this area?*

Oelschlager: Most of the majors. Eli Lilly, Pfizer, and Merck immediately come to mind.

Kazanjian: *Let's discuss financial services. What's the case for that sector?*

Oelschlager: The world is creating a staggering amount of wealth, and this money is going to have to be managed and shifted around. The large insurance companies, such as AIG, or the banks, such as Bank of America and Citigroup, are going to have a strong presence going forward. You've seen Citigroup and Travelers merge, and this trend of banks and brokerage houses joining forces will continue.

Kazanjian: *How long have you been interested in these three themes?*

Oelschlager: I've probably been into financials for 20 years. Tech maybe 10 years. I didn't always have huge positions in tech. When I first moved into the tech area, I started at 5 percent and pretty soon was at 15 percent, then 25 percent. It was an evolutionary process. I've been actively involved in pharmaceuticals for only about four or five years.

Kazanjian: *What are some of the areas you've been in that you no longer think are good places to invest?*

Oelschlager: My two biggest industries at one time were oils and utilities.

Kazanjian: *Are those two areas dead forever, or do you think there's a possibility that they could come back?*

Oelschlager: No one can see the future very well. At least I can't. When you phrase the question that way, they certainly have the possibility of coming back. But, frankly, I don't see anything occurring in those groups on the near horizon.

Kazanjian: *We've talked about how you begin with a theme approach, deciding which sectors you like. How do you then go about finding individual names and putting the portfolio together?*

Oelschlager: You look at different stocks in those areas and try to determine not only good companies but decent valuations. Everything is cheap at a price, and everything is expensive at a price. The trick is knowing the difference.

Kazanjian: *When you're out there looking at a company, what characteristics are most important to you?*

Oelschlager: I want to see that the prospects are favorable for good growth and good earnings and that the stock is selling at a reasonable price for that growth of revenue and earnings.

Kazanjian: *What's a reasonable price to you?*

Oelschlager: It's a floating thing. It's a function of many factors. It's not an absolute number. I don't have a computer screen that I run stocks through. I believe it is more of an art than a science.

Kazanjian: *Can you give us some guidelines for how you determine that?*

Oelschlager: Again, it's more of an art form. It's really hard to quantify. I look at many subjective factors. For instance, I want a company with management that is relatively conservative and not promotional in nature. Some managers hype their company's prospects and then routinely fail to produce what they say they're going to. There are others we run into that generally understate what they're going to do. I prefer the latter group.

Kazanjian: *Are you looking for a certain percentage of earnings growth?*

Oelschlager: Yes, but you have to relate that to the price and multiple on the stock. If it's the difference between a company growing at 10 percent or 20 percent a year, I'll pay more for the 20 percent grower than for the 10 percent grower.

Kazanjian: *Technology stocks make up about 65 percent of the White Oak Growth portfolio. Technology in general tends to be a very volatile area. How do you evaluate these companies?*

Oelschlager: We have a group here that goes around visiting the companies and kicking the tires, if you will. We go to conferences and attempt to find out what's happening out there. We try to develop good long-term relationships with the investor relations people at these companies. We want to keep abreast of what's occurring and what the trends are with the way the world's going.

Kazanjian: *How do you decide how much of the portfolio goes into each stock?*

Oelschlager: On a new account I basically give each stock an equal weighting.

Kazanjian: *How many names do you own at a time?*

Oelschlager: Usually 17 to 22.

Kazanjian: *How frequently are you following these companies?*

Oelschlager: I watch them on a regular basis.

Kazanjian: *Do you sell very often?*

Oelschlager: My turnover is very low. I think the turnover in White Oak last year was about 6 percent.

Kazanjian: *Are you spending most of your time buying new stuff or just following what you own?*

Oelschlager: When your turnover is only 6 percent, you don't really buy a lot.

Kazanjian: *So what do you spend your time doing, just following the companies you own?*

Oelschlager: I just look out the window a lot, you know [laughing]. No, I follow the companies I own. I also track the companies that are on my radar screen, companies I'm watching.

Kazanjian: *What makes you decide to sell a company?*

Oelschlager: There are three reasons to sell a company. One, the company becomes excessively priced, and the valuation is too rich. As we discussed earlier, everything's cheap at a price, and everything's expensive at a price. The second reason is if you just blew it. If the company's results didn't turn out to be what you had anticipated and you made a mistake, you sell it. The third reason, and the most frequent, is if you wake up one morning and you're all excited and you want to buy some new company. Because you want to keep a concentrated portfolio, you look at your portfolio and say, "What do I have in here that, even though I like it, has the least relative potential so I can sell it as a source of funds to buy the new idea?"

Kazanjian: *Do you pay attention to the market and the economy and spend your day watching CNBC?*

Oelschlager: I pay attention to the market and watch things on a regular basis, absolutely. I do watch CNBC every morning while I'm shaving and brushing my teeth but I wouldn't say that's a big source of ideas and information. That's entertainment.

Kazanjian: *Do you adjust, for example, your cash position based on your feelings about the market, or are you always invested?*

Oelschlager: I don't try to play market timer. I basically just buy and hold.

Kazanjian: *The rating services say that White Oak Growth is 90 percent riskier than the average growth fund. That's probably because of your concentrated approach. Do you agree that a concentrated approach is more risky?*

Oelschlager: It depends what time frame you look at. If you want to talk in terms of one hour, perhaps. If you want to take a look at three, four, or five years, which is the way I think you should look at it, I would make the case that this fund has been less risky because it has better returns. The idea is to have good returns over a longer time period, not for a week or a month.

Kazanjian: *Do you think individual investors are better off in funds, or with their own concentrated portfolio of individual stocks?*

Oelschlager: It's hard to say. I will concede that if an individual is ten times as smart as I am, yet doesn't have access to the same information and hasn't been doing it for 30 years as I have, it would be difficult for that person to compete with me. There are many individuals who pick their own stocks and do very well. There are a lot of people who enjoy doing that, and they really get into it. Others could not care less. They just want to have their money grow well. In that situation, they're probably better with professional management.

Kazanjian: *How often do you add a new name to your portfolio?*

Oelschlager: A couple of times a year. I try not to confuse motion with progress, which I think is a big mistake that many managers make. They think active management means a high volume of trading and turnover. I don't think active management necessarily means active trading.

Kazanjian: *Why do you believe so many active managers underperform in the market? Are they confusing motion with progress?*

Oelschlager: I think that's one of the reasons.

Kazanjian: *What are some other reasons very few are able to beat the market?*

Oelschlager: I don't really know why others underperform. I just know why I have outperformed. I'm willing to make concentrated bets in the areas I think are most attractive. I feel high turnover is probably a detriment to your performance. I mean, there is a trading cost. I can also say that my style of low turnover and letting my winners run results in lower short-term tax consequences for taxable investors, and that's another advantage my clients have.

Kazanjian: *Are you purposely tax efficient or is that just a result of not trading a lot?*

Oelschlager: That's just a result of my investment style, which is identical for taxable and nontaxable accounts.

Kazanjian: *I'm assuming that, unless you're extremely brilliant, not all of your stocks go up. You do occasionally have some losers.*

Oelschlager: Not only am I not extremely brilliant, I'm not sure I'm brilliant at all. A lot of teachers from my educational experience would readily agree with me. Of course, I've had some big losers. Everyone in this business makes big mistakes. Babe Ruth hit a lot of home runs, but he struck out a lot too.

Kazanjian: *When do you decide that a stock is just not worth hanging onto anymore?*

Oelschlager: Regrettably, I can make that mistake two different ways. I've given up on some stocks, only to watch them rise from the ashes like a phoenix and soar to new heights. On the other hand, there are some stocks I've held on to for too long, and probably should have dumped sooner. If anything, I probably make the mistake of hanging on to them too long.

Kazanjian: *Let's talk about a stock that typifies the work you do.*

Oelschlager: It would have to be Cisco Systems. That's the stock I'm probably most identified with because I own a lot of it and I've been in it for a long time.

Kazanjian: *What first brought you to it and why do you stay with it?*

Oelschlager: I first bought the stock at the initial public offering. I saw the large potential for being able to network companies together so they could share data and information. Cisco has grown explosively in the nine years it's been public. It is still capable of growing in excess of 30 percent annually for the next several years. I think the prospects are huge out there for the Internet, and Cisco is basically building the backbone of the Internet.

Kazanjian: *When would you get out of a stock like that?*

Oelschlager: I met with the management several years ago and they asked me that same question. I suggested that I expected to be in that company for a long time and thought their prospects were good. I said, however, if the stock was selling at 300 times earnings I would consider that an excessive valuation and would sell even though it was still a great company. I picked a very high number. I didn't want to insult them. I mean, I was in their offices and I didn't want them to pull the trap door.

Kazanjian: *How about another name that's been a big success for you.*

Oelschlager: I suppose AIG, the insurance company.

Kazanjian: *When did you first get into that?*

Oelschlager: That's probably the stock I've had the longest around here. I think I bought that about 12 years ago.

Kazanjian: *What led you to AIG and why do you stay with it?*

Oelschlager: It's a pretty dominating presence in the casualty and business insurance group. It has large international operations, is run by some pretty smart people, and regularly throws out nice earnings.

Kazanjian: *How about a stock that you should have gotten rid of sooner or shouldn't have bought in the first place?*

Oelschlager: Oh, my. I really don't like to say nasty things about companies. I guess I was disappointed in Home Depot. It never provided the earnings I expected and I finally sold it.

Kazanjian: *When was that?*

Oelschlager: I bought it about five years ago and sold it about two years ago.

Kazanjian: *That stock has done well. Do you wish you still had it?*

Oelschlager: No.

Kazanjian: *How about another one?*

Oelschlager: I did sell EMC once and regret having done that. I've been buying it again recently. In this case, I recognized I had made a mistake, which is a hard thing for a money manager to do. We're a pretty egotistical bunch.

Kazanjian: *What caused you to sell EMC originally?*

Oelschlager: EMC was in sort of a price war with IBM. I decided IBM was a big gorilla and the wrong company to be in a price war with. I probably underestimated the strength of EMC's product, which I knew was good. I also underestimated the size of the data storage market that was coming in the years ahead.

Kazanjian: *Has Cisco been your biggest winner of all time?*

Oelschlager: Yes.

Kazanjian: *What was your original cost on that?*

Oelschlager: Split adjusted, I think it was about 16 cents a share.

Kazanjian: *What do you think about the prospects for the overall stock market as we enter the new millennium?*

Oelschlager: I think looking out three or five years, the fundamentals are in place for an extremely good market. The economic dominance of the United States is going to last for a considerable period of time. It really is the Golden Age again. People are going to be surprised by how good things get. Technology is creating the equivalent of another Industrial Revolution.

Kazanjian: *You manage $19 billion. That seems like a lot of money to keep in such a small handful of stocks. Is that a problem at all? Is there a point where size gets to be a problem?*

Oelschlager: Admittedly, $13 billion is a nice size, but there are a heck of a lot of other managers out there running much more money than that. I am basically in large-cap stocks, so I never run into any difficulty.

Kazanjian: *It's pretty obvious that people follow performance. You can see that from what has happened to your fund. You basically kind of came out of obscurity two or three years ago.*

Oelschlager: That's correct.

Kazanjian: *How did that happen?*

Oelschlager: White Oak Growth started showing up in screens and on surveys. I then got a lot of favorable press in various newspapers and magazines, and the money started flowing in.

Kazanjian: *Is that a good thing or a bad thing?*

Oelschlager: I think it's probably a good thing from the standpoint that these articles, by and large, and perhaps your book educates people to some of the funds that are out there that they should take a look at. Many they may never have heard of before. You're right. Our fund went from $25 million about two-and-a-half years ago to $2 billion today. I used to know most of the investors in the fund. I don't anymore.

Kazanjian: *Isn't that bad for your original shareholders? A lot of that new money could quickly pull out if performance starts to lag. If that happened, your remaining shareholders would suffer.*

Oelschlager: I think you've got to stick with it a little bit. If your fund is down for a quarter or six months, I don't think you want to pull out if it has a good long-term track record. There's nobody around that has a good long-term track record that doesn't have some short intervals when performance isn't so good on a relative basis. It's unavoidable. I do think people make a mistake by switching too frequently. That isn't how you make your money investing. You basically make good investments and stay with them for a long time. No hospital wings have ever been endowed by market timers. They've been endowed by people who get into one mutual fund, or one stock, and ride it for a long period of time.

Kazanjian: *Akron, Ohio seems about as far away from Wall Street as you can get. Is that an advantage?*

Oelschlager: Absolutely.

Kazanjian: *How so?*

Oelschlager: I don't want to tell anybody. They'll come here [laughing].

Kazanjian: *Has it ever mattered that you weren't running money on Wall Street?*

Oelschlager: Probably not, and it's becoming less relevant. If you look at the really good mutual funds today, very few of them are head-quartered in New York. The assumption used to be that you had to be in New York if you were going to succeed in this business. With electronics and communications, you can run an investment firm well from anywhere in the country.

Kazanjian: *What do you think about the current actions of individual investors? Internet and day trading have become very popular. Has that had much of an impact on the larger companies that you're spending most of your time on?*

Oelschlager: I don't think so. It's more of an issue for the dot-com and small-cap companies. I think it's a mistake for people to do this kind of day trading. That's not investing; that's gambling. I think that whole phenomenon is going to come to an unhappy ending.

Kazanjian: *You obviously are high on the Internet itself, owning Cisco, but I don't see any Amazon.coms or any e-commerce companies in your portfolios. Does that mean those aren't areas you are interested in? What would it take for you to get on board there?*

Oelschlager: I think the valuations are excessive, and I don't know who the winners are going to be at this time. I think there's going to be a big shakeout, and the valuations are very rich.

Kazanjian: *It's interesting that you talk a lot about valuation because if you look at most of the stocks in your portfolio, the typical analyst would say that, by and large, all of them are overpriced, especially the technology stocks. Are the analysts wrong, or are you just more flexible in your valuation parameters?*

Oelschlager: I don't know whether the analysts are wrong. I could be wrong. Obviously, I've decided that this is the appropriate place to be.

Kazanjian: *What advice do you have for individual investors who say, "I want to pick my own stocks?" How can they develop an art form like yours?*

Oelschlager: First, don't confuse motion with progress. Don't do a lot of trading. Buy stocks that you think will do well and companies you think will do well over several years. Put them in a drawer and don't worry about them.

Kazanjian: *When you look into a company, are you reading the annual report? Are you actually visiting the company? What kind of inspection work do you do?*

Oelschlager: By the time the annual report comes out, it's old news. You look at the numbers, you look at the analysts' reports, you listen to the conference calls after the company reports earnings. The information comes out pretty fast. If you wait for print, it's too late. Yes, we visit companies. We are also seeing a new trend. Company managements come to our offices to make presentations.

Kazanjian: *Do you pay much attention to brokerage recommendations, upgrades, downgrades, etc.?*

Oelschlager: I read that stuff and talk to analysts, but if an analyst says "buy," I don't run out and buy. This just adds more information to the pot.

Kazanjian: *You hold a concentrated portfolio of stocks, but how many mutual funds do you think an investor needs?*

Oelschlager: I've seen people who have 15, 18, 20 funds. I mean, they're just closet indexing. I think it's a mistake to own too many funds. I think probably three or four funds is plenty.

Kazanjian: *What's your suggestion for how people should find a good fund?*

Oelschlager: I would look at the record and the consistency of the record. As we discussed, everybody's going to have some bad quarters. I think you want to find a fund that's had the same manager for a long time, one who has been through some corrections and down markets.

Kazanjian: *How do you invest your own money?*

Oelschlager: A lot of it's in the same stocks that are in the funds. Every stock I own is in the fund.

Kazanjian: *You talk about how you spotted Cisco right away. Do you think there are still success stories like Cisco to come, or are the days of one company being able to have such domination over?*

Oelschlager: I think there are unquestionably other good companies that are going to come and that haven't even been developed yet. But

Cisco is a unique situation. I don't know that I'll ever be smart enough to find another company with that kind of potential, if one exists in our lifetime.

Kazanjian: *I want to end by talking about a few personal things. I understand that you have a battle with multiple sclerosis.*

Oelschlager: True.

Kazanjian: *When did you first find out about that, and how is that progressing?*

Oelschlager: I received the diagnosis in 1973. It's been a continuing deterioration. I've been pretty stable for the last seven or eight years, I guess.

Kazanjian: *Does it run in your family?*

Oelschlager: No. I didn't even know what it was when I got it.

Kazanjian: *You were at Firestone at the time?*

Oelschlager: Right.

Kazanjian: *How did you first find out that something was wrong?*

Oelschlager: I was slowing down on the paddleball court. My partner told me my body knew which way to go but my legs didn't.

Kazanjian: *So you went to a doctor, and they made that diagnosis?*

Oelschlager: Yep.

Kazanjian: *Was it slow in progressing?*

Oelschlager: I walked like a drunk for five years, and then I walked with a cane for five years. Now I'm in a wheelchair.

Kazanjian: *When did you first go into a wheelchair?*

Oelschlager: About 15 years ago.

Kazanjian: *Does it impact you in any other way?*

Oelschlager: My golf game's not so good [laughing]. It's an inconvenience but I'm still able to do everything that's important in life.

Kazanjian: *How long do you think you'll continue to manage money?*

Oelschlager: As long as I live. I love doing what I'm doing. A lot of my peers are retiring. I have no interest in retiring. I'm having more fun than anybody I know. Why should I retire?

Kazanjian: *Do you have a succession plan in place for your firm?*

Oelschlager: I have hired a lot of young, bright people and am trying to develop them in my mode so they can admirably carry on when I get hit by the milk truck.

Kazanjian: *Which hopefully will not be anytime soon.*

Oelschlager: I certainly hope not.

Kazanjian: *You kind of joked about your golf game, but what do you like to do away from the office?*

Oelschlager: My activity is swimming. I swim every day because that's about the only activity I get. My wife and I have a place in the mountains over in Pennsylvania that we like to get to on weekends.

Kazanjian: *Do you work five days a week?*

Oelschlager: I guess I do. I've been known to sneak away on a Friday over to the mountains. I also have a Bloomberg, telephone, and fax machine over there.

Kazanjian: *Money management is a pretty good business, isn't it?*

Oelschlager: It's a fabulous business.

Kazanjian: *Your firm has obviously grown quite large and you've done quite well. Do you think the opportunities are there for young people today in this business?*

Oelschlager: I think the opportunities are greater today than they've ever been in the past. When I first started in this business, they traded 6 million shares on an active day. There wasn't as much wealth, there wasn't as much stock, and there weren't as many people in the business because there wasn't as much money to be managed. You now have more people saving, both in personal accounts and through defined benefit plans. The opportunities going forward are going to be multiples of what they've been in the past.

Kazanjian: *But people seem to be—or perhaps this is a fallacy that we hear in the media—managing their own money now and making their own decisions. We're hearing they don't need investment advisers anymore.*

Oelschlager: For some people, that's true. But you're still going to have a lot of people who want professional management, and you have a lot of organizations, such as hospitals, colleges, and private foundations, that need investment advice. The world has created a staggering amount of money in the last ten years. I don't think a lot of people appreciate the amount of money that's been created.

Kazanjian: *What would your advice be to a younger person getting into the business today?*

Oelschlager: Try to associate yourself with someone who's had a good record and learn from him or her. You learn this business, not so much from a textbook, but from working with people who are reasonably good at the job. The next generation is going to inherit a staggering amount of money. These people will want to do other things than manage their investments. They'll seek out professional management, whether it's a financial planner, investment adviser, or mutual fund.

Jim epitomizes the idea of buy-and-hold investing. His White Oak Growth Fund is by far one of the most tax-efficient in the entire fund universe, since he so rarely makes taxable trades. Technology is clearly his primary area of focus, so much so that he started a fund devoted exclusively to this sector of the market at the end of 1998. As a result, all three of his funds took off like a rocket in 1999, right along with technology stocks in general.

Jim is convinced that being isolated in Ohio gives him a unique perspective on the market. Choosing quality companies is such a natural process for him that he had a difficult time articulating his investment approach. He kept telling me it's an "art form." I suppose all artists have a difficult time explaining their talent to others. What we do know is he looks for companies with conservative management, good growth, and solid earnings. Beyond that, he seems to make his final decision more on intuition than on anything else, a common characteristic among the Wizards.

I also found it interesting that Jim invests his new private accounts in almost equal weightings of each of the portfolio's 20 or so stocks, testament to the fact that, like a good parent, he loves all of his children (or stocks) the same. ■

FREDERICK REYNOLDS

REYNOLDS FUNDS

Fritz Reynolds dreamed of running his own mutual fund from the time he got into the investment business more than 30 years ago. His reasoning from the start was that funds offered inherent efficiencies you don't have with separately managed accounts. They make it possible to manage a lot of money for thousands of shareholders with relative ease.

Fritz finally achieved his goal in 1988 by launching the Reynolds Blue Chip Growth Fund. However, despite excellent returns, it took the general public and the press almost a decade to catch on to Fritz's record. As recently as 1997, the fund had only $60 million in assets, even though it had outperformed the S&P 500 by a significant margin since inception. When reporters discovered Fritz had whipped the S&P by more than 10 percentage points over the three-year period ending in 1998, and 6.4 percentage points over the previous five years, they started to write more about him, and the assets began flowing in at a rapid pace.

Today, Fritz oversees some $600 million out of his office near San Francisco. He runs the show himself, relying on little outside help to keep his fledging fund family going. In addition to Blue Chip Growth,

Reynolds manages a bond fund, a money market fund, and Reynolds Opportunity, a portfolio oriented to smaller companies. Opportunity has also outperformed the S&P 500 by more than 4 percentage points over the past five years, largely by loading up on Internet stocks. He also recently launched another "focused" equity fund called Reynolds Fund.

The 56-year-old manager describes his approach as looking for the "best of the best" companies. He's interested in both well-established names and in those businesses poised to become tomorrow's industry leaders. Fritz was an early investor in Microsoft, which he says typifies his process of buying good companies when they are young and adding to his position over time during market declines. In other words, he's often trying to grab on to tomorrow's blue chips today.

Kazanjian: *I understand you originally planned to become an engineer.*

Reynolds: Yes. I started out in chemical engineering. I always picture Dustin Hoffman getting out of the pool in *The Graduate* and this wise person telling him, "Go into plastics, young man." That was a growth area in the late 1950s and early 1960s. After being in that major for a couple of years I got into more advanced physics, math, and chemistry courses. I didn't have that same schoolboy fascination in college that I had in high school with those kinds of courses.

Kazanjian: *When did you make the transfer to finance?*

Reynolds: I took an economics course to see what that was all about. I enjoyed it, and then I took a course in investments. I figured that some day I might have some money to invest from my career in math and science. I wound up deciding I liked investments better than what I was majoring in, so I switched majors.

Kazanjian: *Then you went on to get an MBA?*

Reynolds: Yes. Once I started taking those investment courses, I knew it was me. I went from not really enjoying the courses to loving them. They have a lot of stock market courses at the University of Madison at Wisconsin. A lot of my classmates went on to become quite well known in the field of investments: Foster Friess, who has the Brandywine funds; Dick Strong of the Strong Funds in Milwaukee; Bill Nasgovitz, who has Heartland Funds; and Ab Nicholas of the Nicholas Funds.

Kazanjian: *Have you crossed paths since then, professionally?*

Reynolds: Yes, we have. I keep in touch with Foster, and I talked to Dick Strong the other day.

Kazanjian: *You were planning to go to New York after school, but the Vietnam War got in the way?*

Reynolds: You got it. I was stationed in San Francisco during the war for a couple of months, and liked it. So I decided to stay in San Francisco. I had some job offers in New York and Chicago. But I interviewed at several firms in San Francisco and wound up taking a job at American Express Investment Management in September 1966.

Kazanjian: *As a broker?*

Reynolds: No. As a junior analyst. American Express was out here because they had just bought Firemen's Fund Insurance Company. Firemen's Fund owned the Commonwealth Mutual Funds that started back in the late 1920s, and they managed Stanford University's endowment funds. So they moved their New York staff out to San Francisco. I worked my way up to senior analyst, then assistant portfolio manager and portfolio manager. By the time I left in April of 1971, I was managing about $100 million in two mutual funds.

Kazanjian: *Did they teach you how to manage money?*

Reynolds: I learned a lot there because I was doing research and analysis from the get-go. I was also very interested in mutual funds at that time. Very early on I appreciated the efficiencies of pooling money and having a net asset value every day. The pooled money saves on commissions and makes it easier for the portfolio manager.

Kazanjian: *Back then I assume not very many people were talking about mutual funds.*

Reynolds: If I remember correctly there were probably no more than 500 or so funds. More than 80 percent of the trades that occurred on either the New York Stock Exchange or what we used to call "over-the-counter" [now known as Nasdaq] were basically individuals talking to their brokers and doing it that way. Only 20 percent were done by professional money managers, including mutual fund managers. The total volume was about 8 million shares a day.

Kazanjian: *What happened in 1971?*

Reynolds: I joined a firm that had been in business for a year called Robertson, Colman and Siebel. Three guys I knew from Smith Barney started the firm. They've all gone on to do great things. The job at American Express was salaried with a small bonus. At Robertson, I had an opportunity to be a partner and share in the growth of the firm. When I joined the firm there were 11 people. When I left in April of 1985, 14 years later, we had changed the name of the firm to Montgomery Securities and it had grown to 350 people. It went to maybe 1,500 after that. I was a senior partner and did a lot of things. It was partially institutional sales. I did manage some money, but was also a liaison between sales and research and corporate finance. We had an investment policy committee that decided the firm's recommended or emphasis list. There were about four or five of us on that committee.

Kazanjian: *From there you decided to go out on your own?*

Reynolds: Yes. I'm at my third stop in life. I always wanted to do this.

Kazanjian: *When did you go out on your own?*

Reynolds: In 1985. Basically from the day I got my MBA, I wanted to have my own mutual funds. I didn't have enough capital to do it right away, nor the experience. It took me a few years to get both. But from day one I wanted to have my own firm.

Kazanjian: *Why?*

Reynolds: I really appreciated the efficiencies and uniqueness of mutual funds. You have an audited track record, and people can put money in and take it out whenever they want. It's easier than managing a lot of separate accounts. You can also have a lower minimum. I started my first fund, Reynolds Blue Chip Growth, in 1988.

Kazanjian: *When did the Reynolds Opportunity Fund start?*

Reynolds: In 1992. The money market fund was the second fund, started in 1991. A year later I launched Opportunity and the Reynolds U.S. Government Bond Fund.

Kazanjian: *Your funds remained in relative obscurity until the past year or so.*

Reynolds: Yes. A couple of things caused that. Number one, we don't have a big marketing staff. We are no-load so brokers don't sell us. I went along for many years figuring if I had a better mousetrap, people would just come. In retrospect, it wound up taking longer for them to come than I thought it would.

Kazanjian: *What turned the tide for you?*

Reynolds: All of a sudden we started showing up on performance records everywhere with great one-, three-, five- and ten-year numbers. People began to realize we were very tax efficient. We also got a five-star rating from Morningstar, and statistics show a high percentage of money goes into five-star funds.

Kazanjian: *For better or worse.*

Reynolds: That's right. But as people began to realize a guy with 30 years of investment experience was managing the fund, it started to grow.

Kazanjian: *You have not participated in a lot of the no-transaction-fee fund supermarkets, such as those operated by Schwab and Fidelity. Why not?*

Reynolds: I guess I haven't made a long-term decision on that yet. I was quite surprised the no-transaction-fee supermarkets took off as well as they did. People like to keep their money at one place and get one statement. They buy mutual funds the way they used to buy stocks. Funds have to pay the supermarkets 35 basis points (0.35 percent) out of their management fees for marketing. I felt that if I had extremely good performance, people would pay the small commission charged by the supermarkets.

Kazanjian: *What kind of staff do you have?*

Reynolds: There's myself and I have a couple of people who act as analysts and do some backup research. But a lot of it is me making the decisions as a portfolio manager. I treat that as a positive for a couple of reasons. I have concluded that it works best if you've got one portfolio manager making the final decision. For example, 30 years ago when I broke into the business, a lot of people brought their money to banks to have it managed. There would be one main person at the bank, but then the money would be delegated to junior portfolio managers who would actually manage the portfolios using the recommended list. I think that usually produces average performance. One reason I've had such good performance over the years is that I personally manage all four of the portfolios. I feel very strongly about that. If I were delegating it to a younger person, he or she might be very bright. He or she might have a Harvard MBA, but there's no substitute for experience.

Kazanjian:　*The risk is, if you get hit by a bus, there's no one manning the store.*

Reynolds:　Yeah, that's basically it. But at most mutual funds, there usually is a point person—a portfolio manager who's making the final decisions, just like me. It's not much of a team management type thing. I think if you look through the funds that have done the best, it's usually one portfolio manager.

Kazanjian:　*What is the difference between Blue Chip and Opportunity?*

Reynolds:　They are somewhat the same right now. The portfolio holdings overlap by about 75 percent. Long-term, however, the Opportunity Fund should own a few more medium-sized companies. The Opportunity Fund might do better of the two, but it's going to be more volatile.

Kazanjian:　*Since inception the opposite has been true. Blue Chip has done better. What's the story?*

Reynolds:　With large-caps in such favor, we've had the wind at our back. That's sure better than having to swim upstream. But, to be quite frank, it's been due to superior stock picking and being in the right industries.

Kazanjian:　*Speaking of superior stock picking, what kinds of companies are you looking for?*

Reynolds:　I'm looking for companies with above-average growth characteristics. I want businesses that have strong unit growth, are well managed, and enjoy good pricing power. Often that might be the number one or two company in the industry. It could also be economies of scale or worldwide growth. Many times it's a very profitable company with high return on equity. It has a balance sheet that's strong, maybe no more than 30 percent debt. I've done a lot of modeling of different companies to see what characteristics make sense and what can hurt a company. I've found that it's okay for a company to have some financial leverage, maybe up to 30 percent debt but I don't want a company that's 70 percent debt. Often the company sells a lower priced product. Wal-Mart stores is a good example. When a company sells a lower priced product, that means they can sell to the wealthiest person in the world, but also to some of the poorest. Warren Buffett and I kind of think alike. We both are fond of Coca-Cola. That's another good example.

Kazanjian: *You said above-average growth and unit-sales growth. Do you have specific parameters you're looking for?*

Reynolds: I will buy a company that has only 13 percent growth if it's really dependable because three years from now those earnings might be 40 percent higher. Many growth stock managers have a cutoff of 20 percent, but I'll go down to 13 percent. Generally I won't go much lower, because I find there are plenty to choose from in this range.

Kazanjian: *What other fundamental analysis do you do?*

Reynolds: I know a lot of these companies well. I've followed them for 30 years. Therefore it's partially a matter of keeping up with what they're doing. I also look for new medium-sized companies that are going to get very large. But before I get into that, it's watching what their market share is. In many cases, the companies are branded and are well known. For example, Coca-Cola's the best-known brand name in the world. There are a lot of consumer nondurable companies like this.

Kazanjian: *What price are you willing to pay for these companies?*

Reynolds: I look at a price earnings ratio relative to the growth rate. That is, saying Microsoft sells for 45 times earnings or Heinz is 20 times earnings doesn't tell you whether it's a good value or not. But if I use the price earnings ratio as the numerator of the equation, and the growth rate as the denominator, I've got a relationship there. Then I have to factor in where we are in terms of interest rates. I found that, over time, if the price earnings ratio relative to the growth rate is 1.25 to 1, and interest rates are very high, stocks are a good value. When interest rates are near a 30-year low, as they are now, the average rate is 2 to 1 or 1.5 to 1 for many of the companies, and they are good values.

Kazanjian: *What's a "blue chip stock" to you?*

Reynolds: It's a combination of the factors we talked about. It usually has a high return on equity relative to its industry and a strong brand. It has a good balance sheet and better management relative to its industry. Money is being spent intelligently on research and development. In many cases it's the largest company. I don't go looking for the largest company, in terms of sales. But as I go through all the other analysis, I usually find that's the case.

Kazanjian: *You also, especially for the Opportunity Fund, say you're looking for the blue chips of tomorrow. How do you know whether a* *company is going to be tomorrow's blue chip, and not tomorrow's dog?*

Reynolds: I'll give you some examples. I've been very early on just about every company that's gone on to do big things over time. Let's quickly go through that analysis. Remember, a lot of portfolio managers are looking for a cheap stock, something undervalued that will maybe go up 20 percent. I'm looking for a company that's going to go up dramatically and get to billions of dollars in sales.

Take Microsoft. I met with Bill Gates two or three times before he even went public. Nobody much cared at the time because the company wasn't even public. They thought, "We'll come back after the stock is trading." At that time, Microsoft already had the DOS operating system, for the IBM PC computers, which IBM—I'm still not sure why—gave to this little company out of Seattle. Prior to that there were all kinds of operating systems out there. Contrast that to another company at the same time, Lotus 1-2-3. There was a world of difference between Lotus 1-2-3 dominating in the spreadsheet software arena and IBM and Microsoft being dominant in operating software on the DOS system. I met with Bill Gates, not one-on-one but at American Electronics Association conferences in Monterey. It was just fascinating to hear him speak and answer questions. I could tell right away this guy was one of the brightest guys I had ever met. I plotted my strategy and have bought Microsoft over 200 times during the last ten years as new money came into the fund. I have never sold it. That's another key thing. Once you've got the company figured out and you're monitoring it, that's 70 percent of the equation. Then you can spend your time figuring out when to buy it and take advantage of the market.

Kazanjian: *What was your split adjusted original price for Microsoft?*

Reynolds: Probably $1. In most of these cases, the companies I buy aren't completely unknown. The next example I'll give you is Wal-Mart. It was a little company in rural, small-town America when I first found it. There were reams of research reports out there from Wall Street, speculating whether the company could continue to do well once it got to medium-sized towns. I thought it could, without a doubt. Sam Walton was very impressive. He had a great inventory system leading the way, was opening a lot of new stores and was discounting what people were interested in buying. Could they compete against Sears-Roebuck or K-Mart? Of course they could. I saw my first Wal-Mart in Florida 15 years ago. The company came to Marin County (where I live) last because land prices here are very high and we have tough zoning laws.

The next one is Home Depot, a category killer. Here the question was different. I was worried because when I first saw the company, it had 60 percent debt. But it had a better store layout than the competition, great inventory controls, everything I look for, except it had too much debt. I reasoned correctly that if earnings grew over time, the company would have earnings with which to buy back this debt or more equity as it sold more stock. Sure enough, that was the case. I bought Home Depot slowly over time.

Next is America Online. Nobody really cared about America Online. It was a little $5 stock that was losing money. It had, at that time, 4 million subscribers. One of them was my 14-year-old daughter. It cost $20 a month. Every time I'd yell upstairs, "Julie, time to do your homework," she'd say, "I'm doing my homework—on the computer." Sure enough, she was browsing around in a chat room. I went up to see what was going on up there. Soon after, the price went from $20 to $10 as competitors brought the price down. In addition, you couldn't get onto the Internet at that time; you were stuck with AOL's content. The question was how were they going to make any money. But I watched as all of a sudden AOL went from four million subscribers to six million and the $10 per month competitors raised their prices. The graphics were very slow, but I felt that eventually there would be faster semiconductor chips out there, which would solve that problem. I figured they could also just add a little button in there to get you to the Internet. AOL was able to get your eyeballs first, which was a major advantage. I correctly figured AOL, Yahoo!, and Microsoft would be the dominant Internet players.

Kazanjian: *You must be a big believer, not only in AOL, but also in the Internet in general. Your funds have a significant portion in this sector. How can you call Internet companies "blue chip" given that they are so new and unproven?*

Reynolds: That's a good point. I think it started when I came to the conclusion that the Internet was one of the biggest things to come along in the last 50 or 100 years. I think it's a major revolution. By the way, I didn't really get caught in the whole biotechnology thing in the 1980s. All through that big run-up I owned only a little bit of Genentech, Amgen, and Chiron, the number one, two, and three companies. By contrast, I think the Internet is a major innovation. I'll give you an example. We have a Web site, Reynoldsfunds.com. The trick is to get people to find the Web site because there are a lot of them out there. I paid less than $15,000 to start the Web site and $200 a month to have it hosted. When we make changes and update a prospectus, I pay another $100–$300. At that price, it isn't really costing me anything. It's a cheap way to do business.

Kazanjian: *It's so cheap to get out there and start your own Web site that the competition is clearly going to be intense as we go forward. How can you pinpoint which companies will be the winners if the competition has just begun?*

Reynolds: We're seeing that the products more uniquely positioned for e-commerce are books, originating mortgages, maybe selling cars, and doing stock trades. I think down the road some of these big blue chips I own, like Wal-Mart, might be dominant companies on the Internet. But that's getting a little off the track from your original question. I think the main answer is I see this as a major industry. It's going to change the way everybody does things.

Kazanjian: *What kinds of companies are you buying? The portals? Those selling merchandise?*

Reynolds: A little of both. Basically what I own are the companies that get your eyeballs first. The bet here has been Microsoft, AOL, and Yahoo!. Then I own smaller amounts of the other portal companies, such as Lycos. I am betting on the companies that I think are going to get large by being diversified. I like E-bay for online auctions, or Excite@Home for delivering the Internet to your home. I can foresee a point in a few years where a lot of people will have Internet access through a little screen on their telephone. New TVs are probably going to have a button giving you access to the Internet, too.

Kazanjian: *When a lot of people think of the term "blue chip," they think of stocks for orphans and widows. Do Internet stocks fit that description?*

Reynolds: I have a very diversified portfolio with a lot of different names. You could argue I've got a higher percentage right now in the Internet. But it may not be as high a couple years from now, as the industry becomes better accepted and mature. I try to be where the new industries are—the industries for the next five or ten years. If you and I were talking in the 1950s, I probably would have a bunch of chemical companies, paper companies, utilities, and such. The growth areas of the next 10 to 20 years look to be things such as re-tailing, leisure time, and health care. In addition, I like the whole area of technology, whether it's productivity improvement, the Internet, telecommunications, or communications. That's where I see the major growth. It's not in chemicals, it's in technology. In addition to Microsoft, AOL, and Yahoo!, we have positions in major technology companies that are helped by the growth of the Internet. These companies include Cisco Systems, Dell Computer, Hewlett-Packard, IBM, Lucent Technologies, Motorola, Nokia, MCI WorldCom, and Texas Instruments.

Kazanjian: *A lot of the bigger companies, like the Wal-Marts of the world, don't have much of a presence on the Internet. Do you think they will eventually catch up with the more aggressive smaller guys?*

Reynolds: Yes, I think they will. There's going to be a lot of commerce being done on the Internet. Most people still like to go down to the mall. It's a fun experience. But it also is an inefficient experience. I see a lot of these companies, such as Wal-Mart, selling through both their normal stores and the Internet.

Kazanjian: *Given that, do you believe your portfolio will look similar or completely different 20 years from now?*

Reynolds: It may be different. It most likely will have a certain component of technology because technology encompasses a lot of different areas. As the world gets smaller, you have an increasing global marketplace. More and more people will be talking to each other. Telecommunications will probably continue to be a strong growth area.

Kazanjian: *Blue chip stocks in the traditional sense are pretty well covered by Wall Street. There aren't a lot of secrets out there. How are you able to get an edge over the rest of Wall Street? The common argument for large-company stocks is that you might as well index this asset class because there are no inefficiencies. You've proven the pundits wrong with your performance. How are you able to do that?*

Reynolds: One edge I referred to before is I have a higher appreciation for the few companies with great growth. I think a lot of Wall Street is still just trying to find cheap stock. They outfox themselves by paying a lower PE ratio. In turn they get companies with poorer prospects.

Kazanjian: *We talked about the characteristics you primarily look for in larger companies. Is there any difference when you're looking for mid-cap or smaller-cap names?*

Reynolds: No, it's pretty much the same. It's kind of an evolving process. It doesn't just happen overnight, in terms of figuring out which companies to go with. Many times these companies go through a 10- to 15-year cycle. It doesn't just last for one or two years. Many people remember a company called Wang Laboratories. It was one of the first companies, if not the first, to offer word processing. I remember working in an office with a whole room full of these things. All you had to do was see the first IBM PC to realize you could do word processing on that in addition to spreadsheets and a bunch of other things. You knew that was going to be the end of Wang. Wang stuck around for another three years or so and the stock came down from 70 to 3.

Kazanjian: *You hold a pretty diversified portfolio.*

Reynolds: Yes. I like to take advantage of opportunities to buy companies I like when their prices lag.

Kazanjian: *How many names do you own?*

Reynolds: Around 200. But many of these are very small positions. If you look closely, you'll see that some of these positions are maybe a couple thousand shares. Partially they're newer stocks I'm keeping my eye on. Some people might ask whether such a little position is worth it. As I've looked back over the years, I've found that if it's a company that can go up 500 percent in price, even a small position can make a pretty good difference. Also, along the way I will probably add to the position. Some of these are stocks I'm just watching to see how the whole story evolves.

Kazanjian: *Your turnover is pretty low. What makes you decide to sell a stock?*

Reynolds: There are several reasons. The most important would be the fundamentals begin to deteriorate. For example, Quaker Oats paid too much for Snapple after making a great buy on Gatorade, and I saw how that could hurt the company's earnings. Another reason would be rising interest rates, which hurt the overall market. That won't impact the fundamentals of many of my stocks, but guilt by association can be brutal. Occasionally I have to sell something to get cash to buy another stock that I think is more attractive. Once in a while I'm forced to sell when I get a redemption.

Kazanjian: *How much attention do you pay to the market, the economy, all those exogenous factors?*

Reynolds: I always have my forecast for the economy. How much growth am I looking at? What's happening with inflation? What's happening with interest rates? How good a job is the Federal Reserve Board doing? Are we heading into a recession? Are there imbalances out there? Within that framework, which doesn't change very quickly, I'm looking at the overall market. When the fundamentals of the economy weaken and the market is correcting, I can turn a negative into a positive. None of us like the market to go down because all of a sudden we're worth less on paper. But I turn it into a positive because it gives me an opportunity to buy some of my favorite companies.

Kazanjian: *How do you react to this information once you get it?*

Reynolds: For example, ideally I want the economy growing at 2 to 3 percent. I want inflation and interest rates to be low. I want the Federal Reserve Board to be fighting inflation. Everything has been really nice the last few years. When we deviate from the ideal, I make some adjustments. The last few years have been pretty easy. The market has gone up most of the time.

Kazanjian: *Sounds as if it goes against the conventional wisdom somewhat that you should buy and hold blue chips forever and not pay attention to the market and what's going on in the world.*

Reynolds: In reality, I don't do that much trading. Among other things, I want to be as tax efficient as I can. I rank in the top half of one percent of all funds for tax efficiency. I think the typical fund manager in the United States manages more for performance and doesn't pay as much attention to tax efficiency. The average portfolio has a 100 percent turnover. I have more recently been averaging 25 percent. I manage some separate accounts, too, and those portfolios have more like a 10 percent turnover. The only way I think you can be highly tax efficient is by owning these blue chip, or world's best, companies that you can bet on for long-term. You can't do that with special situations or stocks you think are cheap. But it's wise to always keep an eye on the market.

Kazanjian: *How about international companies? You talked about the importance of worldwide exposure earlier.*

Reynolds: I get international exposure in two ways. Luckily 80 percent of the world's best companies are headquartered right here in the United States, so all I've got to do is own Procter & Gamble, Colgate Palmolive, or Coca-Cola and I've got a lot of international exposure. Also, almost every really outstanding foreign company trades right here in the United States as an ADR [American Depositary Receipt]. For instance, Sony, Nokia, Vodafone, Ericsson, and Telefonos de Mexico. The Blue Chip Fund can have as much as 15 percent in ADRs. An ADR eliminates two major risks I don't like about owning companies that trade only on foreign exchanges. One is that earnings must be denominated in dollars, so you don't have currency risk. Two, they have to use U.S. accounting, which is among the most conservative in the world.

Kazanjian: *We talked about the successes you've had with Microsoft and Wal-Mart, but there must be some stinkers two.*

Reynolds: Yes. I made a mistake on *The New York Times* years ago. I thought it was growing with all the regional papers in other parts of the country. It was doing more and more in cable. But I didn't realize how much it was dependent on the New York market, which is dependent on finance and retailing. Then there's Oxford Health. My cost was $10, and it went to $40 and back to $20 or so. In this case, I partially let taxes influence my thinking. I said, "If I sell it, I've got this tremendous gain." I also believed in the growth of the HMO industry. I guess I knew all along these were glorified insurance companies, but it was a very small holding. The nice thing about what I do is that when times get really tough, what I call white-knuckle times, I can usually look through my portfolio and not have to make much in the way of changes at all. I can use corrections as a buying opportunity.

Kazanjian: *A lot of people have been comparing today's blue chips to the Nifty Fifty stocks of the 1970s. Do you see any resemblances?*

Reynolds: I looked very closely at this. There is a difference between then and now. One is that these stocks were selling for higher multiples then. Raychem, for example, traded for 70 times earnings. In addition, the market was running out of time because after World War II we had about 20 years of wonderful growth where all you really had to do was own stocks. Then we had a recession, which was the worst since the Depression. There were also negatives specific to some of the most popular companies. Xerox lost its patent on the copy machine. We had housewives going off to work, meaning they weren't at home for the Avon lady. Kodak got competition from Fuji in the film area for the first time. IBM had competition in the minicomputer area from Digital Equipment. Right now, the odds of a fundamental problem on a lot of these companies is nowhere near as high as it was before, and we don't have high odds of a severe recession, as was the case then. I see the potential for a correction over a period of six months, as opposed to that tough period of two or three years that we had in the 1970s.

Kazanjian: *We talked about the Internet and the fact that you've got a lot of money there. Do you follow trends, and try to invest in them, or is it just a coincidence that you have money concentrated in certain areas?*

Reynolds: It's just a coincidence. It's partially me being on this planet and looking at things I like that I believe the masses will use. It's one thing to go shopping at Nordstrom's, and I shop there, but the masses shop at Wal-Mart. So I own far more Wal-Mart. I need to take myself personally out of the equation as best I can. I see the Internet as being a very logical thing, and I want to own it. The other side of the coin is I've learned you don't want to fight the market. If the market is saying something and nobody cares at all, then of course I have to look at that too.

Kazanjian: *Do you actually go out and visit companies?*

Reynolds: Not as much as I used to. I know these companies pretty well. I've followed them pretty closely for 30 years. I start out knowing that beer doesn't have as good a growth prospect as soda pop. I can get the information I need just following and monitoring how companies are doing in terms of share of market, pricing pressure, and demand. That leaves a lot of time for me to find that next big winner. All you need is one home run every couple of years to cover up a few mistakes.

Kazanjian: *Although you are allowed to buy small stocks for Reynolds Opportunity, you don't own many. Does that mean you like the bigger names better?*

Reynolds: Everything else being equal, I would rather own a good big company than a medium-sized or smaller company. They have economies of scale. Stated differently, I would much rather own Microsoft than the company that's competing against Microsoft. If I think two companies, large and small, are equally attractive, then I'll go with the big guy.

Kazanjian: *You mentioned your portfolio 20 years from now might look a little different. Are there any stocks out there that you could feel comfortable buying and holding forever at this point?*

Reynolds: I own many of the same dominant branded companies that are owned by Warren Buffett. I think the odds are Coca-Cola will still be the leading beverage company in the world as far as the eye can see. Coca-Cola is the best-known brand name in the world. Microsoft is a pretty well-branded company also. In the household products area, you could probably stick with Procter & Gamble, Colgate Palmolive, and Gillette. I suppose Wal-Mart could be a forever hold too.

Kazanjian: *The market has done so well for the past decade. Can that possibly continue?*

Reynolds: I think it can. If the economy continues to have a 2 to 4 percent growth, low inflation, and low interest rates, we can continue to do well. We've removed a lot of the economic problems we used to have. In the last 20 years, every single recession we've had has been an inventory recession. Companies didn't have enough feel for end product demand, so they built up too much inventory. Now companies have all kinds of computers to keep track of demand and inventories. Also, the U.S. economy is moving more and more from being a turn-of-the-century railroad and steel-mill economy to a more service-oriented economy. We haven't eliminated the business cycle by any means. We'll still have recessions. A recession really is only two down quarters in terms of GDP growth. But now we can string these things out for six to eight years, instead of having a recession the way we used to.

Kazanjian: *You're clearly optimistic.*

Reynolds: Yes. Capitalism works. I see a lot of positives here. One is that the population of the world right now is about six billion. These are people in China, Russia, and Eastern Europe, where communism is losing and capitalism is winning. There's also a big new emerging middle class in India, Latin America, and South America. The average company over the last 80 years has grown about 8 percent annually in the United States with one percent population growth. The population of the United States was 180 million in the 1950s. It's now 290 million. That's 100 million more people to buy the products. Population growth adds to earnings.

Kazanjian: *It sounds as if I should be buying emerging market stocks too.*

Reynolds: No. The problem with emerging market stocks is these companies have to compete against the big companies we've been talking about. That's tough. And these countries still aren't being run very well.

Kazanjian: *What do you think is the biggest mistake individual investors make?*

Reynolds: They know of a good company, but they take it for granted and say, "It's just overpriced, so I'll come back and own it some other time." You've got to be more appreciative of the fact that you can own these great companies. Studies have shown that investors feel worse about losing money in the market than they do about making money. Take a typical investor. If he or she makes $1,000, he or she feels pretty good. But if he or she loses $1,000 on paper, he or she feels awful. Investors have to get over that. The way you get over that is by staying with really good companies.

Kazanjian: *What's your best bit of investment advice for people?*

Reynolds: Be a good long-term investor. In real estate, it's location, location, location. In stocks, it's quality, quality, quality. Be a good solid long-term investor in the world's best companies, but be diversified. You need to own, I think, 50 of these companies out of the total of 15,000 to take the individual company risk out of the equation. I think a lot of people make this harder than it really is. You just need to sit back and look out the window. Quit taking flyers on stocks and realize there's a reason a stock is $5 a share. Understand that it's hard for a company to turn around. For every Bank of America that turns around there are a bunch of International Harvesters that never do. It's very hard for the number eight company in an industry to become number one.

Kazanjian: *Given how well index funds have done of late, are the days of active managers like you numbered?*

Reynolds: Absolutely not. I'm a big believer in actively managed portfolios. I think there'll be more actively managed portfolio managers beating the market long-term. Eventually more people will figure this out and move to good, solid long-term investing. I like to say that Bill Gates and thousands of other people at Microsoft go to work for me every day. I have to be smart enough to decide to own the stock, but they have to decide what products to sell. My job is easier than theirs. I think more and more money managers will figure that out.

Not long ago, I stopped by the Reynolds Funds booth at a trade show for investment advisors. It made me realize just how much of a one-man-band operation this company really is. The guy working at the booth told me he answered the phones and did a few other chores in the office, but other than that, Fritz *was* the firm. So when you buy any of the Reynolds Funds, you're truly buying into the skills of one man.

There are many advantages to that. For one thing, you don't have to worry about a bunch of internal politics keeping the manager's eye off the ball, which often happens with bigger fund families. On the other hand, there's no one around to watch your portfolio if Fritz decides to go on a three-month safari in Africa.

Incidentally, Fritz recently added a third stock fund to his family: The Reynolds Fund. This "go anywhere" fund will contain, among other things, the best ideas from the other two funds and might be worth considering if you're thinking of putting his skills to work for you. ▪

SPIROS SEGALAS

JENNISON ASSOCIATES

When I first told Spiros Segalas I planned to include him among my panel of Wizards, his response was, "I'll bet I'm the oldest guy you've got in there." As it turns out, he was right. At 66, Spiros, who is known as Sig to his friends, has been navigating his way through both bull and bear markets for some 40 years.

He developed an interest in stocks as a young boy, after his Greek-immigrant father, who couldn't read English well, made Sig look up the prices of his stocks in the newspaper. Sig began his career as an analyst with Bankers Trust, after Merrill Lynch gave him an aptitude test and told him to become an artist instead. I think you'll enjoy reading how he found this job. It was most unconventional indeed.

Sig cofounded New York–based Jennison Associates in 1969, just in time to suffer through the 1973–74 bear market. All turned out well, though. The firm, which has since become a subsidiary of Prudential Insurance, now manages some $59 billion for pension funds, endowments, and a series of mutual funds. The best-known, and best-performing fund Sig runs is Harbor Capital Appreciation, which he took over in May 1990. In addition, he and his team manage the Prudential Jennison

Growth Fund. He's also involved with several other "star concept" funds, in which he and other high-profile managers contribute their favorite stock ideas to a single portfolio.

Sig graduated from Princeton in 1955 and spent two summers as a naval officer in what he thought was preparation for a career in the shipping industry. That endeavor didn't last long, though, and within five years he found his way to Wall Street.

Sig has always favored companies that he feels can grow faster than the overall economy. He has placed a heavy emphasis on technology for years, which he admits is a bit unusual for a manager of his age. It also explains why his portfolio is somewhat more volatile than many of his peers. Sig strays into foreign stocks on occasion and says one of the biggest mistakes today's younger investment managers make is letting their egos get out of control and thinking they know more than they really do.

Kazanjian: *Your father literally made you read the stock pages as a teenager. What did you do to deserve that?*

Segalas: It is kind of interesting. My parents were from Greece. My father was a carpenter who stowed away on a ship back in the 1920s and came to the United States. A lot of Greeks were coming here then. They opened coffee shops, restaurants, floral shops, and luncheonettes in New York. Because my father spoke Greek, other Greeks felt comfortable dealing with him and he became a general contractor. He eventually went back to Greece and married my mother. It was an arranged marriage. My father was totally uneducated. He never made it past the seventh grade. But he was a real hard worker and entrepreneur. By contrast, my mother was the principal of a school and highly educated. It was quite an odd match. He married at 40, and I was born a year later. My mother was about 12 years younger.

Kazanjian: *Were you born in the United States?*

Segalas: I was, as were my brother and sister.

Kazanjian: *I'm still waiting to hear about your initial stock market connection.*

Segalas: My father was a very hard-working man. Day and night he was chasing after plumbers, electricians, and other tradesmen. He worked six days a week and sometimes on Sunday. He owned a few stocks, which he used as collateral to help finance some of his customers. Because he was uncomfortable reading English, after dinner I would read him the stock tables in the newspapers. I found the movement of stocks to be fascinating. I said to myself if I could only learn to pick stocks this sure would beat working like my dad.

Kazanjian: *When did you buy your first stock?*

Segalas: When I graduated from Princeton, my father gave me $1,000, which was like $1 million to me. In college, I subscribed to *Barron's* and *Fortune*. I read that RJ Reynolds was coming out with the first filter-tip cigarette, called Winston. It sounded intriguing, though I'd never smoked in my life. I bought that stock and it went up 50 percent. This convinced me that what I really wanted to do was become an analyst. I was very involved with sports in high school and was extraordinarily competitive. I couldn't stand losing. I had to win. When you think about it, gravitating to this business was very natural. I can't think of a business that personifies or captures the spirit of competition as much as this one does. Your performance can be measured daily, weekly, or hourly. You can't hide it.

Kazanjian: *Do you believe that you can control performance? In other words, in sports you can become a great athlete and really fine-tune your skills with hard work and a lot of practice. In investing, even if you perfect your stock-picking skills, the markets don't always work in your favor.*

Segalas: I think good investors can clearly outperform the market over time. You can't control performance over a short period of time, but, as in sports, hard work and experience matters. You must, however, love what you're doing and have conviction in your methodology.

Kazanjian: *Did you immediately decide to become a professional in this business?*

Segalas: No. I figured the way you made money was by becoming a ship owner. That was the "in" thing for Greeks in those days. I became an officer in the navy, and spent time in Japan and Asia. When I got out, I worked for a shipping company in downtown New York. I wasn't going anyplace. At the same time, my father was now in his sixties. Greeks are brought up on guilt. My mother had passed away, so a lot of relatives told me I had to help my father with his nice little business. I gave in and went downtown to help him. He used me for what I was capable of, which wasn't much. I drove trucks and delivered lumber to jobs. It drove me crazy. At night he would say,

"Spiros, sweep the floors and clean the office." I'd reply, "I'm a Princeton graduate and an officer in the navy." Then he'd ask, "You want me to do it?" So I would end up doing the work. I thought I was getting ulcers. Finally, and you'll probably find this a little hard to believe, I read an article in *Fortune* about the ten most powerful men on Wall Street. I wrote to each one, saying I'd like to become an investment analyst. I didn't get a response from them directly, but I did get responses from the personnel departments of some of these companies. This was around 1960. Merrill Lynch, for one, asked me to take an aptitude test. They wound up telling me to become an artist instead. But Bankers Trust was interested. They offered me either $5,000 to become a junior analyst or $5,500 to go into banking. I took the lower-paying job and became a junior analyst. I was initially quite intimidated because I thought I was old. I was only 27 years old, but didn't have a business degree like a lot of my peers. I was very competitive and had to win. I was fortunate to move up the ranks rapidly and in a few years was promoted to vice president. In 1967 I was asked to start an aggressive small-cap growth fund called the Supplemental Growth Fund. Timing is everything. The market was really hot in those days, and I was buying all kinds of small stocks. The fund did very well, but I can't say my performance had anything to do with talent because the wind was at my back.

Kazanjian: *You obviously knew how to play the game and must have gathered a pretty good reputation.*

Segalas: A couple of brokers tried to hire me, but I wasn't interested in moving to the brokerage side. Then, in 1969, Dick Jennison, who was president of a brokerage firm, told me he was starting a new company. He wanted me to join him. I was intrigued but scared. I had three children and knew only one out of a million of these things work out. I knew Dick was somewhat of a promoter, but I respected him and was very impressed by the other people involved and decided to take a chance. We started Jennison Associates with no assets under management in late 1969.

Kazanjian: *Were you a partner or just an employee?*

Segalas: I was one of the founders. The early days of our company were both frightening and exhilarating. It felt like being thrown in the water and learning how to swim. We grossly underestimated our expenses and overestimated the enthusiasm that people would have for our services. We went after the corporate market, and people would always ask, "Who are your clients and what's your performance?" We had to tell them we were just getting started. After about three months, we got a big break. I had built a fairly decent reputation as an analyst at Bankers Trust. I knew the top management of many companies, including Litton Industries. I think they felt sorry for me. They gave us $5 million in bonds and told us to put them into stocks. That was our first client. Everyone had heard of Litton Industries, so getting additional business suddenly became easier.

Kazanjian: *How was your performance starting out on your own?*

Segalas: In 1970, the market collapsed. Believe me, it was scary. But we got additional accounts from Abbott Labs and Upjohn, followed by such companies as ITT and Mobil, which are big-name companies. Interestingly, Dick Jennison left a year later, but we kept the name. We performed quite well in the beginning but during the 1973–74 bear market, we were down 50 percent in two years. When the market came back, we lagged on the upside. It was definitely uncomfortable.

Kazanjian: *Were people more forgiving of bad performance than they are now?*

Segalas: That's hard to say. Frankly, I find most clients are fairly forgiving. Either they have confidence in you or they don't. Many of the pressures are much more self-induced than client induced. It's the nature of our business. We feel we have to do well all the time. Most clients don't want to admit they made a mistake in hiring you. It's tough to go to your top manager after two years and say, "We hired this fly-by-night investment outfit and they're bombing."

Kazanjian: *How much do you manage now?*

Segalas: We have $42 billion in growth equities, another $1 billion in value, $6 billion in foreign, and $9 billion in fixed income.

Kazanjian: *What's the breakdown of mutual funds versus private money?*

Segalas: The private money is all corporate pension and profit sharing. The mutual funds have grown dramatically. They probably represent about 40 percent of the equities we manage.

Kazanjian: *How many funds do you run?*

Segalas: I'm personally involved in five funds.

Kazanjian: *When did your firm get into the public fund business?*

Segalas: I took over the Harbor Capital Appreciation Fund on May 1, 1990.

Kazanjian: *How did that happen?*

Segalas: One of our clients is the Owens-Illinois Company in Toledo. In their infinite wisdom, this sleepy glass manufacturer decided to get into the fund business, which turned out to be a brilliant decision on their part. The Harbor Capital Advisors, Inc., which they own, has an outstanding reputation and must be extremely profitable. They believed they had some pretty good money managers running their pension plan. They started these funds using pension money. They hired several of their pension-plan managers to run a group of funds. I had been running money for Owens-Illinois since 1972, so they knew a bit about me. That's how we first got involved with the Harbor Capital Appreciation Fund.

Kazanjian: *Wasn't there another manager of the fund before you took it over?*

Segalas: Before me they managed it internally on a quantitative basis.

Kazanjian: *You're also involved in a couple of funds where you are one of a small team of managers. The concept is for you to just pick a handful of your favorite stocks to add to the portfolio.*

Segalas: Right. An investment firm on the west coast came up with a concept called the Master's Select Fund about two years ago. They hired me to run 20 percent of the fund. I specialize in the large-cap growth portion. Someone else does value, small-cap, and international.

Kazanjian: *You run a similar fund for Prudential. What's the difference?*

Segalas: Prudential's is called 20–20. I manage the portfolio independently with their value manager. We can each choose no more than 20 stocks. Subsequent to that, Sun America came out with Style Select. That's run by three growth managers, so you get a somewhat common style. Each of us can own ten stocks. As is the case with all the funds, I don't know what the next person is doing.

Kazanjian: *Harbor Capital Appreciation is your most diversified fund?*

Segalas: By far, and the largest too. That fund has $8 billion and really typifies the Jennison style. It's managed in the same way as our corporate pension accounts.

Kazanjian: *How do you determine which stocks are your favorites for those concentrated funds?*

Segalas: I generally disagree with the concept that in a concentrated portfolio you put your money in your best ideas. I have to be honest with you. I don't believe anyone really knows what their best ideas are. If they did they would invest all their money in them. The way I have approached this issue in the concentrated portfolios is by investing only in those securities with fundamentals that I feel very comfortable with, both on a short- and a longer-term basis. I also need to feel confident they will outperform the market on a 12- to 18-month basis. I tend to have a very quick trigger and sell if I am concerned the outlook has changed.

Kazanjian: *You hold between 60 and 65 names in Harbor. Does that mean you don't have as much faith in the other stocks in Harbor as you do in those 10 to 15 names you select for the other funds?*

Segalas: I have tremendous faith in every stock owned in Harbor. However, with an $8 billion fund it's important to have some diversification.

Kazanjian: *You manage more than $42 billion. That's a number most people can't even fathom.*

Segalas: It's a lot of money. Fortunately, it's an amount we have evolved into. If someone gave us $42 billion to manage tomorrow, we would find it difficult to invest it. But when you start at zero and gradually work your way up, you grow into it.

Kazanjian: *Is there a point where you have too much money to be effective?*

Segalas: Size is a limiting factor. Fortunately, as a mid- to large-cap manager, I don't believe this is an issue. There are many funds, some of which have done well, that are considerably larger than Harbor. I see no reason why we can't continue to find attractive stocks to invest in for some time to come.

Kazanjian: *You have an incredible long-term performance record. In years when you've underperformed the market, what's the most common reason that happened?*

Segalas: It's always a little different, but the common thread is that we're either overexposed in an area that gets hurt, or the S&P 500 has a cyclical recovery. That happens when the companies in the S&P experience earnings growth of 15 percent or more. While our companies are growing faster, the S&P generally starts off the year with a lower PE and has more room to expand on this good news. Fortunately, the market seldom has two or more years of these gains.

Kazanjian: *Let's talk more about the whole process of putting your portfolio together. You said you focused primarily on large- and mid-cap stocks. Is that just a niche you've developed, or is that where you think most people should be investing?*

Segalas: Our focus is in identifying attractively priced companies that will grow earnings at well above average over time. These companies can be any size from small- to large-cap. However, since we manage over $30 billion in equity assets we tend to concentrate our research efforts on large companies.

Kazanjian: *Do you believe people should own small and international stocks in their portfolios?*

Segalas: A diversified portfolio should have some exposure to both small companies and international stocks. There are many opportunities abroad, and you should not limit your horizons—if you look at our portfolio we have large exposure in multinational companies. Most are United States companies but several are foreign, such as Nokia and Vodafone.

Kazanjian: *There's an interesting debate about that going on, because a lot of people like you have talked about how you should just put your money in multinationals, instead of investing directly overseas. Those on the other side say this strategy doesn't make a lot of sense because of cross-correlation. In other words, they say the United States acts differently from foreign markets, so you want to own both. Where do you come in on that? Do you think people even need to have international stocks? Or is the multinational exposure enough?*

Segalas: I don't have a strong feeling either way. I agree there are some differences in local markets. If you have a sizable amount of money you probably should have a little internationally. But when we deal with international stocks, we basically concentrate on multinationals.

I don't like taking country risk. Instead we invest in companies whose products are in demand around the world.

Kazanjian: *Let's talk more about putting the portfolio together. What's the first thing you do?*

Segalas: It's strictly a stock-by-stock, bottom-up process.

Kazanjian: *Do you pay any attention to the market or market forces?*

Segalas: Oh, yes. But I don't let it influence me too much. Every firm has its own personality, its own skills. In this business you have to know your strengths and weaknesses. At Jennison we have a strong bias toward technology. I started as a technology analyst and enjoy investing in this sector. Therefore, the portfolio is likely to have a greater exposure to technology than to other industries.

Kazanjian: *What percent do you have there now?*

Segalas: Thirty-five percent.

Kazanjian: *What traits do you look for in technology companies?*

Segalas: Our approach in researching technology companies is no different from our approach for companies in other industries. We try to get to know our companies very well and make an assessment on their future prospects. Key in this process is getting to know and feel comfortable with the management. Even though we believe we know our companies well, we appreciate our limitations and understand we must rely on management to execute in the future. In addition, we try to identify those companies that are uniquely positioned. In some cases this may mean a strong brand name, superior research and development, or a unique distribution system. Dell, for example, is a superb marketing company with a distribution system that is very difficult for others to replicate. We also have a bias in companies whose products are in demand throughout the world, and we are very sensitive to unit revenue growth, not just to earnings per-share growth.

Kazanjian: *Let's put a number to that. What kind of earnings growth are you looking for?*

Segalas: I hope to end up with growth in earnings of 15 to 20 percent or more. There are a few exceptions, but I generally demand double-digit revenue growth.

Kazanjian: *What about price? How do you decide how much you're willing to pay for a stock?*

Segalas: First, I look at the weighted PE ratio in the portfolio versus the market. We've been as high as a 40 percent premium. We tend to average around a 20 percent premium. On individual names, and this is very much a judgment call, we have internal price targets, but they're not cast in stone. Frequently companies will reach those targets. If we still like the fundamentals and believe the company is going to grow, we tend to shave our positions. In some cases that has hurt us. I've been a net seller of Microsoft and Dell for the last four years because the PEs kept expanding more than I thought they should. We do have a discipline of taking some money off the top when stocks seem to get ahead of themselves on an intermediate basis.

Kazanjian: *How about when you're looking to buy? Do you use the same discipline?*

Segalas: The buy side is always easier than the sell side. When I buy stock I have to be convinced the fundamentals are solid and that the stock will outperform the market. It also must have some of the other characteristics I mentioned. In some cases if a stock is up a lot but seems to have significant longer-term potential I may just take a partial position and add to the holding if it corrects.

Kazanjian: *How do you determine whether a stock is overvalued?*

Segalas: It's a lot of variables, but mostly the PE ratio.

Kazanjian: *Do you have a general rule you follow, such as not buying a stock that trades for a PE higher than its growth rate?*

Segalas: Not always. But that's one of the more important variables I look at. I must emphasize a lot of these decisions are judgment calls, and I make my share of mistakes.

Kazanjian: *Are there certain industries you completely avoid?*

Segalas: I tend to be very skeptical of and cautious about health-service companies. I like the drug stocks, but am less enthusiastic about some of the hospital companies or HMOs. These companies tend to be managed by highly promotional people. The only way they can really grow is through acquisitions. I'm nervous about companies that grow strictly through acquisition. More important, health care is not really free enterprise at work. A drug company can come up with a drug that either works or doesn't. If it works, people will buy it. The problem with the HMOs and hospitals is they want to be efficient, but they also want to grow. I don't think anyone wants his or her doctor to cut corners or not give the right drug to meet earnings estimates for the next quarter. People want the best care and don't care what it costs. As a result, this group tends to get politicized.

Kazanjian: *Any other areas you don't like?*

Segalas: Pollution-control or waste-management companies. They sell a service no one wants but is forced to buy. I don't like that ingredient. People opt for the cheapest way out to meet the government-imposed requirements.

Kazanjian: *When do you sell a stock?*

Segalas: A stock can be sold for several reasons. Any change in fundamentals can dictate a sale, such as a slowdown in revenue growth, or lower margins. If a company has a disappointment that we believe is short-term in nature I may just reduce our exposure. But I find that more times than not I am better off selling the entire holding.

Kazanjian: *Give us some other reasons you might sell.*

Segalas: Perhaps nothing has changed with the fundamentals, but I sense an analyst has less confidence in the stock. That will raise a red flag. My best tool for selling is having no more than 60 to 65 names in the portfolio. While I love every stock, some don't act the way I think they should. When something better comes along, I force myself to sell a stock to buy the new one.

Kazanjian: *What is your turnover?*

Segalas: About 65 percent.

Kazanjian: *You have a reputation for taking more risk than the average large-cap growth manager.*

Segalas: I think people say we're riskier because of our bias toward technology and strong growth requirement. These stocks tend to be more volatile. However, from a qualitative point of view, I believe our stocks are less risky than most. The companies we invest in have above-average profitability and below-average debt. Not to mention, they tend to be strongly entrenched in their industries.

Kazanjian: *What do you like in the technology area?*

Segalas: I like everything. We are broadly diversified within this group. In the component area, our largest holding is Texas Instruments. I have a smaller position in Intel. This is a good example of something I pointed out earlier. Intel used to be a large position, but there have been some short-term concerns about the company. I think Intel will do fine, but I'm sensitive to the market. I'll buy more on any correction we get. In the case of Texas Instruments, it used to be in the commodity memory business. Management has done a remarkable job of developing it into a proprietary company. It's a big beneficiary of what we see going on in the wireless world, and the stock has responded favorably. As a growth stock manager, you have to be involved in technology. It's the only declining cost industry I know of. It costs less to make everything each year. This allows you to constantly develop new markets for your products.

Kazanjian: *By the same token, this also means you're forced to charge less. For instance, computers are cheaper to make, but they're also a lot cheaper to buy. That means lower profits for the box makers, unless they can make it up on the volume.*

Segalas: Absolutely. That's what is exciting about technology. With prices coming down each year, they are constantly creating new markets. There is no doubt in my mind that technology will continue to play a more important role in our lives. Take cellular phones, for example. A few years ago only a few could afford them; now an increasing portion of the world's population can't do without them.

Kazanjian: *What about the Internet?*

Segalas: The Internet is fascinating. I think it's like the Industrial Revolution. It's going to change the way we all do things. I think the potential is phenomenal. Our portfolio is greatly influenced by the Internet. Do I own any Internet stocks? No, except for a position in AOL. I'm caught up in what these things are worth, even though I'm optimistic about their prospects. Our exposure to the Internet is indirect. Virtually all our technology and telecommunications companies are beneficiaries of the Internet, but it doesn't end there. All of our broadcasting holdings, such as Clear Channel and CBS, are being positively impacted. What does that have to do with the Internet? When Internet companies go public, they do a lot of advertising to develop a brand.

Kazanjian: *You've been in this business a long time. Is the Internet just another fad, and how does this compare to past fads?*

Segalas: I think this is real. It's profound. Still, I think some stocks are grossly overpriced. One doesn't have to own an Internet stock to participate in this phenomenon. Many of our holdings such as Cisco, Dell, and MCI WorldCom, are already prospering because of the Internet. Some well-positioned retailers may also succeed. I've seen other speculative moves, as you had in biotechnology, but I think this is much more real. My guess is most of these Internet start-ups will fail. But the concept of the Internet and its implications are here to stay.

Kazanjian: *Are there any other sectors that are heavily weighted in your portfolio?*

Segalas: I have about 12 percent in financials, such as Citicorp, Chase Manhattan, Morgan Stanley, and American International Group. How does that fit in the growth portfolio? Each one of these companies should experience above-average earnings gains over time. This group also provides another useful function. I've tried to put a portfolio together with earnings growing at a weighted average of 15 to 20 percent while keeping a weighted PE premium to the market of no more than 20 percent or so. While I may own Cisco Systems, which has a high multiple, I like to offset that with a company such as Chase, with a much lower PE.

Kazanjian: *How do you find most of your ideas?*

Segalas: I rely a good deal on our analysts. I am fortunate to work with a highly experienced and creative group of analysts. They make me look good.

Kazanjian: *What's a typical day like for you?*

Segalas: I usually get here around 7:15 and start getting calls from brokers. My traders tell me what's happened overnight in Europe and Asia. I then get to read the newspaper. At about 8:45 I meet with our analysts and traders. We discuss what we're thinking of buying and selling. That meeting lasts until 9:30. After that, I meet with companies and clients. It's an exciting day. I usually stick around here until 6:30 or 7.

Kazanjian: *What are the biggest lessons you've learned over the years?*

Segalas: You have to appreciate that this is a humbling business. Be appreciative of your limitations and know what you don't know. Also, gravitate toward what you know and don't get caught up in the current mania.

Kazanjian: *Are individual investors better off in stocks or mutual funds?*

Segalas: Mutual funds make a lot more sense. In fact, I think this on-line trading mania is going to be a disaster. Mutual funds give you the wisdom of a group that is managing a diversified portfolio. I do believe there is some skill involved in outperforming the market.

Kazanjian: *With so many funds out there, how should people find a good fund?*

Segalas: There are more funds than stocks out there. You have to look at the record, although that's no proof of the future. You want to invest your money with a firm or fund that's been in business for a while, not one that's had a hot hand just for the past six months or one year. You also want consistency of performance.

Kazanjian: *What do you think about indexing?*

Segalas: I think it has a role. A lot of money has flown into indexing, which tells me we're probably at the height of that mania and will likely go into a period where most managers outperform the market. Having said that, I have no problem with indexing. The facts show index funds have done better than most managers.

Kazanjian: *You talked about how you're a growth investor. The academics say value outperforms growth over time.*

Segalas: With all due respect, I have to disagree with this statement. There is no doubt in my mind that a good growth stock manager should far outperform value managers over time. Earnings growth does matter. You will find that the best-performing stocks over time will always be companies with well-above-average earnings growth, such as Microsoft and Cisco. Put aside theory and look at the real world. Our investment approach has stood the test of time and has produced superior results. Over the past 30 years that we have managed money we have experienced periods of high and low inflation, recessions and booms, bull and bear markets. In spite of these market gyrations, we have well outperformed the S&P 500, and I have yet to identify a value manager who has done as well during this period. Moreover, we have outperformed the market in each of the 21 trailing ten-year periods ending October 1999. Our first account, Litton Industries, which we have managed for over 30 years, has achieved a compounded rate of return of 16.4 percent versus 13.1 percent for the S&P 500, including dividends. More startling is the cumulative returns, which shows you the power of compounding. Since inception, this account is up 10,516 percent versus 4,292 percent, including dividends, for the market. In other words, on a cumulative basis, it has more than doubled the return of the market. I doubt any value manager has even remotely approached these long-term returns.

Kazanjian: *You sold your firm to Prudential a few years ago. Why did you do that?*

Segalas: Pru approached us at a time when we were insecure about the future of our business. We had lost some $2 billion in assets, even though our performance was excellent, as companies liquidated their pension funds to capture the surplus returns they had earned. We loved the business, and we didn't want to retire. Prudential allowed us to run our business as we had done in the past and also gave us some marketing presence that we didn't have. It has worked out well.

Kazanjian: *A lot of smaller firms are being bought out by the big guys today. Is that good for investors, or does it create an environment where making money and gathering assets is the only goal?*

Segalas: If you're a shareholder in one of these funds that gets bought, it's very important to convince yourself that the principals aren't cutting out. You need to make sure the culture will remain the same.

Kazanjian: *You're 66, which is an age when most people retire. When are you going to hang up your hat?*

Segalas: I can't think of doing anything else. This is too much fun. My golf stinks, my tennis is bad, and I never learned how to sail or ski. I love this business.

Kazanjian: *Do you still work five days a week?*

Segalas: Yes, but I do sneak out on some Fridays during the winter, I must admit.

Kazanjian: *Did your father live to see you succeed in investing?*

Segalas: No. He saw me do well at Bankers Trust. He passed away when I was 32.

Kazanjian: *Is this still a good business to get into?*

Segalas: I would always encourage anyone to get into this business. It's the most exciting, vibrant business around. But it's very competitive, and you've got to love to compete, as I do.

Kazanjian: *What would your best advice be for younger people wanting to get into the business today?*

Segalas: Start out at the bottom and learn to become an analyst. As an analyst you can either stay as an analyst or gravitate toward portfolio management.

Kazanjian: *Do you need an MBA or CFA?*

Segalas: I am not sure these degrees make you any smarter, but chances are you need them because the competition to get into this business today is so fierce.

Sig is right. Today, many Wall Street firms won't consider you for a job in money management unless you have a CFA or MBA, preferably both. Part of that is a function of the number of people looking to work in the business. Had this been true when Sig was looking for his first investment job, he might still be working in the ship-building industry.

As Sig points out, one of the key drivers of his success is focusing on attractively priced companies that he believes are capable of growing earnings at above-average rates over time. Specifically, he hopes to see earnings growth of 15 to 20 percent or more. Sig is pretty aggressive for a manager of his age, but his shareholders aren't complaining. And while he's long past the age when most of his peers on Wall Street decide to work on their golf game instead of battling the ticker tape, he shows no signs of slowing down any time soon. ■

ROBERT TORRAY

ROBERT E. TORRAY & CO.

$\mathbf{B}$ob Torray began his colorful investment career as a retail stockbroker for Alex. Brown and Sons in 1962. He quickly learned he was more interested in researching stocks than in peddling them, and instead moved into pension fund management. He ultimately founded his own firm, Robert E. Torray & Co. Inc., in Bethesda, Maryland, in 1972. While the focus of his business is still on managing large pension plans, he made his services available to you and me in 1991 through The Torray Fund.

While most consultants and fund rating services refer to Bob as a value investor, he disagrees. In fact, this opinionated 62-year-old seems uncomfortable being placed in any particular box. Nevertheless, he admits the price he pays for a stock is important, and he sometimes finds promising ideas by looking through the 52-week new lows list in the paper. In essence, he looks to buy growth stocks when they're out of favor. He gives us several examples of that in the interview.

Bob's investment philosophy calls for buying good businesses run by top-notch managements and then holding on for the long haul. He doesn't run computer screens and is satisfied with finding only two or three new ideas a year. In his view, mutual fund investors have too much information at their disposal, switch around too often, and own too many funds. He doesn't believe in asset allocation and thinks investors would be better off owning just a few well-managed funds—including his. He's also convinced that those who frequently trade stocks are destined to lose.

Ever since he was a little boy, Bob has dreamed of being wealthy. Because of his success in this business, he's been able to accomplish that goal, but insists he's worked "like a dog" to get where he is. When he's not at the office, Bob often flies around on his Gulfstream II Lear jet or stays in one of the several homes he owns around the country.

Kazanjian: *You've been interested in investing since you were a kid. What was the initial attraction?*

Torray: I guess I like making money, and it seemed like the most obvious and easiest way. It isn't easy in the beginning. But once you have some capital, where else can you make so much for really doing nothing?

Kazanjian: *Did you actually buy stocks as a youngster?*

Torray: I did. I can remember buying some when I was in high school. I didn't have much money, but that didn't lessen the excitement.

Kazanjian: *I assume you studied finance in college?*

Torray: No, I was a history major. I took one course in economics. I'm really self-taught. I don't have any advanced degrees, and I'm not persuaded they add value when it comes to investing.

Kazanjian: *Did you have any specific career goals growing up?*

Torray: Financial independence, because it gives you so many options—lifestyle, philanthropy, and so on. I'm very oriented to those activities.

Kazanjian: *What was your plan as to how you were going to achieve financial independence?*

Torray: I didn't have one. I started out to be a lawyer. I went to law school for a year and half in 1961. I also clerked for a law firm that did a lot of SEC work. My boss, who was the senior partner, was an active investor and talked to me a lot about stocks. I always looked forward to our conversations. The market was pretty speculative at the time, undergoing sort of a mini-boom. The Dow had run up to about 700. Brokerage firms were thriving, and there were new ones opening all over town. Some were bucket shops that eventually failed or were closed by the government. I was earning just enough money clerking that I was able to make a few small investments—and I mean small. I didn't know what I was doing. One of them was Agricultural Research and Development. Its claim to fame was that it had found a process to breed disease-free pigs. The stock was $2. I bought 50 shares. In short order it jumped to $4, then $5, $100, and $250 in no time. Of course, I thought I was a genius. But the company was a fraud. It owned a pig farm somewhere in rural Virginia. All it did was slaughter pigs that got sick. It didn't take long for the truth to leak out. When it did, the stock went to zero and I lost my $100. It made an impression on me. I remember it as if it happened last week.

Kazanjian: *Do you think we still have stocks like that today?*

Torray: Oh, sure. There are plenty of them and always will be. Stock schemes are a favorite of con artists. The Internet is probably loaded with them.

Kazanjian: *I take it that halfway through law school you were bitten by the stock market bug. Did you quit law school at that point?*

Torray: I did. I called a lot of brokerage firms trying to get a job. It was strange. In spite of their success and a roaring market, they really weren't in a hiring mood. But, luckily, I finally landed a job with Alex. Brown and Sons. They put me through training in Baltimore and I started work as a retail broker in Washington. That was early 1962. During the first six months of the year, the market dropped like a rock from 735 to 535 on the Dow. IBM sank from $600 to $300. I can still remember the old low-tech tape in our office running at eight o'clock at night. The stock exchange in those days traded only 1.5 to 2 million shares a day. During the collapse, volume swelled to 4 million shares, maybe more. It seemed incredible at the time. Today we trade 300 to 500 times that much on the New York Stock Exchange alone. The Nasdaq's volume is often even bigger.

Kazanjian: *Were you a good broker?*

Torray: I wasn't ideal for the job because I was focused on studying businesses and recommending stocks that I felt people could hold onto for a long time. That doesn't exactly enhance commission income. The nature of the business, then and today, is that brokerage firms don't want salespeople who think too much and become involved in the details of the companies they recommend. They're looking for people who will stay on the phone opening new accounts and selling high-margin products.

Kazanjian: *Years ago, when I first decided to get into the investment business, I went on an interview with a brokerage firm. The branch manager asked me if I liked sales. I told him I didn't, but was really good at analyzing companies and picking stocks. He said that wasn't what he was looking for. He told me to go work at a used-car lot for a few months and then come back so we could talk.*

Torray: I'm not surprised. As I said, brokerage firms want gregarious people who will get out and sell. They're not interested in analyst types except in the research department.

Kazanjian: *Were you a good stock picker in the beginning?*

Torray: It depends on your perspective. I did what I wanted to. I had fun, and it worked out okay. But other approaches would have been better. I guess on a relative basis the answer to your question is no. I tended to like offbeat, obscure situations. I became somewhat of an expert on spur-line railroads, such as the Mahoning Coal; the Cincinnati, New Orleans and Texas Pacific; and the Canada Southern. I seemed to be the only person who'd even heard of the Mahoning, much less knew anything about it. I loved to regale customers and friends with the details. They must have thought I was nuts. People were starting to buzz about computers and software much as they talk about the Internet today. I knew nothing about computers and never bothered to learn what software was. When I look back on that period I feel a little nostalgic. I also have to laugh, though, at the irony of a young man trying to get ahead investing in spur-line railroads which would soon fade into history, instead of computers and software. Things have turned out pretty well anyway, and I wouldn't trade my memories of those old rail lines for anything.

Kazanjian: *What have you learned over the years, and how has your investment approach matured?*

Torray: I've learned a lot of things. One is that investing in obscure companies, special situations and turnarounds, and trying to take advantage of market cycles is a tough way to make a living. My experience over several decades convinced me about 15 years ago that I should forget about all of that. It wasn't that we didn't make money. We actually did very well. But I now believe we could have done about the same, and certainly better after taxes, with less effort, uncertainty, and risk, by simply buying first-rate businesses and hanging onto them for the long haul. To put it another way, early on I was playing the stock market, trying to buy low, sell high, capitalize on turnarounds, breakup values, and so on. Today, I don't trade at all.

Kazanjian: *When you talk about buying quality, does that mean staying away from smaller-company stocks?*

Torray: No. Quality—which to us means strong business economics— is not related to capitalization size. The notion that certain capitalization sizes have advantages over others is baloney. It's as silly as saying companies east of the Mississippi and South of the Mason Dixon Line are better than those in the Pacific Northwest. We have no problem investing in small companies. We don't own any now, but might some day. It's just that over the last ten years it's been easy, profitable, and riskless to buy the big ones. I'm talking about companies such as American Express, which we first invested in nine or ten years ago when it was around $20. There are small-company stocks that have done better I'm sure, but riding from $17 to $125 on American Express is good enough for us. And, of course, we're still riding it, tax and commission free.

Kazanjian: *Speaking of going from one place to the other, how did you go from stockbroker to money manager?*

Torray: In 1967, I moved from Alex. Brown and Sons to Eastman Dillon Union Securities & Co., which is now part of Paine Webber. By that time I had developed a relationship with some labor-union pension funds. I was advising them informally. When they took my advice, they invested through the firm and I earned a commission. They seemed to like my ideas, most of which turned out pretty well. By coincidence, Eastman had an investment management department in New York that also advised unions. Unfortunately, the people who were running it made a lot of mistakes, and when the market broke in 1969–70, its clients lost a ton of money. Boy, were they mad. It was a brutal market in general, but that didn't lessen the sting for the clients. I was offered the job of running that business in 1969. I moved from Washington to New York and became, at age 32, what today we call a "money manager." I was really on the hot seat. But, by that time I was comfortable with what I knew and, luckily, was able to project at least a little confidence. It didn't take long to develop a nice relationship with the clients. Within two years Eastman decided it wanted out of the investment advisory business. Getting new accounts was proving tough. We were dealing with existing clients on a commission basis, but corporate accounts wouldn't go for that because they saw it as a conflict of interest. We tried to convert the unions to a fee, but they wouldn't pay it. For some reason I never understood, the firm wouldn't sell our services both ways—fee or commission. The partners shut down the operation and offered me a job on the West Coast. I didn't want it, so I approached some of our accounts and asked if I went on my own whether they would hire me. Five said yes, and that's how I got started.

Kazanjian: *That was the end of 1971, which is when you started Robert E. Torray & Co.?*

Torray: Well, it took until May 1972 to get up and running.

Kazanjian: *Your firm still specializes in pension funds, right?*

Torray: Yes. We also manage endowments, foundations, and other institutional assets. We've had them on average for 18 years. My relationship with a few dates back to 1969 when I first took the job in New York.

Kazanjian: *What's the average portfolio size?*

Torray: They range from $20 million to around $700 million and average probably $150 million. They're always getting bigger. The economics of this business are good. If you do a credible job, and earn double-digit returns over decades, your business grows steadily, and you don't have to keep adding more people. Our staff totals only 14 including my partners—Doug Eby and Bill Lane—and me.

Kazanjian: *So, you're finally achieving the financial goals you dreamed about as a youngster?*

Torray: I've done pretty well for a long time now. But I don't focus on that aspect as I did in the beginning. I'm an investor at heart. I've taken my own advice over the years. I just keep buying stocks. I'm up to my ears in stocks. They're the best investment you can make.

Kazanjian: *How much do you manage all together now?*

Torray: About $6 billion.

Kazanjian: *Tell me about The Torray Fund.*

Torray: We opened it on January 2, 1991. People, including some we work for on the pension side, had been suggesting we start a fund for years. I had never wanted to be in the individual account management business. It's inefficient, and the overhead tends to be high. Even so, I have friends who do very well at it. They've got 400 or 500 clients. From my perspective, that's a lot of paperwork, phone calls, and hand-holding. A mutual fund eliminates those problems. In 1990, I thought: "What the heck? Maybe we should give it a try—there certainly must be a lot of people out there who would like what we do." Deep down I really didn't expect much of a response, and that proved to be the case for a few years. We financed the start-up, invested personally, and also entrusted our company profit sharing plan to the fund. Our trustees invested as well as some family members and a few close friends. That was about it. We didn't advertise or promote it in any way and haven't to this day. The performance eventually began to attract the attention of financial publications and fund rating services such as Lipper and Morningstar. It took us three years to get up to $30 million, which is the minimum size required for listing in the financial section of papers around the country. During that period our shareholders had to call us for the price. But once we were listed and our performance was publicized, the fund began to grow. The next thing you know, it's up to $1.7 billion, and we probably have 50,000 shareholders. It's been an exciting and rewarding business.

Kazanjian: *You wrote in your 1996 annual report that if the fund got to between $500 million and $1 billion, you'd consider closing it.*

Torray: That was a mistake. Cash flow is a huge advantage. It enables us to make new investments without selling existing holdings and to adjust portfolio weightings without incurring transaction costs and tax liabilities. Right now, we're happy with things the way they are. The group think on this subject is that a portfolio manager's job is to be nimble, jumping in and out of stocks, moving from stock to stock, sector to sector, and so on. While this is probably an accurate picture of what's going on in the fund industry as a whole, it's certainly not a pretty one. All the motion is a waste of time and shareholder money. The record proves it. We don't do any of that. Our approach is deliberate. We don't trade, and we don't change our minds very often. We get paid for results, not activity. At this point, we're invested in big companies. We couldn't buy 3 percent of the Walt Disney Company if we spent the whole fund on it. Most of our investments have capitalizations of 500 million, 1 billion, 2 billion shares, and up. The Torray Fund's assets are just a drop in the bucket compared to these

numbers. So size just isn't a factor for us, but cash flow is. And negative cash flow is the worst. It forces you to sell stocks at a time when
you may want to buy more. This is obviously not good for shareholders. So, we think it's an enormous advantage to have a steady inflow
of new money, and we're certainly not going to shut it off—at least
not for now.

Kazanjian: *You said you were somewhat reluctant to start the fund.
Are you glad you did it now?*

Torray: Oh, yes. It's been a great experience. It's a fantastic business
and very rewarding in many ways. I especially enjoy helping people.
We've got a strong following among our shareholders. There's a small
group that is happy only when the price is rising—the types who are
always jumping from fund to fund and in and out of the market.
They're wasting their time. But, by and large, we have thousands of
accounts that we've had for a long time. People call, write letters.
They're so appreciative. We've made a significant difference in the
lives of quite a few people. That's probably the greatest reward I've
had from being in the investment business. Everyone in our company
feels it. We're proud of what we do, excited by it, and thankful for the
way things have turned out.

Kazanjian: *Obviously, a lot of these shareholders came in because of
your performance. Do you think they'll jump out as soon as performance dwindles?*

Torray: Some will. It happened in 1998. After advancing an average of
39 percent a year from 1995–97, the fund was up only 8.2 percent
compared to 28.7 percent for the S&P 500. I'm sure the results surprised and disappointed a lot of shareholders even though we warned
in several previous reports that a slowdown was inevitable. I got a
few nasty calls and letters. But I'm resigned to the fact there's nothing
I can do about that. You just can't please everyone. A certain percentage of people love to buy a rising price. Once the trend reverses, they
get upset and sell. It's kind of sad. All these types lose in the long
run—every single one of them.

Kazanjian: *Let's talk about your investment approach. How do you
begin the process of putting your portfolio together?*

Torray: We don't have a process. It's not a construction project. We
just look at businesses on a case-by-case basis and select those we believe have the best long-term prospects and management. We always

visit the managements of companies we invest in. We have to feel comfortable with them and the business. If those tests are met we sometimes invest. It's that simple.

Kazanjian: *Does that mean you don't pay attention to the market?*

Torray: I don't think about the market except to the extent that it serves up opportunities to invest in good businesses at a fair price.

Kazanjian: *Are you always 100 percent invested, then?*

Torray: Pretty much. We sometimes have 2 to 3 percent in cash, but that's about it.

Kazanjian: *Where do you find your ideas?*

Torray: I've never been able to explain it. They just present themselves. If you've been in this business a long time, you know something about hundreds of businesses from a cross-section of industries. It takes very little time to bring yourself up to speed, if you're so inclined. I'm in the habit of periodically scanning the new low list. Every now and then a name catches my eye, and then maybe I'll check it out. We're looking for a good business facing challenges that cloud the near-term outlook. When that happens in today's market, the stock often takes a brutal pounding. We analyze the business fundamentals and if they look strong for the long haul we may invest. Sometimes our ideas take a few years to work out, but that's okay. We're willing and able to wait longer than a lot of other institutional investors because we're not under pressure to perform on a quarterly basis.

Kazanjian: *How do you know the names on the new low list won't go lower?*

Torray: A lot of them do, but we're really not concerned about that. Short-term price movements are irrelevant to us. We figure out what we think a business is worth and that's what we'll pay for it. The short-term performance after that is not important, except if the price drops we may buy more. To put it another way, we're not trying to buy at the bottom just so we can flip the shares to somebody else when they go up. We also don't need the reassurance of a rising price to confirm our judgment. The idea is to get in and stay put.

Kazanjian: *Let's say a stock you like shows up on the new low list. What research do you conduct on the company?*

Torray: In many cases we're likely to know quite a bit about the situation to begin with. The typical approach, though, is to analyze company reports, review Wall Street research, and consult the best analysts. If things check out, we meet with management. There's nothing magic about it. Sometimes we don't need to know every last detail. Take AT&T, for example. In the spring of 1997, the stock, adjusted for splits, dropped to the low $20s from the mid-$40s in early 1996. We had been studying the company off and on for about two years, but the price always seemed too high, given the considerable uncertainty surrounding the future of the long-distance business, management turmoil, and other factors. As the stock sank lower and lower, we began to develop a clearer picture of where we thought the situation was headed. Some of it was the result of analysis, some was intuition. In the end, although we didn't know everything about the company, we certainly knew enough to make an informed judgment. The assets were sound, it had an AA balance sheet, and it was still number one in long distance, though its position was eroding. Earnings and cash flow were declining moderately, but we thought a recovery would occur within a few years. We also felt the company's huge customer base was relatively secure against the competition. In the end, we concluded AT&T was a great investment and made it one of our top five holdings. The return, factoring in the Lucent Technologies and NCR spin-offs, has been outstanding. This is a good example of the type of opportunity we like. More recently we made an investment in Franklin Resources, manager of the Franklin Templeton and Mutual Series funds. Assets under management total about $220 billion. When the Asian situation blew up in the fall of 1998, Templeton was hit by withdrawals. Then value investing fell out of favor, causing withdrawals at Mutual Series. Franklin stock dropped from a 1998 high of $57 to $27 in February 1999. That's when we first invested. It's a business we know a lot about because we're in it. My partner Doug and I made up our minds on this one in pretty short order.

Kazanjian: *Do you always try to get out and visit the company in person?*

Torray: Yes, sooner or later we do. Sometimes we buy first and get around to the visit later, but that usually happens with major companies where the reporting is good and the issues are clearly defined. We do talk to a lot of Wall Street analysts. They're well informed and very helpful. The bottom line is, if you're experienced, it's relatively easy to reach informed judgments on most companies.

Kazanjian: *In the final analysis, it doesn't sound as if you have a specific price discipline that's set in stone.*

Torray: No. We're not interested in disciplines. You can't value businesses that way. But I think our instincts and judgments have been pretty good. As far as I can recall, all of our big investments have worked out eventually. On the other hand, look at the market over the last decade. How could you have gone wrong?

Kazanjian: *You mean to tell me you haven't had any stocks that haven't worked out?*

Torray: Oh, there have been plenty of them over the last 28 years. Most, though, occurred during the period I mentioned earlier when the approach centered more on market dynamics, turnarounds, breakups, and so on. The business fundamentals of the companies we bought then were generally weaker than are those we own today. As a result, the chances of our being wrong were higher. We swung at a lot more pitches, and the batting average was lower. But, the results were still good. When I said all of our big investments have worked out I was referring more to the last decade, a period during which we've taken much larger positions in top companies and held onto them. Time, a great economy, and strong business fundamentals have been on our side. All investors need to know is that first-rate companies make great long-term investments. Inferior companies don't, even if they're bought at a low price. Our job is to know one from the other.

Kazanjian: *Clearly, you focus on company fundamentals, not the stock market.*

Torray: We're fond of saying value derives from businesses, not stocks. That's so because businesses generate earnings and earnings have economic value. Stocks don't earn money, they evidence ownership. Day by day, their price tells us one thing: how much investors are willing to pay for those earnings. Unless we're selling, why do we care about that? Measured over decades, though, the daily quotations strung together in a line track corporate earnings in a one-to-one ratio. It is earnings that determine the long-term performance of stocks, not the other way around. Take, for example, the Walt Disney Company, one of our largest investments. Its long-term record is outstanding, but recent results have been disappointing. As a consequence, investors are willing to pay less than 60 percent as much for Disney shares today as they were early last year. The issue for us is whether the company's long-range prospects are intact. We think they are. But, if we're wrong, buying the stock at $26 instead of $42 won't make that much difference ten years from now. Put differently, the business can move the stock but the stock can't move the business. Thus, the daily fluctuations of Disney shares have nothing to do with Disney World attendance, ABC ratings, or the fortunes of the Anaheim Angels baseball team. Can you imagine Coach Terry Collins of the Angels telling Michael Eisner they didn't make the World Series because the stock's down 40 percent? Of course not. This is why we say value is in the business, not the stock. Corporate earnings drive stocks, not vice versa. Our job is to invest in the best businesses we can find, at a fair price, and hold onto them as long as their fundamentals remain sound. I'll add one more thing. Just as stocks don't make money, portfolio managers don't make money for funds. We're merely intermediaries, and the more we intermediate, the worse things get for shareholders. There is a disconnect in the public's mind among businesses, stocks, and money managers. It is the businesses that count. Yet most people pay little or no attention to them. Instead, everyone talks about what the stock is doing, and, if it's not doing well, what the portfolio manager is going to do about it. But, portfolio managers can't do anything. They don't run the companies they invest in. So, in most cases, if a stock falters, they sell it and move on to another they hope will do better.

Kazanjian: *How patient are you willing to be waiting for a stock to rise?*

Torray: We've held stocks that didn't move much for three or four years. Some eventually turned out to be among our best investments.

Kazanjian: *What makes you decide to sell?*

Torray: The realization we've probably made a mistake. Sometimes we get into a situation where the recent record has not been good, yet we have reason to think things will revert to the favorable long-term trend. This doesn't always happen. Also, if we need money to buy a more attractive opportunity, we'll sell.

Kazanjian: *What if the price of a stock appreciates? Is that another reason to get rid of a holding?*

Torray: No. The mere fact of appreciation is meaningless. It's an ongoing process with good companies. As long as a business performs, the stock will appreciate forever. There are cases where it may make sense to sell if you find a better opportunity and need money to buy it.

But we're leery of making those comparisons. I can't recall an instance in which we've sold one of our core holdings to buy something else.

Kazanjian: *You hold a pretty concentrated portfolio.*

Torray: We have 31 investments now. That's more than enough to get the job done.

Kazanjian: *Is that because you purposely want to stay concentrated?*

Torray: Yes.

Kazanjian: *That goes against the conventional thinking that having more stocks is better because of the diversification factor.*

Torray: Believe me, in this context more is worse. I've never known anybody whose fortunes improved through diversification. Warren Buffett is by far the most successful investor of all time. Most of his fortune can be traced to a handful of astute investments. Some say he is an anomaly. I don't agree. And as far as conventional thinking is concerned, it produces conventional results. We're certainly not interested in that.

Kazanjian: *Do you believe risk increases if you don't have a larger portfolio?*

Torray: Only if you don't know what you're doing. A handful of top-notch companies held for a decade or more will produce returns far superior to a list of hundreds, and at less risk. As I've pointed out, risk has nothing to do with stock price fluctuations. It is a function of business fundamentals. If you buy a lousy company and hold it long enough, you're probably going to lose money, no matter how low a price you pay for it. But that's not so with a good company, even if you pay a little too much. Time dilutes both the advantage and disadvantage of the entry price.

Kazanjian: *Do you consider yourself to be a value investor, which is how many people classify you?*

Torray: No, I don't. That's what the mutual fund rating services and consultants say. I don't argue with them. They've made up their minds. As I see it, "value investing" means paying a below-average price for an asset. Value stocks typically sell at less-than-market PE ratios and above-market yields. Proponents believe the low price creates economic value that's absent at higher levels. We don't see things that way. Most of the businesses that pop up on value screens tend to be low, slow, or no-growth situations. Everyone knows that, which is why their prices seem modest. Our view is that while the low price may add "value" for the buyer intent on flipping the shares to a sucker at a higher level, the long-term investor will be stuck with the lackluster fundamentals. The longer he or she holds on, the more certain the unfavorable impact of those fundamentals will become. As I said earlier, value is in the business, not the stock. The bottom line is that value investing appeals to people who like to play the market, buy low, sell high. And that's fine. I started out that way myself. But it's not our approach now.

Kazanjian: *Wait a minute. You have said you're looking for stocks on the new low list. Obviously there is some sort of a value bias there.*

Torray: Not exactly. It may seem like splitting hairs, but I say again, value is in the business. In the long run the price paid—within reason, of course—will have very little impact on the return. The value of a business is related to the stream of earnings it generates. The share price will reflect those earnings but cannot alter them. We're simply saying we want to buy at a fair price, and sometimes we find that on the low list. Every stock ends up there sooner or later. A lot of our investments are not on that list when we acquire them. One, Clear Channel Communications, was close to an all-time high when we bought it in early 1991. It's risen about 100 times over the last decade. The difficulty with investing in first-rate companies is that their identity is well known, they're always in demand, and, as a result, remain relatively expensive unless something goes wrong with the fundamentals. When it does, the stock is likely headed for the low list. Some of these situations will be of interest. But that's a small part of the picture for us. It's really the business we're focused on, not the price.

Kazanjian: *Do you believe individuals should own mutual funds or stocks?*

Torray: They're better off with funds if they can identify a few that are intelligently managed. Unfortunately, that's not easy. Despite all the propaganda, the fund industry is not about long-term investing and competitive returns. It's about marketing, asset-gathering, and customers. The record is clear. John Bogle, chairman of the Vanguard Group, says the industry has underperformed the S&P 500 for the last ten years by 2.5 percentage points per year. If this continued for 30 years, the underperformance would cancel half of an investor's gain. To make things worse, it's been estimated that taxes on gains have cost taxable shareholders an additional 3 percentage points per year during the last decade. A 5.5 percentage point annual penalty just can't be overcome by clever portfolio management.

Kazanjian: *Do you consider yourself an exception to this generalization?*

Torray: Yes. Our company has done better than the market for nearly 27 years, and The Torray Fund is slightly ahead since we started it in 1991.

Kazanjian: *How is an investor supposed to find a good fund, then?*

Torray: It's a dilemma. Most people get advice from either financial planners, investment advisers, or brokers. From what I've seen, the results are not good. People end up with too many funds, and there's a lot of switching from fund to fund—"rebalancing the portfolio"—as they say. This is a terrible concept. If I weren't in the business and didn't know what I know, I'd probably buy an index fund. If I could find one with about 50 or 100 of America's best companies, I'd take it. But an S&P 500 fund would be fine too. Expenses and taxes are virtually zero, saving 5 1/2 percentage points annually on the fund industry's experience of the last decade. If history repeats itself, I'd make 10 percent to 12 percent a year long-term, doubling my money every six or seven years. That's a lot better than most people I know have done.

Kazanjian: *But that goes against the conventional asset-allocation argument, which says you need small stocks, international stocks, etc.*

Torray: Why do you need them? Asset allocation is nonsense. It keeps thousands of people employed talking, writing, and advising, but that's about all. The only asset worth owning is stock in successful companies. I tell anyone who'll listen to never buy bonds and to stay away from commodities and options, futures, derivatives, strips, straddles, spiders, and all the other concoctions Wall Street's dreamed up over the years. Every one of them is a loser. As I pointed out earlier, the return on bonds over the last 70 years has been about 2 percent annually after inflation, but before taxes. Why would anyone buy that record? I guarantee you that any portfolio emphasizing asset allocation hasn't a chance of matching one invested in 10 or 20 top-notch companies. And the more the portfolio is reconfigured, the worse the results will be. *The Wall Street Journal* recently ran an article headlined "Flight to Cash by Strategists Has Paid Off." It reported on the performance of asset-allocation blends recommended by 13 major brokerage houses for the three-month, one-year, and five-year periods ended September 30, 1999. The headline obviously refers to the three-month results, a period during which the broker's model portfolios lost an average of 3.8 percent, but an all-stock portfolio would have dropped 6.6 percent. For one year, however, the brokers made 15.3 percent, but a 100 percent stock account was up 27.3 percent; and over the five-year period the brokers averaged 122.7 percent, but stocks climbed 206.6 percent. Looking at the big picture, it's easy to see asset allocation didn't pay off at all. In fact, quite the reverse is true. Why pay someone fees and commissions to shuffle your money around based on their reading of the tea leaves when the end result is you make 122 percent instead of 206 percent? Are we supposed to feel good because we did relatively well for three months (even though we lost money), when over five years this crazy strategy cost us 84 percentage points of gain? And, believe me, if the sharpest minds on Wall Street can't beat this game, the financial planners and investment advisers don't have a prayer. So, we say forget about asset allocation and invest for the long haul in top-notch equities. That's a game you can't lose.

Kazanjian: *What about growth versus value?*

Torray: It's not even a close call. Growing companies make far better investments. That's why their prices are higher.

Kazanjian: *Right now you're heavily invested in financials and consumer stocks. Do you like those two areas in general?*

Torray: Yes. They're relatively stable and they're growing, although not at the rate of a Microsoft or Cisco. The prospects for Citigroup with its 100 million customers worldwide are outstanding. American Express and J. P. Morgan are also well positioned. We believe they'll be worth a lot more in ten years, but we don't try to gauge how much. Our interest is more in the certainty of the outcome than the extent.

Kazanjian: *How about the consumer area?*

Torray: We like companies with proprietary products that have appeal around the globe. Gillette, for instance, fits that bill. We think Gillette is a good investment if you have a five- or a ten-year perspective, which we do. As far as the near-term is concerned, we don't even think about it.

Kazanjian: *You talked about low turnover. Are there any stocks you own that you'll never sell?*

Torray: No, situations change. For instance, many of the businesses that were important when I first started investing in the early 1960s don't amount to much now, and quite a few don't exist. None of them compares to today's technology giants such as Microsoft, Intel, and Cisco Systems. General Motors, still the world's largest company in terms of sales, is now valued in the stock market at $42 billion. Microsoft is worth 11 times that much. There are always companies expanding while others are cresting or in decline. We want to be in the first group.

Kazanjian: *You said you don't really pay much attention to the market, but how well do you think the market will do over, say, the next decade?*

Torray: Measured annually, the market has risen 75 percent of the time over the last 50 years. It was up in each of the five decades and every two out of three years since 1915. So, the odds favor an advance between now and 2010. How much is anyone's guess. Given the high level we're starting from, though, I find it implausible the record will match the 1990s.

Kazanjian: *There was a report a few years ago basically concluding that younger fund managers produce higher returns than older fund managers. Do you buy that?*

Torray: No. That's a preposterous notion. I don't know of any business where inexperience creates an advantage. The thesis of the study is that young people are more aggressive and more willing to take chances than older investors are. These are not favorable characteristics when it comes to investing. In fact, given enough time they're likely to produce a disaster.

Kazanjian: *Your partner and co-portfolio manager is 40. Is that too young?*

Torray: Not at all.

Kazanjian: *How long are you going to stay in this business?*

Torray: As long as I can think straight. Every day I'm talking on the phone, studying businesses, looking for opportunities, attending meetings, and so on. It's exhilarating. I often find it hard to switch gears and think about anything else.

Kazanjian: *I know you have a couple of homes and a jet plane. You travel a lot.*

Torray: That's true.

Kazanjian: *Do you fly the jet yourself?*

Torray: No. I used to, but I stopped about 15 years ago. It's not a job for part-timers. We have a terrific crew. We probably fly 250,000 miles a year. I just love to get onto a new investment, fly out to see management, and then, if things check out, pour in the money. It's hard to explain. I guess it's just in the genes, although no one else in our family has been in this line of work, as far as I know.

Kazanjian: *I'm sure people are thinking you have a great lifestyle, but you told me before you've worked like a dog for everything you've got.*

Torray: This is the toughest game in the world. It looks easy only from the outside. A lot of people seem to think we're just sitting around buying and selling stocks for a living. Nothing could be further from the truth. Unfortunately, the aspects of money management that have the greatest superficial appeal are of no importance and provide no professional satisfaction. In order to succeed, you have to be wired up a certain way. If you are, you get to a point where you just know things, sometimes even before you've really thought about them. It's like a sixth sense. But, from what I've observed, few people possess it, and it's not a teachable trait.

Kazanjian: *What three attributes do you need to succeed in this business?*

Torray: Aptitude, determination, and the power of persuasion. As I said earlier, you must have that certain feel or affinity for the business. Successful investors are born, not made. You must also be willing to dig in your heels and be prepared for a long and difficult uphill battle that may not end for two or three decades. And finally, while it may not be an absolute requisite, it certainly makes life easier if you're persuasive. Trust and confidence play a big role in this business. Without it you may be the smartest guy in the world, but you'll have no clients to practice on.

Kazanjian: *Anything else you would like to add?*

Torray: Keep it simple. Ignore the preachings of academia and avoid the advice of market strategists. Much of the investment industry believes that profit lies in the process, that wealth can be amassed by trading around in the stock and bond markets, always landing in just the right place at the right time. Of course, it never turns out that way, so don't fall for this ruse. The market and the process are irrelevant. Businesses are the foundation of a successful investment operation. If you buy and hold the good ones, you'll be a big winner.

The academics must be cringing. Bob makes a convincing argument against all of the theories they hold so dear—diversification, asset allocation, and value stock investing. That's what makes Bob such a refreshing voice in the industry. He always tells it like it is.

It's interesting to note that even though most of the industry views Bob as being a value manager, he resents this label. I think it has to do with the way most people define value. Based on his investment approach, I still think it's fair to say Bob uses value techniques for selecting his investments. But, like Bill Miller, he doesn't like being viewed as a value purist.

A few years back, Bob was quoted in an investment-industry publication as saying he had no intention of advertising his fund through any means. If investors were interested in what he did, he surmised, they could find him for themselves. Based on his track record, that search may very well be worth the extra effort. ■

HOWARD WARD

When Howard Ward took the reigns of the Gabelli Growth Fund on January 3, 1995, he had some tough shoes to fill. Star manager Elizabeth Bramwell had just quit following a bitter dispute with her boss, Mario Gabelli, leaving behind a fund with a terrific track record. Many media pundits questioned whether Howard, a far less known manager, was up to the challenge. He was. In fact, Howard has smartly outperformed the fund his predecessor launched after setting up shop on her own.

Howard joined Gabelli after 12 years at Scudder, Stevens and Clark, where he led the large company growth team and managed the Scudder Large Company Growth and Balanced funds. While it seems awkward for a growth manager to be at a value shop such as Gabelli, Howard says he feels right at home, since he follows his own valuation discipline and won't pay any price even for his favorite stocks. He focuses on dominant businesses capable of growing earnings by at least 12 percent annually for several years. That often leads him to the bluest of blue chips.

Howard combines both bottom-up and top-down analysis. From the bottom-up, the 43-year-old manager looks for companies with competitive advantages, such as brand names or proprietary products. These businesses must also have above-average or expanding market shares and profit margins. From the top-down, Howard looks at broad trends—such as the aging of the population and the technology revolution—and then seeks out companies well positioned to benefit. He's a big believer in technology, although he stays away from pure-play Internet stocks, which at the time this interview was concluded were in a phase that he referred to as a "classic mania."

This 1978 graduate of Northwestern works out of Gabelli headquarters in Rye, New York. While his boss Mario Gabelli's picture is on the front of the annual report, this is clearly Howard's fund. He calls all the shots and insists the buck starts and stops at his desk.

Kazanjian: *Like a lot of folks in the investment business, you were once an aspiring attorney.*

Ward: Yes. At Northwestern University, I majored in economics with the intention of becoming a lawyer. After taking a class on the legal and constitutional history of the United States, I decided studying the law was more interesting than practicing it, and studying the law wasn't that interesting to begin with. My senior year, in 1978, I really wasn't sure what I wanted to do. I started interviewing with companies such as IBM and Procter & Gamble. I remember my interview with P&G well because two men interviewed me at the same time, which I didn't think was fair. The weekend before my interview, I was driving with a friend to Cincinnati and noticed an incredible stench coming from a P&G lye plant. I asked these two men from P&G what they intended to do about that. Needless to say, I didn't get a job offer.

Kazanjian: *Where did you ultimately wind up?*

Ward: I wound up at Brown Brothers Harriman and Company, which I had never heard of before. I had no interest in the stock market at the time, but figured if the job didn't work out, I could always quit and go to California in my Ford Econoline van. Brown Brothers put me in its executive-development training program. It was geared toward people without master's degrees. The firm discovered that people without master's degrees didn't cost as much as people with them, yet could often perform their functions equally well. I spent my first six months learning what Brown Brothers did. Then I was supposed to pick a specialty from one of three choices: foreign exchange trading, bond trading, or their money position, which was essentially managing and tracking the checkbook of the bank itself. I ended up going to the bond department and worked for one of the pioneers of active bond management back in the 1970s. Brown Brothers was a very hot investment boutique for active bond management at that time. It was quite exciting in those days, because interest rates were going up and there was a lot of action in the fixed-income world. I really started getting turned on to Wall Street and the investment side of the business.

Kazanjian: *I trust you eventually went over to the equity side. How did that happen?*

Ward: After 13 months in the bond department, I went on to further my education and worked as a banker, which entailed sitting at a desk wearing a jacket and doing what they called credit agendas all day long. A credit agenda is a report that gets presented to the credit committee every Friday morning. They would determine, based on your report, whether it made sense to extend credit to whatever company you were analyzing. Preparing credit agendas really didn't get my juices flowing. I went to the head of personnel, Bill Goodman, and said I wanted to pursue a career on the equity side in sales. I became an institutional salesman in training. My first day, Hank Goss, manager of institutional sales, collected all the research reports written by Brown's analysts over the previous 12 months and told me to read all of them. That was how I started. After a couple of years of learning about companies and how the stock market operates, I reached the point where I wanted to get on to the other side of the table and be an actual money manager.

Kazanjian: *What was your first step?*

Ward: Another fellow in my department at Brown who was about ten years older confided that he had interviewed for a job at Scudder. They were looking for someone with my kind of background. He felt he was too old for what they were looking for, but thought I might not be. He gave me the name of the recruiter handling the job. We met, and two weeks later I had a job offer as a junior portfolio manager. That was in June 1982.

Kazanjian: *Scudder was probably managing only about $12 billion in those days with around 100 employees in the New York office.*

Ward: That's right. It was a tight-knit firm run by George Johnston. He and the other senior partners had a great sense of character, morality, and principles. It was a wonderful laboratory to work in. They didn't have a training program per se. You were assigned to work with five or six partners, so you could learn different styles. You were responsible for all of the grunt work and made recommendations to the partners. Over a period of time, the partners would gain confidence in you and assign you as the primary contact for some of the smaller accounts. I ended up working with all different kinds of clients, from both foreign and domestic individuals, to endowments, foundations, pension plans, and insurance companies. In those days, you not only did the stocks, but also the bonds and asset allocations.

Kazanjian: *You moved up the ranks and eventually got your own mutual fund?*

Ward: Early in 1991, George Johnston wanted to start a fund that was, in essence, Scudder's large-cap growth institutional product. So, on May 15, 1991, the Scudder Quality Growth Fund was launched. Sadly, George developed prostate cancer in 1990 and died before the fund was launched.

Kazanjian: *You focused exclusively on large company stocks?*

Ward: The distinction between large-cap, mid-cap, and small-cap wasn't as strong then as it is now. The focus was on blue chip growth companies, but the cut-off point for market capitalization was pretty small, around $200 million. But, yes, it was predominately a large-cap offering.

Kazanjian: *This was the first time your record was on public display. That must have been nerve wracking.*

Ward: Not really. The sense at Scudder was that performance comes and goes, but we will always support you within your style because we believe in the style and we believe in you. Performance pressure was less intense than at places such as Fidelity.

Kazanjian: *Performance clearly is important, though. How did the fund do?*

Ward: We shot out of the box very quickly, because large-company growth stocks did very well that year. I think we were ahead of the

S&P 500 by about 11 percent during the first seven months. Then 1992 came around and concerns about health-care spending started to emerge. We always had a pretty significant investment in drug stocks. We decided we needed to protect ourselves against the potential for falling drug prices and the overall health-care problem. We invested in some companies that were supposedly going to be the private-market solutions to these problems, like Medco Containment Systems, Surgical Care Affiliates, United Healthcare, and U.S. Healthcare. As the Clintons took office, the threat of federal health-care and drug-price regulation hurt not just the drug stocks, but also the private-company solutions to the problem as well. If the government was going to tell everyone what they could charge for what kind of service, you didn't need the private companies that were going to work and lobby on behalf of their customers to get lower prices. As a result, all of these stocks got slammed. I believe the private solutions got hurt even more than the drug stocks. It was the beginning of a two-year slide in the relative performance of a lot of growth stocks. Then, in April 1993, we had Marlboro Friday, when Philip Morris cut the price of Marlboro cigarettes by 40 percent overnight. Investors clobbered not only Philip Morris, which was probably our largest holding at the time, but also all of the consumer staples stocks.

Kazanjian: *Without question, 1992 and 1993 both were difficult years for you. What did you learn during that time?*

Ward: I learned that leading brands are valuable assets. All of the private label consumer-brand companies failed to have a lasting or measurable impact on the blue chip multinationals. I remember there was American Safety Razor, which was going to knock off Gillette with cheap razors. The company didn't do very well. The biggest disaster of all was Cott's beverages of Canada, which was practically a joke. They were going to take on Coke. They failed. Perrigo, a private-label provider of over-the-counter medication and household products, was another land mine. All these different companies were going to take on the Procter & Gambles, Cokes, and Philip Morrises of the world. Of course, none of them worked out. The overall impression it left on me was simply to be more paranoid about making sure a company's growth prospects were solid, that they weren't deteriorating in any sense of the word. Marlboro Friday itself was a function of the cigarette industry and the absolute dependence the cigarette industry had on raising prices in order to generate profit gains. I think the problems that were somewhat peculiar to the cigarette industry should not have been viewed as problems for other consumer staples companies as well. Philip Morris was addicted to raising prices. After years of raising prices, consumers started to balk. At first, the head of Philip Morris, Mike Miles, was strongly criticized by Wall Street for the 40 percent price rollback. He called it Marketing 101—in order to stimulate and kick start demand for something you cut the price significantly. Wall Street thought it was a terrible idea that would result in a big hit to earnings. The way it turned out, Miles lost his job in the ensuing feud, but was actually correct. Marlboro's market share came roaring back. Yes, there was a one-time hit to Philip Morris earnings, but the company ended up thwarting the private-label industry offensive in the process. The stock did well until getting bogged down in litigation. That shows you brand names are very powerful and won't just disappear overnight, although there is a limit to what consumers will pay.

Kazanjian: *How did you get hooked up with Mario Gabelli?*

Ward: I met Mario through a mutual friend. When Liz Bramwell [the previous manager of the Gabelli Growth Fund] quit in February 1994, my friend told me to talk to Mario. That began a series of meetings that lasted for over six months.

Kazanjian: *In the meantime, Mario was managing the fund on his own. Were you interested in taking it over?*

Ward: I thought it was a special opportunity. In those half a dozen or so meetings I had with Mario, I felt we would get along really well. We both were stock junkies and loved the market. The idea of working for somebody who was a strong money manager in his own right appealed to me. In fact, when we were having breakfast at one point I said to Mario, "I had really lousy results in 1993, don't you want to talk to me about that?" He replied, "No. All large-cap growth managers had a bad 1993, so I know what happened. If you had a good 1993, then I'd want to find out what you did because you probably weren't doing what you should have been doing." I knew I could get along with this guy.

Kazanjian: *But Mario is known for being a hard person to get along with.*

Ward: That's not true for everyone and certainly not for me. I think Mario is a demanding workaholic. He takes his responsibility seriously. He sets very high standards for himself and others. I can honestly say that Mario's a good friend outside the office as well. At this point in my career, I would not work anywhere else.

Kazanjian: *What was it like replacing Elizabeth Bramwell? There was a lot of publicity surrounding her departure, and she was a highly regarded manager. [Bramwell left the fund following a highly public bitter dispute with Gabelli. She went on to start her own fund, The Bramwell Growth Fund.]*

Ward: She had developed a good reputation here as a money manager. I was not nearly as well known. A lot of people wondered whether I could do as good a job as Liz. I remember a reporter interviewed me at the time and asked how I felt about the pressure of having to fill her shoes. My answer was the same I'd give anybody today. If you really want to be good in this business, and probably any other business, you put that pressure on yourself. It's an internal desire or pressure to do well. It doesn't come from the outside. That was true then, and it's true now. You must block out the noise that's in the press or industry, focus on doing your job, and let the chips fall wherever they may.

Kazanjian: *I interviewed Bramwell for another book,* Growing Rich with Growth Stocks. *She talked about how her performance was often better than Mario's. She claimed that would make him angry, especially when the press gave her attention at his expense. It looks as if it's the same situation with you. Your fund is significantly outperforming his. Does this cause any tension between the two of you?*

Ward: Not at all. There's never been any inkling of that whatsoever. He's very, very happy that the size of the fund has grown from $470 million to $2.4 billion since I've been here. We have different styles that perform differently relative to the market.

Kazanjian: *Do you watch Liz's fund at all? You must consider her to be a prime competitor.*

Ward: I watch about 60 other funds, including hers. I've done much better than she has. The only year she outperformed me by a hair was in 1998. In all fairness, it's not an apples-to-apples comparison because we have different styles.

Kazanjian: *What is the difference in the environment between Gabelli and Scudder?*

Ward: There is a significant difference. Part of that is simply size. At Gabelli, we're much smaller in terms of assets and people. [Gabelli Asset Management has $18 billion under management. Scudder has more than $200 billion.]

Kazanjian: *Do you have more freedom as a money manager?*

Ward: I have absolute total freedom to manage the portfolio as I feel it should be managed within my charter as a growth manager with a large-cap bias. The Scudder decision-making framework is geared more toward consensus, both in terms of having teams of people working on portfolios and having a research department where the analyst has significant input into the process. I didn't like that because I had differences of opinion with some analysts from time to time. That often led to friction. At Gabelli, I basically run my own firm and do exactly what I feel is in the best interest of shareholders. I'm one of the shareholders. The bulk of my own personal family savings is invested in the fund. I tell people I have a great job. I get paid to manage my own money.

Kazanjian: *Do you work by yourself?*

Ward: I have a couple of people who help me, and some of the analysts here lend a hand. But we're very lean. We don't have committees. My name is in the prospectus as the fund manager, and I make the decisions.

Kazanjian: *How do you begin the process of putting your portfolio together and finding investment ideas?*

Ward: People say they are either top-down or bottom-up in their approach to managing money. I believe most people are really a combination of the two, and I'm no exception. I very much combine a top-down with a bottom-up view of the world. I start by asking a lot of questions. What makes a company great? What allows a company to grow its earnings at an above-average rate over a period of years? The answer is that a company must have a competitive advantage in the marketplace. Then you've got to define competitive advantage. I've noticed there are a few basic competitive advantages that tend to surface. One is that you have a proprietary product. That's something you run into with drug or technology inventions that are patented.

Another competitive advantage is having a dominant brand name, which we already talked about. Dominant brands aren't just consumer staples. Intel's a dominant brand in PC microprocessors. Microsoft is a dominant brand for software. Another advantage is being in a business where you don't have a lot of competitors, due to the high levels of technology, expertise, capital, or labor required. It could be you're in the broadcasting business, where there are only so many licenses available. You can find these little monopolies or oligopolies that have been carved out as industries have consolidated over the years. These are franchise companies, the kinds I want to own.

Kazanjian: *What* don't *you want to own?*

Ward: Commodity companies. They have no power over what they charge in the marketplace. They are basically victims of a farmer's market where supply and demand is instantly at work dictating the prices they can charge. The first leg of my process is finding companies with competitive advantages that I feel can grow earnings by at least 12 percent annually. Commodity companies can't do that. The 12 percent number may change when economic growth is stronger or weaker. But for the last five years, I've used 12 percent as the number. In reality, that doesn't sound like much. But in the large-cap world, where corporate earnings in the United States have compounded at a rate of around 6.5 percent in the last 50 years, that's really double what the average company is capable of doing.

Kazanjian: *Do you also take a look at the market, different sectors, the economy, any of that?*

Ward: Not yet. The next thing I want to do is introduce this top-down part of the process. This is one of the lessons that got drilled into me during the turbulence with the health-care stocks and what was going on with brands in the early 1990s. I decided I needed to pay more attention to what was going on in the social and political arenas. From a top-down standpoint, I want to see if there are major trends at work that would give me a wind at my back if I were invested in a company benefiting from such a trend. There are several such trends today. One is the aging of the population. This is definitely something that's going to be in place for a number of years. We know today, for example, what our labor pool is going to look like for the next 16 years because those people are already born. It's a labor pool that shows almost no growth, both in the United States, Europe, and Japan. That will have an impact on how we spend our time and money. One reason the stock market is where it is is because the aging boomers earn and save more and spend proportionally less than they did when they were younger. That's a big theme, and it's an important part of my portfolio. It impacts not just financial services and technology, but also companies that use technology to make better products. In fact, you can also think of it in terms of the increasing substitution of capital for labor. We have a situation today where the unemployment rate is at a 30-year low and yet the economy isn't even that strong. It's likely to stay that way. Instead of having people answer phones, we have voice mail; instead of having tellers give us our cash, we have ATMs; instead of having porters at airports to help us with our bags, you slide your credit card through a machine and you get your own little cart to put your luggage on and do it yourself. You're increasingly seeing these trade-offs, where instead of having a human being perform a service function, you're apt to do it yourself or have some piece of technology do it for you. I think this trend is going to continue.

Kazanjian: *What's another major theme?*

Ward: The information revolution. The technological changes in the world are huge. The labor shortage is forcing companies to invest more and more in technology to improve productivity. It's changing the way we do things. The Internet is the biggest new medium since probably the telephone. It's going to have profound effects on the way we live and work. The information revolution is important. It has a huge wind at its back as companies spend big sums to build up their productivity and deliver enhanced goods and services. It's an area you simply cannot ignore as an investor.

Kazanjian: *I assume that tied into this is your third major theme—globalization.*

Ward: Yes. Capitalism has won, and we've got a global economy. Roughly 95 percent of the people on this planet do not live in the United States. As these large companies grow, they've got to expand beyond our borders and go after huge new markets in Europe, Latin America, Asia, and even the Middle East. You're going to get this huge globalization where modern technology makes it easier to handle global communications environments and computer networks. There are probably other big trends out there, but these are the ones I think will really be the meat and potatoes of my portfolio for the fore-seeable future.

Kazanjian: *Getting back to the baby boomers, what types of companies do you think will do best?*

Ward: Health care is going to be huge, and especially the pharmaceutical companies, because the vast majority of expenditures on drugs occur in the later stages of life. In your first 40 years, you consume almost nothing compared to what you consume in the next 40. You've already seen the number of prescriptions being written and filled growing very nicely over the last few years. Part of that has to do with changes in how drugs are paid for, but it's also because of the expanding population of people needing drugs.

The financial services sector is also very significant. You have two things happening here. First, a whole new generation of investors is getting turned on to the stock market. Second, as their parents pass away, you'll have a massive transfer of wealth to the boomers. This will enrich them even further, even after the government takes its big share of the pie. The outlook for financial services companies is very good, although at some point you'll have more competition, which may start eating into margins. Life insurance, brokerage, and asset-management companies will do well.

Finally, technology will be wonderful, from the standpoint that companies are being forced to invest greater amounts in technology to stay competitive and be low-cost producers.

Kazanjian: *Are you buying Internet companies?*

Ward: I'm playing the Internet by investing in the companies that build the Internet. I don't own the straight pure-play Internet companies, such as America Online, because I cannot make economic sense out of those valuations. I play the Internet through Cisco Systems, IBM, Sun Microsystems, EMC, Microsoft, Intel, Lucent Technologies, and MCI WorldCom. Computer services companies are another way of participating in the Internet, as are companies providing outsourcing services to those that don't have the expertise to manage their own technologies.

Kazanjian: *I want to talk more about valuation in a moment. First, tell me how you're playing the globalization theme.*

Ward: This feeds nicely into a number of U.S. companies, especially those in technology and health care. In fact, the drug companies were really the first industry in the United States to go global. They had a larger percentage of their revenues coming from overseas than did any other industry 20 years ago. That's still true today.

From the standpoint of financial services, there are several companies that fit neatly into the globalization theme. AIG, for example, is one of my longstanding investments. AIG has enjoyed 30 years of 15 percent growth in an industry where most of its competitors have done much worse. AIG has a large presence outside of the United States and is actively going after business in Asia and Europe. Merrill Lynch is going into Japan and buying brokerage firms. State Street Boston similarly has a strong global presence providing financial services to institutions and mutual funds. Marsh and McLennan, another one of my large holdings, is the world's largest insurance broker. One thing people forget is that no commerce can take place without insurance. Everything's got to be insured. If you believe in globalization, you believe in more ships, planes, trucks, and trains transporting things across borders. All of these must be insured.

Kazanjian: *What else do you look at when examining specific companies to determine whether they are good investments?*

Ward: The caliber and quality of the CEO. I don't believe that Wall Street pays enough attention to this, but character and leadership qualities can make a big difference. Look at AT&T. Under Bob Allen, AT&T was losing market share every month and going nowhere fast. It was a sinking ship. He's replaced by Michael Armstrong. In 18 months, Armstrong turned AT&T into a completely different company. Almost overnight it became the biggest cable TV operator in the United States. Another example is Steve Jobs. He comes back to Apple, and you have strong results very quickly. Lou Gerstner at IBM. I could go on and on.

Kazanjian: *Do you actually go out and visit companies?*

Ward: Oh, yes. I think that's a very important part of the process in getting a feel for the culture of the company and the character of the management.

Kazanjian: *Is there anything you completely avoid?*

Ward: I stay away from stocks that look statistically super cheap. When a stock looks super cheap, it's generally for a good reason. People should think twice before buying something that looks too good to be true. I also try to avoid commodity companies and those dependent on acquisitions for growth. Sooner or later, that ends badly. It's one thing to enhance your growth rate from 10 to 12 percent through acquisitions, but if almost all of your growth is because of acquisitions, you've got a real problem.

Kazanjian: *What about valuation? How do you figure out how much you're willing to pay for a stock?*

Ward: I've developed an earnings valuation model that tries to tell me what the logical price for a stock is using a five-year time horizon. By the way, models don't work well for cyclical stocks. I take the current year's earnings estimate and grow the earnings by five years using a five-year growth rate. Sometimes I'll use what is, in essence, a consensus growth rate. Putting a five-year growth rate on a stock has its risks, yet the market does it. Some might wonder how I can use a five-year number with a lot of confidence. When the market prices a stock, it discounts many years of future growth and is itself putting a growth rate on the company. I have to do the same thing to compete with and understand the market. The case of Automatic Data Processing is a good example. That's a company with a highly predictable earnings stream. The company is expected to earn $1.23 this year. Given the high degree of predictability with that company, that's probably a pretty good estimate. I think earnings will grow at 15 percent annually over the next five years. I'll use that number in the model. If I grow earnings at 15 percent for five years, the $1.23 becomes $2.47. Then I look at what kind of price-earnings multiple the market is willing to pay for ADP stock. I see it's trading at 34 times the current estimate. I will typically use a PE number in my model that's 10 percent lower than what the market is currently paying and won't use any multiple in my model that exceeds 30. That's because I don't think any of these large-cap companies are capable of sustaining a multiple north of 30 for more than a few years, including Microsoft. In the case of ADP, the current multiple is 34. I'm using a multiple of 30. I take the 30, multiply that by $2.47, and end up with a value of $74.22. Then I have to calculate the present value of that $74.22, because that's something I'm not expecting for five years. To find out what it's worth today, I discount that number back for five years using the ten-year Treasury rate plus 2 percent. The plus 2 percent part is the equity risk premium. That gives me a fair value on

ADP stock of $51. So $51 divided by the $42 share price shows me the stock is currently about 21 percent below its fair value. My target price, if you will, is $51, or 21 percent above the current price.

Kazanjian: *Does that mean you sell when it reaches your target price?*

Ward: No. These models always have a degree of error built into them. One of the things I know from experience is that a stock price that is rising rapidly is frequently a leading indicator of an up-side earnings surprise. You want to avoid the situation where the stock hits your price target, you sell it, and the next day the company reports a big up-side earnings surprise. You've got to be a bit of an artist in how you approach these models. I don't typically start reducing a position until the stock is at least 10 percent overvalued, and I won't eliminate a position until it's about 20 percent overvalued. A recent case in point is my investment in Charles Schwab. In the first quarter of 1998, my models showed the stock was worth $60. Because it started trading like an Internet stock, the price soared to $60, $70, $80, and then $90 in a matter of a few weeks. As it blew through $60 and $70, I reduced my position. As it got to $95, I sold what was left. A week later, it ran up to $150. At $120, the Morgan Stanley analyst, Henry McVey, increased his rating to a strong buy and headlined his report by saying "The Best Is Yet to Come." That drove the stock to $150 in two days. Mind you as I was clearing off my desk, I came across Henry's report on Schwab from the previous April where his target price for the stock was $40. [The stock has since split two-for-one.]

Kazanjian: *That's an interesting point. Wall Street analysts tend to go with the flow, just like your average investor. Do you pay much attention to them?*

Ward: No. I think Wall Street analysts can provide a lot of good information, but it's dangerous to buy into their ratings. Their primary job is to generate transactions and securities underwriting business. They're not necessarily going to tell you the optimum time to get in or out of a stock. You've got to be independent in how you look at companies. You must go with your beliefs and experiences. It takes many years of doing this to develop a belief in your own abilities and not feel scared about doing something other than what the Wall Street crowd tells you.

Kazanjian: *Good point, Howard. The consensus of a lot of folks I've interviewed is that the Internet is going to be huge. Does that mean everyone is wrong?*

Ward: I agree the Internet is going to be huge. But I think you should avoid pure-play Internet stocks. That has been a classic mania. Most of the money is going into these stocks after they've already reached exorbitant, indefensible levels.

Kazanjian: *Besides exceeding your price targets, what are some other reasons you'll sell a stock?*

Ward: If I feel that a company's fundamentals are deteriorating, which could be management not executing or a problem with the business itself, I'll sell the stock. You've got to be willing to take the risk of being a bit early, because if you're late, it can be ugly.

Kazanjian: *What percentage of the time are you right versus wrong in your decisions?*

Ward: I'm probably two-thirds right, one-third wrong.

Kazanjian: *What's the most common reason you're wrong?*

Ward: Because I go into a company without knowing management well enough.

Kazanjian: *You keep your portfolio pretty diversified.*

Ward: I have this self-imposed limit of not putting more than 25 percent in any one industry sector. In my 20 years in the business, I've seen people get too carried away with a particular idea, theme, or industry and overstay their welcome. I believe the average retail investor in this fund is seeking professional diversification. I don't think it's my right to give them a sector fund in drag.

Kazanjian: *How many stocks do you typically own?*

Ward: With all the studies that have been done on investing, no one's been able to statistically prove what the optimum number of stocks should be. You have Peter Lynch owning hundreds of stocks and doing well, and you have Warren Buffett owning eight. One of the challenges is determining what's right for you. You've got to walk a fine line between having too many stocks to beat the market and having too few, in which case your volatility scares people away. When I took over, there were 130 names in the fund. Having 50 now gives me good diversification and real exposure to what are, I hope, my best ideas.

Kazanjian: *Do you have a limit on how much you'll keep in a single stock?*

Ward: I don't like to see it get up much above 5 percent. The top 15 holdings are probably 40 percent of the portfolio.

Kazanjian: *How do you define a growth stock?*

Ward: It's a company that can grow its earnings year in and year out. Instead of having earnings that go up and down or up and sideways, they just go up like a staircase every year.

Kazanjian: *Do you believe in indexing?*

Ward: For most people, no. If you are the State of California and have many billions of dollars to invest, from a practical standpoint you probably don't have any choice but to do some indexing. But I think you can do better than indexing. This fund has done better than the S&P during my tenure of managing it, and it did better under Liz Bramwell's tenure.

Kazanjian: *Are individual investors better off in individual stocks or funds?*

Ward: Most people are better off in funds. They don't have the education or training to be investing on their own. To the extent they have the time and interest and want to pursue that education, it's fine for them to choose stocks.

Kazanjian: *You've been complimented in the media for writing shareholder-friendly annual reports. Is that a job you take seriously?*

Ward: Yes. It's a job I enjoy because I like writing and I like to express myself. I use those shareholder reports as a communication, to make a connection with the shareholder, and to let them know there really is a human being managing their money. I may sometimes write things in those reports that are not always 100 percent politically correct, but I think it's okay to express a point of view.

Kazanjian: *Do you think most shareholders read the reports?*

Ward: My guess is that most shareholders don't have the time or interest to read them. I think they should, though.

Kazanjian: *When should people sell a fund?*

Ward: Every fund's got a performance time frame that people need to take into consideration. I think if a manager is not meeting his objective over a three-year period, then you should probably move on. Everyone's entitled to have a bad year. If you've got two years where maybe you're mediocre, you deserve that third strike. But after three strikes I think people should move on.

Kazanjian: *That's ironic because most fund managers would not give a company three years.*

Ward: They wouldn't give them three quarters. When there's a change in a portfolio manager, people need to investigate what that's all about and determine whether or not it makes sense to continue their investment in the fund. Frequently, when a new portfolio manager takes over you may see a lot of turnover, a change in style, and taxable gains. I think that's a red flag.

Kazanjian: *How do you spend your time away from the office?*

Ward: My family keeps me pretty busy. I've got three kids, and they have very active sports and social lives. I'm a terrible golfer, I have a 32 handicap, and I don't have the time to focus on that.

Kazanjian: *Is there anything else you'd like to add?*

Ward: It's very important to have a lot of conviction in this business. Otherwise you're constantly going to be chasing your tail trying to generate performance. I think people need to make distinctions between good stocks and good companies because there are plenty of good companies that are in bad industries that you don't necessarily want to invest in. People need to really get a sense as to when it's a good time to cut their losses and move on. You don't want to be a martyr about your ideas. Don't be afraid to make a mistake and don't be married to a stock. Making mistakes is simply part of this business. Just like trying to hit a baseball, you're going to miss it a lot. Patience is a virtue in this business. All too often we are impatient in our buys and sells. Investors should do whatever possible to avoid selling into panics. We've had several panics in the last 15 years. No one's ever been rewarded for selling out. I frankly think reading charts is a bunch of garbage that will mislead you into investing in companies that have real problems. People should try—as hard as it is in this very short-term-oriented world—to focus on the long haul and not get so wrapped up in every little economic statistic and quarterly report. Otherwise you'll end up really missing the big picture, and you can get into big trouble. Don't be a slave to a model or a point of view. Things change. That's why we do research.

Howard is one manager who has unquestionably learned from his mistakes, and he's not afraid to admit it. One of the most crucial lessons I learned from him is the importance of investing in companies with dominant brands. Although you might be able to get the stocks of private-label competitors at cheaper prices, chances are you'll get what you pay for.

Among Howard's other major insights: Be wary of Wall Street analysis, since it often has some kind of bias; avoid commodity companies, since they can't grow their earnings very fast; look for businesses with a clear competitive advantage; and stay away from stocks that are statistically too cheap (often the price is low for a good reason). ■

PART TWO

INVESTING LIKE THE WIZARDS

WHAT THE WIZARDS
HAVE IN COMMON

As you've no doubt figured out from reading these interviews, every manager owes his or her success to something a bit different. No one Wizard picks stocks in precisely the same way, nor have they taken the same road to the top on Wall Street. But I have found several common threads these managers share.

Unbridled passion for their job. You get a clear sense that every Wizard has a real love for the work he or she does. Picking stocks is both a hobby and a profession. In fact, even though it didn't get into every interview, I asked all the managers what they did outside the office. Almost universally, they replied, "I'm always working. I don't have time to do anything else." And they really meant it. Many were hard-pressed to come up with much else they enjoyed doing, aside from spending time with their family and taking part in occasional sporting events. They are passionate about their work and are always on the lookout for tomorrow's promising investments.

Adherence to a specific discipline. Every manager has a clear and distinct process for finding new investment ideas. They all stick to this process, regardless of how they are performing or what's happening to the market. You likely gathered from several interviews that developing your investment discipline is an evolving process. Few pick stocks today in exactly the same way they did when they first got started. They have honed and refined a process that works. They don't stray from it even when the going gets tough. For instance, those who follow a value approach don't abandon their discipline of paying attention to price just because the market currently favors high-priced growth stocks. That may cost them shareholders and harm their egos in the short run, but they know sticking to their knitting will pay off over time.

A concentrated approach. There are some exceptions to this, but the Wizards, by and large, hold very focused portfolios of 50 names or less. Many contend that the fewer names you own, the greater your chance of outperforming the market. The exception seems to rest with managers who specialize in small company stocks. Because these companies are inherently volatile, managers such as Jim Callinan and Neal Miller feel more comfortable owning a larger roster of names in this area of the market. But even they keep a significant portion of their assets in their top ten holdings, in essence putting their money in what they deem to be their best ideas. As several experts point out, the more names you own, the more likely you are to be below average and/or perform in line with the indexes.

Life experience, versus fancy degrees. Ever since I got into this business, I've been amazed at how the most successful managers on Wall Street are not necessarily those with MBAs and CFAs. In fact, while several of the Wizards do, in fact, have business degrees, few are Chartered Financial Analysts. Many investment firms today screen out candidates without these degrees, but that may be a mistake. Being well schooled doesn't necessarily translate into being a good stock picker. We know that's true, since a lot of CFAs are among the 90 percent of managers who fail to outperform the S&P 500. Instead, the best managers have good instincts and broad backgrounds, which enable them to get a solid understanding of many different industries. I've always thought journalism was a great degree for an investment manager. I'm probably biased, since that's what one of my degrees is in. But when you think about it, a good manager is like a journalist—always sniffing around for new ideas, asking tough questions, and disseminating data in a defensible way for shareholders. You don't necessarily learn those skills in school, even at the top universities.

Belief in the Internet. Every Wizard, without exception, has an undying faith in the Internet. They believe it will have profound ramifications for investors and will impact every company doing business today. While they all agree it's unclear exactly what will happen at this stage of the game, they all embrace the Internet and want to own companies that do the same. This doesn't necessarily mean they own pure-play internet upstarts, such as the many new e-commerce companies. Although the Wizards are occasionally willing to take a chance on these businesses, they often play the Internet through more established technology companies. Some even invest in this space through blue chip retailers and other corporations that effectively use the Web to improve their bottom lines.

Eating their own cooking. The Wizards almost universally invest their own money in their funds, some to a greater degree than others. I think it's extremely important for investors to stick with managers who eat their own cooking. After all, no one cares more about your money than you do. Therefore, managers with their own money on the line are going to be more careful about how they run their portfolios. As William Oates admits, "It's hard to forget about number one," meaning him. He's the largest shareholder in his fund. If a manager doesn't invest in his or her fund, you should ask yourself why. After all, if the fund isn't good enough for the manager, why should it be good enough for you?

10 KEYS
TO BEATING THE MARKET

As I interviewed these Wizards, I started jotting down the stock-picking techniques they seemed to have in common. In all, I came up with what I call the "10 Keys to Beating the Market," or 10 things you should keep in mind when choosing stocks or funds for your portfolio. Granted, not every Wizard follows all these rules. But these market-beaters kept bringing up these themes during our conversations:

1. **Do your homework.** Whether you invest in stocks or funds, it's essential that you do plenty of research before investing your hard-earned dollars. Kevin Landis equates this to being a good detective. "You get the [company's] story and then go check it out," he says. "If all detectives did was get somebody's story and never check it out, they wouldn't be great detectives, would they? You talk to customers, competitors, suppliers, and figure out if they are as locked in as they think."

    David Alger agrees it's crucial to dig deep inside your potential investments. "I want to know their products, their management, and their competitors," he maintains. "We like to think we know our companies better than anyone."

    Every expert in this book goes through a specific process of investigating each company before it gets added to his or her portfolio. You should do the same. That could mean just paying more attention to the research you already do on a regular basis. For instance, Neal Miller is constantly taking notes as he reads through the many periodicals he receives. "I subscribe to more than 300 magazines," he says. "I'm always looking for anomalies, things that don't fit into

an existing pattern, with the idea that this can suggest a coun-
tertrend or a new wedge of future opportunity."

2. **Rely on your instincts.** Time and again, the Wizards point out the
importance of going with their instincts and note how straying from
them often proves to be costly. That's true no matter how much
homework you have done. Background research gives you the data
you need to make intelligent decisions. But, more often than not,
your instincts will tell you whether an investment ultimately feels
right for *you*.

Perhaps no one illustrates that better than William Oates. "I
think the best money managers have a lot of instinct and feel, like a
really great surgeon," he offers. "Have you ever asked a surgeon
how he does an operation? He can't tell you because he gets the
knee, hip, or heart open and just starts doing it. I do investment
work for a tremendous orthopedic surgeon and he couldn't possibly
tell me how he does it." That's because much of the operation, and
the decisions he makes, are done on instinct.

Applied to investing, if you're considering the purchase of a company that just doesn't feel right, chances are it isn't.

3. **Stick with dominant industry leaders.** Almost without exception, the
Wizards invest their money in companies with dominant market
shares and a number one or two position in their industry. This is
true regardless of whether they buy small or large companies.

Along these lines, brand recognition is another invaluable asset.
Howard Ward learned that early on in his career. In the early 1990s,
he tried buying several private-label consumer brand companies,
since they were selling at much cheaper valuations. However, they
failed to have a lasting impact on their blue chip multinational competitors, and many failed.

"I remember there was American Safety razor, which was going
to knock off Gillette with cheap razors," Howard recalls. "The company didn't do very well. The biggest disaster of all was Cott's beverages of Canada, which was practically a joke. They were going to
take on Coke. They failed. Perrigo, a private-label provider of over-
the-counter medication and household products was another land
mine. All of these companies were going to take on the Procter &
Gambles, Cokes, and Philip Morrises of the world. Of course, none
of them worked out."

4. Rely on a good support team. Even though most of the Wizards work alone, many are backed by strong research teams and have established networks of analysts they can turn to for input.

"I have three analysts who report directly to me," says Jim Callinan. "They focus on broad areas of concentration in the emerging growth areas. We have a hardware person who does just technology hardware, from semiconductors all the way to telecom equipment. Then we have somebody who does software, the Internet, and computer services. I do business services as well as biotech and finance. Someone else does consumer products and medical devices." All contribute ideas to the RS Emerging Growth portfolio and have helped to fuel its spectacular growth.

At Janus, all of the fund managers share ideas in an effort to make the entire team successful. They also have a group of analysts beneath them. "There's great give and take on ideas and a financial incentive for us to work together," notes Warren Lammert. Perhaps you, as an individual investor, can't hire your own research staff. But you can build your own support team of helpful Internet sites and research publications that will give you the additional information you need to make smart investment choices.

5. Concentrate your portfolio on a handful of your best ideas. Several managers point out that their secret to beating the market is placing big bets on their favorite ideas. You'll notice that, by and large, the Wizards don't own many stocks in their portfolios. Even Ron Canakaris, who runs $31 billion, holds fewer than 40 names. Even those with larger portfolios tend to keep a big portion of their total assets in a relatively small number of positions. "It's not unusual for my largest position to be in the high single digits and even into the double digits," Kevin Landis shares.

"We typically own 30 to 35 stocks," adds Bruce Behrens. "We don't own a little bit of everything. We own just what makes sense to us. We really don't believe in the Noah's ark approach where you have two of everything until you get a whole zoo of stock."

As for Richard Lawson, "I keep 25 to 35 names in the fund," he offers. "If I were managing a portfolio just for myself, I'd be comfortable with between 10 and 15 stocks."

The outspoken Bob Torray goes one step further. "I've never known anybody whose fortunes improved through diversification," he maintains. "Warren Buffett is by far the most successful investor of all time. Most of his fortune can be traced to a handful of astute investments. Some say he is an anomaly; I don't agree. And as far as conventional thinking is concerned [about the importance of heavy diversification], it produces conventional results. We're certainly not interested in that."

I believe concentration is even more important for investors who use mutual funds. Regardless of the size of your portfolio, you can comfortably own four or five funds run by great managers and have all the diversification you need.

6. **Follow a disciplined approach.** My observation is that most individual investors decide which stocks or funds to buy based on hot tips, input from friends, and by chasing performance that's reported in the media. Few have a disciplined approach. By contrast, every Wizard has a clearly defined strategy for choosing investments.

"I'm looking for companies with above-average growth characteristics," says Fritz Reynolds. "I want businesses that have strong unit growth, are well managed, and enjoy good pricing power. Often that might be the number-one or -two company in the industry."

Bill Miller agrees that having a proven investment approach is much more important than trying to predict the direction of the market, economy, or any other factors that are out of your control. "I think too many people underperform because they have a money management style that makes no sense," he insists. "Namely, they try and forecast variables that are unforecastable. Nobody can forecast interest rates or GDP numbers."

The Wizards know exactly what kinds of companies they are looking for, based on predetermined criteria, and actually avoid paying attention to all of the "noise" that most individual investors focus on.

7. **Buy good businesses, not gambling chips.** Too many investors treat the stock market like a casino, especially in this era of day trading. The managers in this book view it differently. They consider stocks to be fractional ownership in businesses, which is exactly what they are. Warren Buffett, whom many of the Wizards refer to, has sent out this message time and again. He's not interested in trading stocks. He buys ownership in companies, using stocks as a proxy, with the intention of remaining with these businesses for a very long time.

"I do think people make a mistake by switching too frequently," Jim Oelschlager maintains. "That isn't how you make your money investing. You basically make good investments and stay with them for a long time. No hospital wings have ever been endowed by market timers. They've been endowed by people who get into [stocks or mutual funds and ride them] for a long period of time."

8. **Have an exit strategy.** By the same token, even though all of the Wizards go into their positions with a desired holding period of forever, they all have a sell strategy in place.

Ron Canakaris has a twofold sell discipline. "When a stock gets to a 20 percent premium to (what we consider to be) fair value, we either cut back or sell," he says. "Our rule is that when a company has an earnings disappointment, we analyze the situation. If we're not willing to add to our position, we sell the stock."

As for Sig Segalas, he'll unload a stock for a number of reasons. "Any change in fundamentals can dictate a sale, such as a slowdown in revenue growth, or lower margins," he reveals. "If a company has a disappointment that we believe is short-term in nature I may just reduce our exposure. But I find that more times than not I am better off selling the entire holding."

The most common reasons the featured managers sell is if a stock gets overvalued, their original thesis for buying proves wrong, or they find a more attractive investment idea and want to swap from one company to another. One of the major lessons that other managers have learned from Bill Miller is that you don't want to sell your biggest winners too soon. If you own a truly great company, its up-side potential is unlimited. (Those who have proclaimed that Microsoft was severely overpriced for the past decade can certainly testify to that!)

But, as Howard Ward points out, it's also important not be a martyr about your investments. You should be willing to get rid of stocks that clearly turn out to be stinkers. "Don't be afraid to make a mistake, and don't be married to a stock," he cautions. "Making mistakes is simply part of this business. Just like trying to hit a baseball, you're going to miss a lot."

9. **Never underestimate the importance of management.** Whether buying a stock or fund, the person running the show is critical. The key, according to Chris Davis, is to figure out whether those in top management are doers or bluffers. "That's a funny characteristic to look

for," he admits. "You know it when you see it. Do they have a record of doing what they say they're going to do? Therefore, can you rely on them and are they credible? We can analyze the quantitative side of the business, but we really have to know if the information that we're getting from management, our partners, is credible. "That doesn't mean they don't make mistakes," Chris adds, noting that there are different ways to find out how credible management is. "Talking to competitors, customers, suppliers, and looking at the record helps."

Glen Bickerstaff goes one step further. "I need a good understanding about who's making the decisions," he insists. "You can't get away from the fact that these are the human beings making the most critical decisions. There are many managements out there that can tell a wonderful story but can't ever bring it to the bottom line."

Even great products will fall flat without top-flight leadership. "Taking it to its extreme, Coca-Cola says it has an incredibly unique product and a magic formula nobody knows about. Really, the company sells sugar water," says Amy Domini. "Why is Coke such a successful company? Because management put the factory in the right place, distributes the product in the right place, and makes good decisions about advertising." You should also place a heavy emphasis on management when selecting your mutual funds. I think one of the biggest mistakes fund investors make is buying funds based solely on performance, without even researching who's pulling the trigger. Often the manager who generated the advertised performance isn't even at the fund any more, which negates any meaning those numbers had in the first place.

10. **Don't try to outfox the market.** Individual investors collectively spend millions of dollars annually subscribing to newsletters and other services designed to help them time when to get in and out of stocks. Talk about money down the drain! The Wizards put almost no emphasis on "the market" when choosing investments for their portfolios.

   For starters, it's impossible to predict what the market will do. Only those trying to peddle market-timing newsletters would disagree with that. Second, focusing on the market's day-to-day gyrations makes you lose sight of what's really important, namely paying attention to the specific investments you own and those you are thinking about buying. In the short run, everyone is impacted by the market. But in the long run, it's the fundamentals that will win out. And since you can't predict what the market will do in the short run, why spend any of your time worrying about it? So, while the Wizards admittedly are aware of what's going on from day to day, they don't get worked up over it.

"The one thing the market contributes is opportunity," adds Glen Bickerstaff. "Sometimes in market declines you get the chance to buy a business at a price you think is extremely attractive. Paying attention to what's going on in the market is helpful in identifying opportunities that you might have one day versus another. But the market itself is significantly less interesting to me than are individual companies.

ABOUT THE AUTHOR

Kirk Kazanjian is a nationally recognized investment expert, stock and mutual fund analyst, bestselling author, and lifelong entrepreneur. He is the former director of research and investment strategy for one of the nation's largest fee-only investment management and financial planning firms, and spent several years as an award-winning television news anchor and business reporter. Kazanjian now appears regularly as a guest on radio and TV stations across the country, including CNBC, CNNfn, and Bloomberg. In addition, he is a popular teacher and speaker on investment topics.

Kazanjian is the author of many books, including *Growing Rich with Growth Stocks,* and the popular annual investment guides *New York Institute of Finance Guide to Mutual Funds* and *Wall Street's Picks.* He has been featured in numerous publications, including *Barron's, Your Money, USA Today, Entrepreneur, Mutual Funds Magazine, First,* and *The Christian Science Monitor.*

The author welcomes your comments and feedback. He can be reached at KirkKazanjian@aol.com.

INDEX